Ecumenism, Christian Origins and the Practice of Communion

The theology of communion, or *koinonia*, has been at the centre of the ecumenical movement for more than thirty years. It is central to the self-understanding of the Anglican, Roman Catholic, and Orthodox Churches, and has been prominent in the work of the World Council of Churches. This book, based on the 1996 Hulsean Lectures, examines the significance of *koinonia* for contemporary ecumenical theology, tracing the development of contemporary understanding in critical engagement with the thought of Plato, Aristotle, the Hebrew Scriptures, the New Testament, the Cappadocian Fathers, and Augustine. In each case, reflection on community life is related to actual communities in which texts were produced. The importance of conflict and the place of politics for the *koinonia* that constitutes the Christian churches is a major theme throughout. Communion is seen as a gift to be received and a discipline to be cultivated in the continuing practice of ecumenism.

Nicholas Sagovsky is the William Leech Professorial Research Fellow in Applied Christian Theology at the University of Newcastle upon Tyne. He is a member of the Anglican–Roman Catholic International Commission and delivered the Hulsean Lectures at Cambridge University in 1996.

ECUMENISM, CHRISTIAN ORIGINS AND THE PRACTICE OF COMMUNION

NICHOLAS SAGOVSKY

William Leech Professorial Research Fellow in Applied Christian Theology,
University of Newcastle upon Tyne

CAMBRIDGE
UNIVERSITY PRESS

CAMBRIDGE UNIVERSITY PRESS
Cambridge, New York, Melbourne, Madrid, Cape Town, Singapore, São Paulo, Delhi

Cambridge University Press
The Edinburgh Building, Cambridge CB2 8RU, UK

Published in the United States of America by Cambridge University Press, New York

www.cambridge.org
Information on this title: www.cambridge.org/9780521772693

First published 2000
This digitally printed version 2008

A catalogue record for this publication is available from the British Library

Library of Congress Cataloguing in Publication data
Sagovsky, Nicholas, 1947–
Ecumenism, Christian origins and the practice of communion /
by Nicholas Sagovsky.
p.   cm.
Includes bibliographical references and index.
ISBN 0 521 77269 9
1. Ecumenical movement – History.
2. Christian union – History.   I. Title.
BX6.5.S25   2000
262'.001'1   99–042143   CIP

ISBN 978-0-521-77269-3 hardback
ISBN 978-0-521-09053-7 paperback

Contents

Acknowledgements

The first full draft of this book was the text of the Hulsean Lectures, given in Cambridge in the Michaelmas Term 1996. I must therefore thank the electors for the honour they did me when they gave me the opportunity to develop my thinking in such a context. I hope that John Hulse, who endowed the post of 'Christian Advocate' in 1790 that there might be someone to 'compose some proper and judicious Answer or Answers every year, to all such new and popular or other Cavils and Objections against the Christian or Revealed Religion, or against the Religion of Nature, as may. . . seem . . . most . . . to deserve or require an Answer' and who required 'such his written answer to be in English, and only against notorious Infidels, whether Atheists or Deists, not descending to any particular Controversies or Sects among Christians themselves', would not have found the concern in these lectures with the *reconciliation* of Christians to be misplaced.

Two of the Hulsean electors in particular I must thank for their encouragement with this project and friendship over many years: Nicholas Lash, who, as Norris-Hulse Professor in the University of Cambridge for nearly twenty years resisted all manner of Cavils and Objections to the Christian Religion with the seriousness (or otherwise) they deserved, and David Ford, who, as Regius Professor, makes it his business to see that the Faculty of Divinity may properly be called a community, making its contribution fully within the scholastic community of the University.

Sections of the text were also read at a conference of the Council for Christians and Jews, two meetings of the London seminar of the Society for Ecumenical Studies, a 'Bishop's Study Day' in Birmingham, as a College Lecture at Cranmer Hall, Durham, and as a Lecture in the Department of Theology at Durham University.

It is no coincidence that my theme should have matured amongst the friendships of Clare College, Cambridge. In this book there are echoes of conversations with Valentin Dedji, the late Roger Hooker, Jonathan Lear, C. F. D. (Charlie) Moule, Stephen Plant, Malcolm Ruel, Mark Santer, Dominic Scott, Robin Steinke, Stephen Sykes, Douglas Templeton, Nicholas Tustin, and John Zizioulas, conversations I remember with delight. The Master and Fellows of Clare gave me sabbatical leave for two terms in 1993 and one in 1997, for which I am profoundly grateful. The support of Tim Brown and the generosity of Jane Charman and Jo Bailey Wells, covering for me in my absence, made those times possible, as did the tolerance of my family, my closest and most beloved *koinonoi*.

In October 1997, I became William Leech Research Fellow in Applied Christian Theology at the University of Newcastle. When interviewed, I blithely assured the Trustees that the redrafting of this book would be finished before I took up the appointment. My timetable proved hopelessly optimistic. The task occupied much of my research time through my first year in the new post. The indulgence and support of the Trustees has enabled me at last to finish the work and to look with confidence towards a second volume on 'Justice and The Common Good'.

John Orme Mills OP, Ben Quash, Rowan Williams, Alex Wright, and three anonymous readers appointed by the Cambridge University Press read the typescript in full, offering searching and perceptive criticisms which I tried to bear in mind as I revised the text. Others who read or heard part of the text and helped me with their comments were Stephen Barton, David Carter, David Chapman, James Dunn, Paul McPartlan, and William Telford. Michael Root helped me by procuring material from the Institute for Ecumenical Research, Strasburg. Mistakes that remain after so much help are, of course, 'mine own'.

Two very different groups can have little idea how much I

owe to the many hours spent in their company. I owe an immense debt to those in the group that first met to consider our response to The Community Charge, and then went on meeting to support one another in work for those at the margins of our community: Gabrielle Cox, Chris Moss SJ, Alan Murdie, Paul Nicolson, Louise Pirouet, Hannah Reed, and Graeme Walker. Members of the group have so often spoken of situations in which they are expending their energies in practical concern for the poor, while I have been silent. If they in any way hear the echo of their voices or find helpful theological reflection in this book, I shall be delighted. The other group without which this book could not have been written is that which meets every year as ARCIC (The Anglican–Roman Catholic International Commission). Those annual nine-day seminars, not only in theology, but in Christian living, have been one of the great privileges of my life. Within the Commission there has been a special *koinonia* amongst the drafting group that met more frequently through several years. I owe an exceptional debt of gratitude to John Baycroft, Peter Cross, and Jean Tillard OP for all I have learnt working together with them.

I hope my sisters and brothers in ARCIC will accept my dedication of this book to them, in gratitude for the communion that we share and in longing that the Lord's petition may be fulfilled, '*ut simus consummati in unum*'.

NOTE ON TRANSLATIONS

Throughout this book I have used and quoted a variety of translations of key texts, indicating in the notes which translation is being used, or adapted, for a particular quotation. Unless otherwise indicated, the translation of the Bible quoted, including for Apocryphal texts, is the Revised Standard Version or New Revised Standard Version.

Abbreviations

ANCF	Ante-Nicene Christian Fathers Series (Edinburgh: T. and T. Clark; Grand Rapids: Eerdmans)
CD	*De Civitate Dei* (Augustine)
CWS	Classics of Western Spirituality Series (London: SPCK; New York: Paulist Press)
FC	The Fathers of the Church Series (Washington DC: The Catholic University of America Press)
GS	*Gaudium et spes* (The Pastoral Constitution on the Church in the Modern World, from The Documents of the Second Vatican Council)
LCL	Loeb Classical Library
LG	*Lumen Gentium* (The Dogmatic Constitution on the Church, from The Documents of the Second Vatican Council)
NEB	New English Bible
NIV	New International Version (of the Bible)
PCPCU	Pontifical Council for Promoting Christian Unity
PNCF	Post-Nicene Christian Fathers Series (Edinburgh: T. and T. Clark; Grand Rapids: Eerdmans)
PG	Migne, J. P. (ed.), *Patrologia Graeca*
RSV	Revised Standard Version (of the Bible)
SC	*Sources Chrétiennes* (Paris: Cerf)
TDNT	Kittel, G. (ed.) *Theological Dictionary of the New Testament*, 10 vols. (Grand Rapids: Eerdmans, 1964–76), translation of Kittel, G. (ed.) *Theologisches Wörterbuch zum Neues Testament*, 10 vols. (Stuttgart: Kohlhammer, 1933–79)
TWOT	Botterweck, G. J. and Ringgren, H. (eds.) *Theo-*

logical Dictionary of the Old Testament, unfinished, 8 vols. (Grand Rapids: Eerdmans, 1974–), translation of *Theologisches Wörterbuch zum Alten Testament*, 8 vols. (Stuttgart: Kohlhammer, 1973–5)

UR   *Unitatis Redintegratio* (The Decree on Ecumenism, from The Documents of the Second Vatican Council)

WM   Gadamer, H.-G. *Wahrheit und Methode*, revised edition (Tübingen: J. C. B. Mohr, 1986)

CHAPTER I

The common life

The theme of this book is the life of God. It is about the shared life that God engenders and the God whose very being is a sharing. Christians are used to speaking of the life that God engenders within the Church as '*communion*', of the Christian life as a *participation* in the life of God, and of the life that is God as *love*. There is one Greek word that can be used for all three: *koinonia*, of which the Latin translation is *communio*. This book is an exploration of *koinonia/communio* as the terms have been used in current ecumenical discussion and in the formation of the Christian tradition. There has in recent years been a ground-swell of interest in 'community' and in society as a 'community of communities'. An exploration of what it means for the Church to be that unique human community which is explicitly constituted by its communion in God, Father, Son, and Holy Spirit, is potentially a resource for the renewal of secular social thought, and the insights of secular social thought of the greatest value in renewing our understanding of the common life of the Christian Church.

In much ecumenical literature, the Latinate *communion* or *communio* is used interchangeably with the Greek *koinonia*.[1] These two words do, however, have differing resonances because of their differing provenance: the very different history and understanding of the churches and societies in East and West. One of the central points at issue in this book will be the losses and gains in translating Christianity, which first took institutional form in the Greek-speaking Hellenistic world, into

[1] See, for example, *Communio/Koinonia*, A Study by the Institute for Ecumenical Research (Strasburg, 1990).

the institutional forms and language of the Latin-speaking West. It will be important to explore in depth the conceptuality associated with the Greek term *koinonia*, a term which is prominent in both Plato and Aristotle. It will also be necessary to explore Jewish conceptuality that fed into the use of *koinonia* and associated terms in the New Testament. The thread of the specific use of the word *koinonia* leads on to Ignatius of Antioch, Justin Martyr, and particularly to the Cappadocians. The thread of *communio* leads by various routes to Augustine and to Jerome's translation of the Bible into Latin, the Vulgate. In the chapters that follow it will be possible only to take soundings, to suggest a range of uses and some of the questions they raise for contemporary theology and ecumenical discussion. The wider aim, though, will be to demonstrate *communion* as the central reality of the Christian life, indeed of all life.

This approach raises a serious methodological issue, of which I have been acutely aware in writing this book. The first research was a word-study, using articles in Kittel's *Theological Dictionary of the New Testament*, the *Dictionnaire de Spiritualité*, and other standard sources.[2] The exposition that follows is marked by this approach, which has its uses and its dangers. One major use is the careful tracing of linguistic links that have been lost in translation. It is simply not possible from any of the standard English translations of the Bible to discern where words of the root '*koin-*' are used and so to pick up some of the allusive links offered to the Greek reader of the New Testament. Nor is it possible to pick up, behind identically translated words or words with associated English roots, differences in the original Greek vocabulary, which may have suggested shades of meaning that have been lost in translation.

The dangers of word-studies are as great as the benefits. We

---

[2] *TDNT*, vol. 3 (article by F. Hauck), pp. 789–809; *Dictionnaire de Spiritualité* (17 vols., Paris: Beauchesne, 1937–95) vol. 8, '*Koinonia*', cols. 1743–69. Other general studies which remain valuable include: H. Seesemann, *Der Begriff Koinonia im Neuen Testament* (Giessen: Alfred Töpelmann, 1933); J. Y. Campbell, '*Koinonia* and its cognates in the New Testament', *Journal of Biblical Literature* 51 (1932), 352–82, reprinted in *Three New Testament Studies* (Leiden: E. J. Brill, 1965), pp. 1–28; J. Reumann, '*Koinonia* in Scripture: Survey of Biblical Texts' in T. F. Best and G. Gassmann eds., *On the Way to Fuller Koinonia*, Faith and Order Paper 166 (Geneva: WCC, 1994), pp. 36–69. Reumann's article and comprehensive bibliography are particularly useful.

may think that because we have studied a word or group of cognate words, we have understood a concept, when we ought to take into consideration the broader linguistic context, the phrases or sentences in which words are used; the semantic field, the broader conceptuality, to which words contribute; and the actual social context in which they are used.[3] For this study, it was necessary to decide how the focus could extend to 'communion' as a semantic field and a theological reality. The intention is to use linguistic study as a way into the latter. Hans-Georg Gadamer, to whose thought I am greatly indebted, once remarked, 'The history of concepts seems to me a precondition for responsible critical philosophising in our time, and it is only along the route of the history of words that the history of concepts can move forward.'[4] This book is intended to be an exercise in 'critical theologising' along the lines sketched by Gadamer.

The need for such a study is generated by the widespread use of *koinonia* and *communion* in recent ecumenical discussion, often without sufficient regard for the history of these concepts and these words in the communities from which, over a thousand years, Christianity was formed. It is striking how often these words are used in their Greek or Latin form: there is no English word that translates them adequately. In a whole range of ecumenical documents it is the theology and the ecclesiology of '*koinonia/communio*' which is offered as a way forward. This book is written in the conviction that there is indeed a way forward in this ecclesiology and that we can tread it confidently. It is a way, as far as this study is concerned, that has led by a narrow and specific linguistic path through broader semantic fields, which reflect experience of community as a fundamental Christian, Jewish, and human reality. Though we may deal with a word, and with words, these words are the precipitate of life in

---

[3] These points are trenchantly made by James Barr in his critique of Kittel's *TWNT*. See *The Semantics of Biblical Language* (Oxford: Oxford University Press, 1961), especially pp. 210, 231–4, 281.

[4] H.-G. Gadamer, *Philosophical Apprenticeships* (Cambridge, Mass. and London: MIT Press, 1985), p. 148.

community and a stimulus to the deepening of communion within and between contemporary Christian communities.

Since 1965, when the Second Vatican Council concluded, there has been a striking ecumenical convergence around certain basic notions of what it is to be 'Church'. More than that, there is widespread agreement that this understanding of what it is to be 'Church' is at the heart of the Christian faith. This consensus has been expressed through some of the key documents of the Second Vatican Council, through official statements and reports of various Christian traditions, through the reports of bi-lateral ecumenical discussions, and through the multi-lateral statements of the World Council of Churches. At the centre of all these documents is an understanding of the Church as communion, of this communion as a sharing or participation in the life of the Trinity, and of the vital contribution this understanding can make to the ecumenical goal of 'visible unity in one faith and in one eucharistic fellowship expressed in worship and in the common life of Christ'.[5] With this emerging consensus has gone a consensus about method: that we must build on the communion Christians already experience by virtue of shared participation in Christ, a shared participation that can be made explicit by 'going behind disagreements' or finding from the tradition reconciling language in which both parties can recognise their own faith.[6] Central to this understanding and this method is the theory and practice of communion – or, to use the Greek term, *koinonia*.

It will be clear from what follows that I warmly support the ecumenical rapprochements that have taken place in recent years and wish to promote genuine consensus amongst Christians who are working for visible unity. I am thus concerned to prevent the term *koinonia* being used in a slovenly and over-general fashion to paper over ecumenical cracks, and wish to sound a note of warning against this or similar terms being used

[5] Statement of the Fifth Assembly of the World Council of Churches (Nairobi, 1975). See N. Lossky *et al.* eds., *Dictionary of the Ecumenical Movement* (Geneva: WCC; London: CCBI, 1991), p. 1085.

[6] See G. R. Evans, *Method in Ecumenical Theology* (Cambridge: Cambridge University Press, 1996), especially pp. 102, 134ff, 177ff.

ideologically to promote (and conceal) the very opposite of true communion. *Koinonia* is a term which, used with care, can be of immense power and suggestiveness, an invaluable ecumenical resource. Words, however, relate to human living and the use of a word like *koinonia* must be tested against the realities of human life. Though my approach will be in part through a discussion of language, tracing continuities in translation and usage, my concern remains equally and fundamentally the concrete life of communities from the past which have struggled with the problems of unity and diversity, and communities which do so today. Throughout this book I shall, I hope, be developing grounds for a critique of the way in which the language and ideology of *koinonia* is properly used to sustain the unity and to promote the reconciliation of the Christian churches.

Ecumenical theological discussion does not usually make much of the extensive use of the term *koinonia* in pre-Christian Greek literature, especially that of Plato and Aristotle, which was so influential for the early formation of Christian theology and for its development in the Middle Ages and at the Reformation.[7] Nor does this literature usually reflect upon the actual life of communities, whether Hellenistic, Jewish, avowedly Christian, or a mixture of all three. Though much discussion of communion relates this explicitly to Trinitarian theology, it does not do so by reference to early Christian experience of *koinonia* (both the powerful experience of the Spirit and the intense struggles for unity and fidelity to tradition).[8] Closer reflection upon actual Christian experience within actual Christian communities is vitally important if ecumenical theology is

---

[7] Discussion of the influence of Plato on the formation of Christian theology can be found in A. Louth, *The Origins of the Christian Mystical Tradition* (Oxford: Clarendon, 1981); of Plato and Aristotle in A. H. Armstrong ed., *The Cambridge History of Later Greek and Early Medieval Philosophy* (Cambridge: Cambridge University Press, 1967); for the fresh infusion of Aristotelian and Platonic texts to the scholarly life of the West, especially in the twelfth and fifteenth centuries respectively, and for their dissemination by translation see R. R. Bolgar, *The Classical Heritage and its Beneficiaries* (Cambridge: Cambridge University Press, 1954), especially pp. 161–74, 277–88.

[8] A striking and creative exception is *The Niagara Report* of the Anglican–Lutheran Consultation on Episcopacy (London: Anglican Consultative Council; Geneva: Lutheran World Federation, 1987).

not to remain at a level of high abstraction remote from the concerns of believing Christians in their local churches.

Attention to such issues has led me to identify five themes, each of which is implicit in all that follows. The first is *translation*. Christianity is from beginning to end an exercise in translation as the Word of God is heard afresh in new ways and in new situations.[9] In following the progress of the Gospel towards the English-speaking world, we must trace a linguistic trajectory from Hebrew and Greek to Latin to various forms of English. These linguistic shifts have been necessary to present the un-changing Word of God faithfully, in such a way that people can hear it as addressed directly to them, and to sustain Church life as a living expression of contemporary faith, not a museum piece. However, just as there are norms of fidelity in linguistic translation, so there are norms of fidelity in the development of the life of the Church. The linguistic norm is the text of Scripture itself, where (in the New Testament) the word *koinonia* and its cognates are to be found extensively. What one might call the 'living norm' is the actual life, the actual *koinonia*, of the apostolic communities of which the words of Scripture are the precipitate that is left to us. It is clear from the linguistic norm of Scripture that continuities can be traced from the life of the synagogue, from the household and the *polis* within the Hellen-istic world, to this 'living norm' of Christian community.[10] As for those early Christian writers known as 'The Fathers', they 'made their own the categories in which the Greeks habitually interpreted their own experience'.[11] They did so because the life of the local church, the life of the Christian household, was itself both a translation and a transformation of whatever went before. The community was newly formed about Christ, but the experience of *koinonia* was not new: to the Hellenistic and the Christian mind it was a condition of being human. In the writings of Plato and Aristotle and their followers, and in Jewish

[9] Barr (*The Semantics of Biblical Language*, p. 4) rightly talks of the problem 'not only of translation but of transculturation'.

[10] *The Niagara Report*, para. 46, speaks of the way that 'Churches increasingly found that political or quasi-political terminology expressed their sense of their own identity.'

[11] Bolgar, *The Classical Heritage*, p. 26.

sources, both those which were translated into Greek and those which were not, there is a rich tradition of reflection on the experience of *koinonia* and on the social conditions under which humans flourish. As we consider these traditions, we shall discover they have important lessons to teach us about the functioning of human communities, including churches. It is, after all, from such sources as these that we have drawn again and again in theological reflection, and we need to investigate them afresh as resources for critical reflection on the ecumenical effort to translate the Gospel and the life of the Church for the cultures of our time.[12]

The second theme is *politics*. I have tried to bear in mind throughout that the texts with which we have to deal are the precipitate of life in historical communities. Certainly, the texts, both scriptural and non-scriptural, are formed by and bear witness to the life of communities in many different ways, but it is important to remember that they are not theoretical treatises composed in abstraction from the abrasions and the conflicts of everyday life. Wherever there are communities of human beings, power is deployed and conflict is either contained or it tears the community apart. Issues of leadership, representation, communication, education, division of resources, justice, fidelity are integral to the life of every human community. In negotiating these issues, whether in a local church or a local community, in an ecumenical encounter or as citizens of a modern state, we engage in politics. Politics and *koinonia* are interwoven. One outstanding teacher of the importance of recognising the proper role of politics in every human community has been Bernard Crick, who writes with characteristic economy:

---

[12] My position would differ sharply from that of Alan J. Torrance, who writes in *Persons in Communion* (Edinburgh: T. and T. Clark, 1996), pp. 254–5: 'There is absolutely no conceptual or ontological connection between the Greek interpretation of participation conceived as *methexis* and the New Testament interpretation as *koinonia*.' This claim, which he reiterates frequently, drives a wedge between the language and conceptuality of the New Testament and the Hellenistic culture to *and from* which it spoke. For cognates of *methexis* and *koinonia* used within the NT as synonyms, see Luke 5:7–10, 1 Cor. 10:16–17. Reumann finds in his survey of biblical texts ('*Koinonia* in Scripture' p. 43) that *metechein* emphasises 'have a share in', but concludes that 'it is difficult to establish a clear distinction from *koinonia*'.

A political doctrine is . . . just an attempt to strike a particular harmony in an actual political situation, one harmony out of many possible different (temporary) resolutions of the basic problem of unity and diversity in a society with complex and entrenched rival social interests.[13]

The point must be spelt out with care if it is to be applied ecclesiologically, for the issue of temporary or permanent resolution of disputes and the constraints upon diversity if unity is to be maintained must appear in a distinctive light within the Christian Church, but the 'attempt to strike a particular harmony' and the 'basic problem of unity and diversity in a society with complex and entrenched rival social interests' goes to the heart both of Church life within particular traditions and of the ecumenical enterprise.

The third theme is a development of the second: it is that of *conflict*. Implicit in the notion of politics is the recognition that conflict is integral to life in community. It is not the presence of conflict that is unhealthy for communal life, but the premature suppression of conflict in the interests of an in-authentic unity. Serious, impassioned conflict, where the protagonists are committed to apparently irreconcilable positions, is characteristic of humans living in community. The Church is not immune from this fundamental datum of human sociality. On the contrary, where Christians have a proper depth of conviction, it is inevitable that those convictions will clash. Dietrich Bonhoeffer was right to put this point starkly: 'Conflict as such is not the consequence of the fall, but arises on the basis of common love for God.'[14] The issue for Christians within the Church is not whether such conflict is present but how it is handled within the Body of Christ. Where Christians remain in communion, there is potentially a security to face disagreement and a resource to sustain debate in a climate of trust until there is some resolution which is

---

[13] B. Crick, *In Defence of Politics* (fourth edition, London: Penguin, 1992), p. 33.
[14] D. Bonhoeffer, *Sanctorum Communio* (London: Collins, 1963), p. 41. Stephen Sykes argues from the evidence of the New Testament for the 'inevitability of conflict in Christianity' in *The Identity of Christianity* (London: SPCK, 1984), pp. 13–26. Compare his *The Integrity of Anglicanism* (London: Mowbrays, 1978), p. 89: 'A dispersed authority implies recognition of the probability of conflict.'

satisfactory to all.[15] Where trust and communion have broken down, but there is the desire for reconciliation, there can only be a more cautious handling of contentious issues. Serious conflict is a much more dangerous threat to the unity of those who are not bound in communion. This is why a change in perception whereby communion is seen as taking many forms within the life of the Church, and the recognition of other Christians as truly bound in that communion, has revolutionised the basis for ecumenical discussion. Recognition of a fundamental unity in Christ, though that unity is not yet made explicit in eucharistic communion, has made it possible to handle old conflicts in a new light – even to see the protagonists of contrary views, and those views themselves, as contained within the diversity that goes to make up the variegated unity of the Church.

A fourth theme is *dialogue*. This will be addressed explicitly in the chapter on Plato, but it is implicit in both the discussion of ecumenism and the use that I have made of my sources. Plato above all teaches us that to read is to enter into dialogue with the text, that reading is a participatory activity. It is an emphasis reinforced by hermeneutic practitioners of the stature of H.-G. Gadamer[16] and George

---

[15] For a powerful description of such decision-making among the Thembu people of South Africa, see N. Mandela, *Long Walk to Freedom* (London: Abacus, 1995), pp. 24–5: 'The meetings would continue until some kind of consensus was reached. They ended in unanimity or not at all.'

[16] H.-G. Gadamer consistently stresses the importance of dialectic for shared understanding, taking as his model Plato's Socratic dialogues. This insight, which he often expresses in terms of Heidegger's fundamental notion of *Dasein* ('Being as manifest in the world') revealing itself in dialectic, is applied to reading and the 'experience' of 'understanding' between text and reader (see *Truth and Method*, second, revised edition, London: Sheed and Ward, 1989, pp. 163–4 (German, *Wahrheit und Methode*, revised edition, Tübingen: J. C. B. Mohr, 1986, pp. 168–9), pp. 367–8 (*WM*, pp. 373–4), pp. 378–9 (*WM*, p. 384)). R. E. Palmer builds on a fine study of Gadamer when he writes, 'An interpretative "act" must not be a forcible seizure, a "rape" of the text, but a loving union that brings to stand the full potential of interpreter and text, the partners in the hermeneutical dialogue' (*Hermeneutics*, Evanston: Northwestern University Press, 1969, p. 244). Gadamer's concern with the ontology of the experience of understanding meets with a central concern of this book: the ontology of communion (compare the English title of J. Zizioulas' *Being as Communion*, London: Darton, Longman and Todd, 1985). Furthermore, Gadamer's concern for the actuality of dialogue is splendidly relevant to the *praxis* of ecumenical dialogue: 'In a successful conversation [the partners] come under the influence of the truth of the

Steiner.[17] I would go beyond Gadamer (on theological grounds) to say that the construing of a text brings about a dialogue between the reader *and the writer*, in which there is a kind of meeting, a communion. The text of this book for me represents a kind of communion with Plato and Aristotle, the biblical writers, the Cappadocians and Augustine, though their words and thought as interpreted here may be as historically inauthentic as, in all probability, are the words of the participants at Plato's banquet. The dialogues we sustain with and through classic texts take their place among the many conversations that we sustain with other people and other sources. To exist in such a network of communication is in one mode to exist in communion, or in community. This dialogue, or these dialogues, with classic texts, principally but not exclusively the Scriptures, is one means by which the life of the Church continues as a life in dialogue. To identify my methodological indebtedness a little further: the discussion at Plato's banquet moves from individual statement towards an exposition of the way of love in communion with God and so, I hope, does this book.

A fifth theme is *symbols*. This is particularly important in a study of *koinonia* because of the tendency to think that communion or communication takes place at a level above or behind the physical (at the 'spiritual' level). *Koinonia* as 'mutual sharing' or as 'fellowship' is often spoken of in this way. The position taken here is that there can be no *koinonia* without shared participation in symbols and that such participation is a corrective to any 'spiritualising' which overlooks or excludes the place of the physical in communion.[18] For Plato, objects in the world

---

object and are thus bound to one another in a new community (*Gemeinsamkeit*). To reach an understanding in a dialogue is not merely a matter of putting oneself forward and successfully asserting one's own point of view, but being transformed into a communion (*Gemeinsam*) in which we do not remain what we were' (p. 379; *WM*, p. 384). See also 'Conversation and the Way we come to Shared Understanding' in *Plato's Dialectical Ethics* (London and New Haven: Yale University Press, 1991), pp. 17–65.

[17] See especially 'The Uncommon Reader' in *No Passion Spent, Essays 1978–96* (London: Faber and Faber, 1996), pp. 1–19; *Real Presences* (London: Faber and Faber, 1989). Also relevant is Steiner's essay on translation, *After Babel* (Oxford: Oxford University Press, 1975), especially pp. 296–413.

[18] I have dealt with this briefly in *Liturgy and Symbolism* (Bramcote: Grove Books, 1978).

carry a 'surplus of meaning' which is attributable to their participation in a higher world of fuller reality. They are symbolic. Beginning with the critique of Aristotle, the 'higher world' may for many people have evaporated, or may now be differently understood, but the symbolic intensity of objects, their 'surplus of meaning' within an ecology of *koinonia*, remains.

To be human is to inhabit a world of symbols in which language is only one (secondary) mode of symbolic communication. More, perhaps, than the giving and receiving of *a word*, more than 'something understood', the physical giving – and receiving – of *a gift* is a paradigm of *koinonia*.[19] How is it that we know in particular circumstances what is the appropriate gift – one that can be received? Such knowledge is often made explicit in religious or social codes. The giving, and receiving by God or the gods, of appropriate sacrificial offerings is at the heart of what we would think of as 'religion' (that is the 'cult') within the Graeco-Roman world, and within the world of the Hebrew Scriptures.[20] Sacrifice as that which effects *koinonia* with the deity, the benefit of which may be appeasement, or reconciliation, empowerment, or blessing, is widely recognised throughout the ancient and modern world. Within Judaism, the symbolism of sacrifice was articulated by an elaborate code, in which the various dimensions of *koinonia* effected by the sacrifice, whether between the sacrificer and God, or between the sacrificer and others who participated in the sacrifice, were spelt out. In tension with this, however, was the prophetic appeal to the covenantal *koinonia*, sealed in the past with

---

[19] Marcel Mauss, *The Gift* (translated by W. D. Halls, London: Routledge, 1990) is fundamental. In her Foreword, 'No Free Gifts', Mary Douglas explains, 'A gift that does nothing to enhance solidarity is a contradiction' (p. vii).

[20] Of many studies, one anthropologically informed recent treatment (with good bibliography) is L. B. Zaidman and P. S. Pantel, *Religion in the Ancient Greek City* (Cambridge: Cambridge University Press, 1992), pp. 28–39: 'Bloody animal sacrifice of alimentary type . . . simultaneously gave expression to the bonds that tied citizens one to another and served as a privileged means of communication with the divine world' (p. 29). Anthropological and biblical material is brought together in M. F. C. Bourdillon and Meyer Fortes eds., *Sacrifice* (London: Academic Press, 1980). The discussion in S. W. Sykes ed., *Sacrifice and Redemption* (Cambridge: Cambridge University Press, 1991) has a more theological focus.

sacrifice but thereafter operative in the ethical demands made upon a people in relationship with their God.

This tension within Judaism is reproduced within Christianity. There is in Christian tradition a move towards concretion, towards the development of a rich, sacramental economy of water and bread and wine, of the bishop, the liturgy, the community gathered in one place (*epi to auto*). There is also within the tradition a deep prophetic alarm at any suggestion of religious mechanisms which detract from or short-circuit the ethical, the intellectual, the life of the Spirit. The development by which the Christian community is called (as by Pachomius) *the Koinonia*, or the eucharist becomes known as *the communion*, represents a major shift towards the concrete, with significant implications for ecumenism today. For those who accept that such a development was not misplaced, and that sharing in the one eucharist with the one bishop in some sense 'makes the Church',[21] so that it is right to speak of a visible Christian community as a '*Sharing*' (as in 'The Anglican *Communion*') it is clearly inadequate to engage in an ecumenism of 'reconciled diversity'. Since the one *koinonia* of the Spirit is broken into ecclesial fragments that do not fully recognise one another, what is required for the reconciliation of the Church in its wholeness is a convergence or reconvergence of communities, in all their diversity and particularity, on the eucharist as the central symbolic act of the Church (which does not at all exclude a correlative convergence in the interpretation of Scripture). In the ecumenical movement today, we continue to seek ways of realigning our ecclesiastical and liturgical symbols by means of translation, politics, conflict, and dialogue. In one sense, the enterprise takes place within the shared life of the Church, in *koinonia*. In another, the goal remains 'visible *koinonia*': shared participation in the visible symbol of the eucharist. If Mary Douglas is right in saying that 'the perception of symbols in general, *as well as their interpretation*, is socially determined',[22] the

---

[21] Paul McPartlan takes up this phrase of Henri de Lubac in *The Eucharist Makes the Church: Henri de Lubac and John Zizioulas in Dialogue* (Edinburgh: T. and T. Clark, 1993).

[22] Mary Douglas, *Natural Symbols* (Harmondsworth: Penguin, 1973), pp. 27–8, my emphasis.

way forward can only be by means of convergent and inclusive social *praxis*. Not to ask what *praxis* will draw together the communities in which the traditions that sustain those variant interpretations are carried, is to misunderstand the complex and concrete functioning of symbolism.

Each of these five themes – translation, politics, conflict, dialogue, and symbols – is related to human life in actual, human communities, and therefore to the practice of *koinonia*. Though much of the discussion in this book will be about language, there will be hints that my concern is equally to reflect upon the actuality of *koinonia* as lived, human experience in living, human communities. So strong has been the renewal of interest in community in recent years that the theme has at times been all but done to death. Nevertheless, the search for authentic expressions of community continues. Alasdair MacIntyre's conclusion to *After Virtue* has been particularly influential:

What matters at this stage is the construction of local forms of community within which civility and the intellectual and moral life can be sustained through the new dark ages which are already upon us.[23]

MacIntyre acknowledges his debt to Christianity: 'We are waiting not for a Godot, but for another – doubtless very different – St Benedict.' His conclusion is echoed by other recent writers of moral or social philosophy. Richard Bernstein concludes his study of Arendt, Gadamer, Habermas, and Rorty by saying:

What we desperately need today is . . . to seize upon those experiences and struggles in which there are still the glimmerings of solidarity and the promise of dialogical communities in which there can be genuine mutual participation and where reciprocal wooing and persuasion can prevail.[24]

Bernstein concludes his study with an impassioned plea for

---

[23] A. MacIntyre, *After Virtue* (second edition, London: Duckworth, 1985), p. 263. For MacIntyre, tradition plays a vital role in the life of healthy communities (a point of convergence with Gadamer), as does conflict (a point of convergence with a significant theme in this book). As he puts it, 'Traditions, when vital, embody continuities of conflict' (p. 222).

[24] R. J. Bernstein, *Beyond Objectivism and Relativism: Science, Hermeneutics and Praxis* (Oxford: Basil Blackwell, 1983), p. 229.

dedication to 'the practical task of furthering the type of solidarity, participation, and mutual recognition that is founded in dialogical communities'.[25]

'Dialogical communities' of various sorts – the Athens of Plato and Aristotle, the synagogue in Hellenistic Judaism, the Essene community, the earliest Christian churches and monastic communities, the churches of today engaged in ecumenical discussion – are presupposed throughout the chapters that are to follow. I have already hinted at the pervasive influence of Hans-Georg Gadamer, with his exploration of the dialogical reading of texts leading to a 'fusion of horizons'.[26] Gadamer's hermeneutical account of the emergence of meaning and the communication of truth within a tradition presupposes the existence of communities in which the responsible interpretation of texts and the appropriation of tradition takes place. His focus, however, is on the text, on truth known in literary and artistic interpretation. He has, accordingly, been criticised for lack of critical reflection on the composition of the communities in which he finds truth-ful interpretation. Gadamer, it is argued, offers no account of the realities of conflict, power, the ideological use of tradition, the *politics* of interpretation, and fails to address the issue of the universal validity of truth disclosed in the interpretation of particular texts within particular communities. Despite his regard for Gadamer's 'magnificent actualisation of the humanist tradition, which is oriented to the formation of the free spirit',[27] Jürgen Habermas finds a weakness at this point.[28]

Habermas' own consistent concern, as expressed in his earlier work, is for human emancipation from 'systematically distorted communication', for 'communication free from domination'.[29] The utopian caste of his thought is evident when he writes:

[25] *Ibid.* p. 231.
[26] Gadamer, *Truth and Method*, pp. 269–74 (*WM*, pp. 307–12).
[27] J. Habermas, *Philosophical–Political Profiles* (London: Heinemann, 1983), p. 186.
[28] See the excellent analysis by Alan How in *The Habermas–Gadamer Debate and the Nature of the Social* (Aldershot: Avebury, 1995), which defends Gadamer against the criticisms of Habermas.
[29] J. Habermas, *Knowledge and Human Interests* (second edition, London: Heinemann,

Only in an emancipated society, whose members' autonomy and responsibility have been realised, would communication have developed into the non-authoritarian and universally practised dialogue from which both our model of reciprocally constituted ego identity and our idea of true consensus are always implicitly derived.[30]

The realisation of such communication is, for him, an ethical possibility implicitly present in all linguistic utterance. 'Our first sentence', he writes, 'expresses unequivocally the intention of universal and unconstrained consensus.'[31] Habermas asserts the universal possibility of such consensus (though it is not clear that he ever points to the realisation of such consensus in actual human communities).[32] The value of his work lies in his identification and exploration of transcendental conditions for non-exploitative human community (for true *koinonia*), and his finding within every act of human speech the possibility of an intention towards that 'undistorted communication' which would be the hallmark of such a community. Duncan Forrester writes appreciatively: 'His "discourse ethics" points in the direction of participation, equality and community. And he proposes a thoroughgoing hermeneutic of suspicion of social structures.'[33]

Habermas has developed his theory of communicative action in an extended critique of modernity.[34] His discussion of reason and the 'rationalisation' of society follows Weber's discussion of the growing application of instrumental reason throughout society, for example in the growth of bureaucracy and the

---

1978), p. 53. I am indebted to Duncan Forrester, who encouraged me to return to Habermas with *koinonia* in mind.

[30] Habermas, *Knowledge and Human Interests*, p. 314.

[31] *Ibid.*

[32] Paul Lakeland, in *Theology and Critical Theory – the Discourse of the Church* (Nashville: Abingdon Press, 1990), measures the practice of the Roman Catholic Church against the critical theory of Habermas. See especially, 'The Church: Community of Communicative Action', pp. 103–37.

[33] Duncan B. Forrester, *Christian Justice and Public Policy* (Cambridge: Cambridge University Press, 1997), p. 174. Forrester also notes that Habermas believes theology to have become irrelevant, and (*tu quoque!*) criticises Habermas for the way that his theorising 'has become increasingly remote from any identifiable field of practice' (p. 182).

[34] See especially, J. Habermas, *The Theory of Communicative Action* (2 vols.: vol. 1, *Reason and the Rationalization of Society*, Boston: Beacon Press, 1984; vol. 2, *Lifeworld and System, A Critique of Functionalist Reason*, Boston: Beacon Press, 1987).

spread of what we now call consumerism. The growth of individualism, together with the split between 'facts' and 'values', has been a disaster for our understanding of what it is to be human. Habermas identifies a widespread split in capitalist society between 'institutions effective for social integration' and 'systemic mechanisms' such as those of money, power, and the market.[35] 'Without the brackets of a lifeworld centred on communicative action', he writes, 'culture, society, and personality fall apart.'[36] His critique is intended to illuminate the rational conditions for their being reunited. Though his work is a profoundly critical analysis of the failures of modernity, it is also a vigorous attempt to further the Enlightenment project of universal emancipation in the face of the pessimism of post-modernism, where there can be no rational arbitration between competing concepts of 'culture, society and personality'. Habermas' critique of modernity and his commitment to universal human emancipation in mutual understanding ('communicative action') itself provides a basis on which the discussion in this book can engage with the concerns of contemporary thought. The reflection on Christian understandings of *koinonia* offered here is intended to be more than an intensification of understanding within Christian tradition. It is intended to contribute to and draw from wider discussion of the conditions for authentic human community.

Nevertheless, the focus in the chapters that follow will not (with Habermas) so much be on conditions for the realisation of true humanity or authentic hope, as on the life of *particular communities* which have claimed in some way to realise emancipatory *koinonia*. Habermas' emphasis upon the human need not just for communicative speech, but for communicative *action*, opens a perspective on life in community which goes beyond that of Gadamer, with his commitment to disclosure of truth in the responsible reading of texts within a humanistic tradition. Together, however, they remind those involved in Christian

---

[35] *Lifeworld and System*, p. 163.
[36] *Ibid.*, p. 225. Habermas discusses at length the concept of the 'lifeworld', engaging particularly with the work of Alfred Schutz. He describes the 'lifeworld' as 'the horizon within which communicative actions are "always already" moving' (p. 119).

ecumenism, which is so often a matter of the reappropriation of classic texts within a convergence of tradition, that ecumenism (including the responsible interpretation and re-interpretation of texts) is first and foremost a *praxis*.[37] What they illuminate are the conditions for an authentic ecumenism that is not inturned upon the needs of the Christian community, but which finds its integrity in dialogue with the world. Where specifically Christian understanding of *koinonia* goes beyond what either of them can offer as philosophers is in the claim to something radically new. The Christian claim is that there is about the *koinonia* of the Spirit (2 Cor. 13:14) an element of radical novelty, the need for which is apparent to human reason, but the realisation of which is a matter of gift and the incarnation of the Gospel in the Body of Christ. The Christian practice of *koinonia* is seen as a practical participation in the love of God, which can be entered upon only with repentance and is normally sustained within or by reference to confessional Christian communities. Only by the activity of the Spirit can we live, in its fullest sense, 'the common life'.

---

[37] That is to say, an exercise of practical rather than theoretical reason, in Aristotle's terms an exercise of *phronesis* rather than *nous*.

CHAPTER 2

Communion: Anglicans, Roman Catholics, and ecumenical consensus

In the last thirty years, ecumenical discussion of every kind has proliferated. During that time – broadly speaking, since the Second Vatican Council (1962–5) – the theology of *koinonia/ communio* (to set the Greek and Latin terms side by side) has all but swept the board. Here is a way of presenting the Christian faith that takes in a fundamental concern with God as Trinity (*koinonia* in God), with human beings as made for *koinonia*, with ecclesiology and the doctrine of salvation (*koinonia* with God and with other human beings), and ethics (living in and for *koinonia*). It engages with much wider debates in society about community, about what it means to be a person, and about human relations. The theology of *koinonia* is a theo-logy (a study in the working, in the 'logic', of God) which comes to a focus in study of that unique community, or community of communities, which is the Christian Church. This ecclesiological focus is, perhaps, why it has been so widely developed and so much drawn upon within the ecumenical movement.

Within the ecumenical movement, with Roman Catholics[1] and Orthodox as active participants, Christians have been forced to reflect in new and creative ways on what it means to

---

[1] The Decree on Ecumenism of the Second Vatican Council (*Unitatis Redintegratio*) was of the greatest significance in opening the way for much fuller Roman Catholic participation in the ecumenical movement. It spoke of those non-Catholics who believe in Christ and have been baptised as 'in some, though imperfect, communion with the Catholic Church' (3) and frequently referred to 'separated brethren', but also maintained that the unity which Christ wills for the Church 'subsists in the Catholic Church' (4). Roman Catholics participate fully in almost all programmes of the World Council of Churches, including the Faith and Order Commission (J.-M. R. Tillard OP is one of five vice-moderators), but the Roman Catholic Church is not as such a member of the WCC.

be Church; that is, on what grounds we (I write as a Christian) recognise others as Christian, on what grounds churches make that claim of themselves or recognise it when made by others, how we determine whether we share 'the same' faith, how we determine the permissible diversity in expressions of faith, what would have to change for Christians to admit one another to be, in the fullest sense, 'sisters and brothers', and how we progress towards that longed for goal in which Christians, with all their diversity of tradition, work and live together as one Church in the world. Faced with questions such as these, ecclesiology can no longer be seen as an appendage to the rest of Christian doctrine. In a 'theology of communion' ecclesiology moves centre stage.

There is now a powerful ecumenical consensus that in *koinonia/communio* we have a reconciling and fruitful way of understanding what it is to be Church, and so of understanding what it is to be a Christian. This understanding can be extended to include fundamental statements about what it is to be human, and what we understand of the life of God. In this chapter I intend to discuss recent ecumenical dialogues in which Anglicans have been involved (for this is where my own roots lie), some Roman Catholic documents indebted to the Second Vatican Council, and the work of the World Council of Churches, to illuminate this consensus. Though the approach will be through a discussion of texts, my concern remains equally and fundamentally the actual life of those communities which have ultimately generated these texts, and which look to them today. I hope that this discussion of the 'logic' of *koinonia* will in and of itself constitute an encouragement to a renewed *praxis* of communion within the life of actual Christian communities. When in later chapters I trace some of the conceptuality associated with the emergence of distinctively Christian communities, or churches, in the past, I shall, I hope, be at the same time developing a constructive and supportive critique of an emerging consensus amongst fragmented Christian churches today; of the steps they are taking to strengthen and develop their *koinonia*.

ANGLICANS AND COMMUNION

The first report of a bi-lateral ecumenical discussion woven around the theme of *koinonia* was *The Final Report* of the Anglican–Roman Catholic International Commission (ARCIC 1) in 1982.[2] The introduction, which has been widely quoted in other ecumenical documents, stresses that *koinonia* is the 'governing concept' of all that follows and 'fundamental' to all the statements included in the report:

The *koinonia* is grounded in the word of God preached, believed and obeyed. Through this word the saving work of God is proclaimed. In the New Testament it is clear that the community is established by a baptism inseparable from faith and conversion, that its mission is to proclaim the Gospel of God, and that its common life is sustained by the eucharist. This remains the pattern for the Christian Church. The Church is the community of those reconciled with God and with each other because it is the community of those who believe in Jesus Christ and are justified through God's grace. It is also the reconciling community, because it has been called to bring to all mankind, through the preaching of the Gospel, God's gracious offer of redemption.[3]

The theme of *koinonia*, used with increasing prominence and confidence, runs through all the statements included in *The Final Report*. The eucharist is seen as the effectual sign of *koinonia*, *episcope* as serving *koinonia*, and primacy as a visible link and focus of *koinonia*.[4] This theme was carried forward into a statement by the second ARCIC (ARCIC 2) in 1991 on *Church as*

---

[2] *The Final Report* (London: SPCK/CTS, 1982) is published with official responses and critical discussion in C. Hill and E. Yarnold eds., *Anglicans and Roman Catholics: The Search for Unity* (London: SPCK/CTS, 1994).

[3] *Ibid.*, Introduction, para. 8; compare 'The Helsinki Report' of the Anglican–Lutheran European Regional Commission para. 49 (*Anglican–Lutheran Dialogue*, London: SPCK, 1983, p. 21), where this paragraph is quoted at length. 'The Meissen Common Statement' of the Church of England, the [then] Federation of Evangelical Churches in the German Democratic Republic and the Evangelical Church in Germany, para. 5 (*The Meissen Agreement*, The Council for Christian Unity of the General Synod of the Church of England Occasional Paper 2, 1992, p. 10) and 'The Fetter Lane Common Statement' of The Church of England and the Moravian Church in Great Britain and Ireland para. 23 (*Anglican–Moravian Conversations*, The Council for Christian Unity of the General Synod of the Church of England Occasional Paper 5, 1996, p. 13) are both based upon this paragraph.

[4] *Ibid.*, Introduction, para. 6.

Communion[5] where 'communion' rather than *koinonia* is used almost throughout but in such a way as to make it clear that the two words are interchangeable.[6] The same theological framework is also used in *Life in Christ, Morals, Communion and the Church*,[7] the first major bi-lateral ecumenical statement to venture into ethics. Throughout the work of ARCIC, work which continues, *koinonia* or communion has been a key concept. *Church as Communion* is probably the best short presentation of an ecumenical ecclesiology of communion.

The Anglican Communion is distinctive amongst world churches in the way that it is structured as a communion of autonomous provinces with primates ('a communion of communions'), the Archbishop of Canterbury having a special responsibility as a pastor in the service of unity but having no legal power over other Anglican Archbishops.[8] The ordination of women to the priesthood, beginning on a major scale with the first regular ordinations of American priests in 1976, and then the ordination of women bishops, beginning with Barbara Harris in Massachusetts in 1989, has tested the unity of the Anglican Communion severely. The Lambeth Conference of 1988 called for the Archbishop of Canterbury to set up a Commission which would examine the situation and make recommendations in the light of this deep threat to unity. The result was the Eames Commission, which produced three reports, using *koinonia* as a central theological theme.[9] The framework is thus the same as that of ARCIC, here applied to

---

[5] *Church as Communion* (London: CTS/ACC, 1991).
[6] *Ibid.*, para. 43.
[7] *Life in Christ: Morals, Communion and the Church* (London: Church House Publishing/ CTS, 1994).
[8] The understanding and practice of authority within the Anglican Communion is well described by 'The Virginia Report' of the Inter-Anglican Theological and Doctrinal Commission (J. M. Rosenthal and N. Currie eds., *Being Anglican in the Third Millennium*, Harrisburg: Morehouse, 1996, pp. 223–85), which was 'welcomed' at the Lambeth Conference 1998. In a series of affirmative resolutions, the Conference requested a decade of study on 'whether effective communion, at all levels, does not require appropriate instruments, with due safeguards, not only for legislation, but also for oversight' as well as on the issue of 'a universal ministry in the service of Christian unity' (Resolution III.8). This was a clear signal of an interest in stronger structures to sustain communion within Anglicanism, and more widely.
[9] Collected in *Women in the Anglican Episcopate* (Toronto: Anglican Book Centre, 1998).

the maintenance of unity *within* the Anglican Communion rather than the building of unity where eucharistic communion has been broken and parallel juridical structures have grown up. The Eames Commission argued strongly that the decision to ordain women was a necessity for mission, and that care has now to be taken not to set up within the one Church parallel jurisdictions, one for those who accept the ordained ministry of women and one for those who do not, for to undermine the authority of the one diocesan bishop would amount to 'institutional schism'.[10] They cite Cyprian to the effect that:

In the event of disagreement no compulsion should be brought upon the dissident bishop or bishops. The Church, while still preserving unity, will be obliged to live with the fact of disagreement.[11]

The Commission argues that the ordination of women can only be 'provisional' until there is a wider process of reception in the Church. They do not suggest how wide that process of reception should be, but the painful ecumenical issue is clearly the extent to which it can include the Roman Catholic and the Orthodox Churches, which remain strongly opposed to the ordination of women, or, conversely, and almost inconceivably, whether the Anglican Communion could reverse the flow of the tide towards priestly and episcopal ordination of women and receive the current teaching of those sister churches that are opposed.

---

[10] The Eames Commission does not discuss in detail the appointment of Episcopal Visitors to provide alternative episcopal oversight for parishes that do not accept the ministry of ordained women. Such proposals have been implemented in the Church of England and the Church of Wales. For some critics, the appointment of Provincial Episcopal Visitors ('flying bishops') amounts to nothing less than 'institutional schism'. Defenders of the practice point out that PEVs exercise their ministry at the invitation of and on the authority of the diocesan bishop, and that they remain in communion with all the other bishops. Opponents argue that this is not adequate to the unity of the church, which requires that all members of the diocese, lay and ordained, be fully in communion with each other and with their one diocesan bishop.

[11] *Women in the Anglican Episcopate*, p. 36. A similar attribution to Cyprian of generosity *within communion* comes from E. W. Benson, who quotes Augustine's teaching, 'that Christian men must be able to differ in opinions without forfeiting or withholding from each other the rights of intercommunion', specifically attributing both the words and the thought to Cyprian, in *Cyprian, his Life, his Times, his Work* (London: Macmillan, 1897), p. 533. In the quote from the Eames Commission Report, 'while preserving unity' must then be taken to mean 'while preserving communion'.

The issue has been sharpened by statements from Rome which made it clear that in current official Roman Catholic understanding the issue of the ordination of women to priesthood and episcopate is not a matter of church discipline, which could be changed by church authorities, but of 'the deposit of faith', which the magisterium does not see itself as at liberty to change.[12] For those who look at the question in this light, there can be no question here of 'living with the fact of disagreement', or of 'legitimate diversity'. To grant that would be to undermine *koinonia* in truth, which is the basis for sharing at the eucharist. The Eames Commission writes on the presupposition that a significant degree of communion between those who differ remains intact. Where unity (of which the sign and sacrament is sharing in the eucharist) is strained but unbroken, the maintenance of *koinonia* must require 'charity' and 'patience' in the process of reception. To those who do not accept that this is a matter on which there can be 'legitimate diversity' within the Church, *koinonia* between those of opposite views can only be maintained at a reduced or 'impaired' level. The reconciling breakthrough is to concede that since communion is many-faceted it can at some level survive deep disagreements of principle. The Lambeth Conference of 1988 had spoken of provinces of the Anglican Communion 'maintaining the highest possible degree of communion with the Provinces that differ'.[13] The Eames Commission developed this by applying the principle of Cyprian, '*salvo jure communionis diversa sentire*' ('provided the law of communion is respected, diversity of opinion (is permitted)').[14] This brings into sharp focus a further principle: the '*ius communionis*' ('law of communion'). Whatever the issue, to press ahead without sufficient consensus would, in Cyprian's terms, amount to a breach of 'the law of communion'. The Eames Commission stressed the 'law of communion', that is to

---

[12] *Ordinatio Sacerdotalis*, *Origins* 24:4 (9 June 1994), 50–2; Congregation for the Doctrine of the Faith, 'Reply to the *dubium* concerning the teaching contained in the Apostolic Letter *Ordinatio Sacerdotalis*', *L'Osservatore Romano*, 22 November 1995; *The Tablet*, 25 November 1995.

[13] Resolution 1. See *The Truth Shall Make You Free*, The Lambeth Conference 1988 (London: Church House Publishing, 1988), p. 201.

[14] Benson, *Cyprian*, p. 533.

say the need to accept the widest diversity of views possible within full communion; it also stressed the imperative of mission, which is a key motivating factor for adventurous change in the life of the Church; and the importance of reception, which is the means by which the Church comes to accept or to reject such change. The Commission appealed explicitly to the theology of *koinonia* to hold together all three principles in the life of the Church, in a situation where they (and the Christians who appeal to them) come into conflict. How the Church changes, with integrity and without schism, is a major question for the ecclesiology of communion.

The theology of *koinonia* has also been vital for the drawing together of Anglican and Protestant Churches. In 1988, representatives of the Church of England and the Evangelical Churches in Germany agreed 'The Meissen Common Statement', including 'The Meissen Declaration', which was formally accepted by both communions in 1991. This agreement, which represents a significant step on the way to 'full communion',[15] draws explicitly on a common understanding of the Church as *koinonia*:

Underlying many of the New Testament descriptions of the Church, such as 'the people of God', 'the body of Christ', 'the bride', 'the temple of the Spirit', is the reality of a *koinonia* – a communion – which is a sharing in the life of the Holy Trinity and therein with our fellow-members of the Church. The Church is the community (*koinonia*) of those reconciled with God and with one another.[16]

A key paragraph acknowledges the differences over understandings of episcopal ministry which account for the limited nature of the sharing in the eucharist and in ordinations.[17] At

---

[15] The statement provides for continued mutual participation in the eucharist 'in a way which advances beyond mutual eucharistic hospitality but which falls short of the full interchangeability of ministers' and provides for mutual participation by bishops in ordinations with a *caveat* relating to the unresolved problem of 'historic succession': it is made clear that, 'For the Church of England . . . a participating bishop or priest may not by the laying on of hands or otherwise do any act which is a sign of the conferring of Holy Orders. He may take part in a separate laying on of hands as an act of blessing.' ('The Meissen Common Statement', para. 17 in *The Meissen Agreement*, pp. 22–4).

[16] *Ibid.*, paras. 4–5.

[17] *Ibid.*, para. 16. The Lutheran, Reformed, and United Churches, 'though being

this point the statement breaks through the barrier: it provides for diversity. It recognises that 'personal and collegial oversight (*episkope*) is embodied and exercised in our churches in a variety of forms, episcopal and non-episcopal, as a visible sign of the Church's unity and continuity in apostolic life, mission and ministry'. The Church of England and the Evangelical Churches of Germany here take the line of Cyprian, affirming on the basis of their common understanding of the nature of the Church and what they describe as 'communion already shared' that their differences are not sufficient to hold them back from further steps towards unity. Joint acceptance that oversight as a function in the service of the communion of the Church may *not necessarily* be exercised by a bishop in historic succession has been crucial in opening the way to a deepened common life between the participant churches both here and in other significant ecumenical agreements. We shall trace a little more of the theological background to this crucial ecumenical move when we consider the groundbreaking report of the Faith and Order Commission of the World Council of Churches, *Baptism, Eucharist and Ministry*, below.

Two further significant agreements have taken place between Anglican and Lutheran churches. The 'Concordat' proposed in 1991 between the Evangelical Lutheran Church in America and the Episcopal Church moved swiftly over the agreement in doctrine that had already been affirmed to set out the steps to 'full communion' – to mutual sharing in ordinations, at the eucharist, and in a deepened common life.[18] The 'Porvoo Common Statement' of 1992 sets out in

increasingly prepared to appreciate episcopal succession "as a sign of the apostolicity of the life of the whole Church"' do not make this particular form of *episcope* a condition for 'full visible unity', whereas the Anglican understanding of 'full visible unity' includes 'the historic episcopate'.

[18] James E. Griffiss and Daniel F. Martensen, *A Commentary on 'Concordat of Agreement'* (Minneapolis: Augsburg; Cincinnati: Forward Movement Publications, 1994). The proposal to enter into 'full communion' with the Episcopal Church failed by the narrowest of margins to win the requisite two-thirds support at the assembly of the Evangelical Lutheran Church in America in August 1997. A subsequent vote overwhelmingly endorsed the reintroduction of the proposal in 1999 (see 'Called to Common Mission, A Lutheran Proposal for a revision of the *Concordat of Agreement*', Chicago: Evangelical Lutheran Church in America, 1998).

detail the agreement in faith between the British and Irish Anglican Churches and the Nordic and Baltic Lutheran Churches, some of which (like the Church of Sweden) have maintained episcopal succession from before the Reformation and some of which (like the Church of Norway) experienced a break.[19] In both cases the underlying theological agreement is rooted in a common understanding of communion. The Porvoo Statement draws attention to the broad ecumenical convergence to which Orthodox, Roman Catholic, and Protestant churches have contributed, expressing the relevance of this in the following terms:

Of particular importance is the understanding of the mystery of the Church as the body of Christ, as the pilgrim people of God, as fellowship (*koinonia*), and also as participation through witness and service in God's mission to the world. This provides a proper setting for a new approach to the question of the ordained ministry and of oversight (*episcope*).[20]

Like 'The Meissen Common Statement', 'The Porvoo Common Statement' moves from agreement on the nature of the Church as *koinonia*, through a detailed account of 'what we agree in faith', to a plan of action. The chapter on 'The Nature and Unity of the Church' is detailed and significant. It speaks of 'the maintenance of unity and the sustaining of diversity', which are 'ultimately grounded in the communion of God the Holy Trinity', being served by 'bonds of communion':

Communion with God and with fellow believers is manifested in one baptism in response to the apostolic preaching; in the common confession of the apostolic faith; in the united celebration of the eucharist which builds up the one body of Christ; and in a single ministry set apart by prayer and the laying on of hands. This unity is also manifested as a communion in love, implying that Christians are bound to one another in a committed relationship with mutual responsibilities, common spiritual goods and the obligation to share temporal resources.[21]

Anglicans and Lutherans have long been close in their

---

[19] *Together in Mission and Ministry* (London: Church House Publishing, 1993). For discussion of episcopal succession in Norway see pp. 94, 158–9.
[20] *Ibid.*, p. 7; *The Porvoo Common Statement*, para. 5.
[21] *Ibid.*, p. 14; *The Porvoo Common Statement*, para. 14.

understanding of the visible Church.[22] The breakthrough has been to set this understanding of the Church as constituted by word and sacrament in the context of an ecumenical theology of communion. The Porvoo Statement affirms that 'the communion of the Church is constituted by the proclamation of the word and the celebration of the sacraments, served by the ordained ministry' and it speaks of the unity of the Church as 'a joyful communion with the Father and his Son Jesus Christ, as well as communion among its members'.[23] Commenting on the proposed Episcopal–Lutheran Concordat, Daniel F. Martensen writes that, 'Serious consideration of the Concordat invites us Lutherans to explore anew the Church as *koinonia*.'[24]

'The Meissen Agreement', the 'Concordat of Agreement', and 'The Porvoo Agreement', have all been made possible by a shift in understanding of the relation between apostolicity and episcopacy, setting both in the context of a wider understanding of communion within the Church. A supportive paper by the Bishops of the Church of England stresses that apostolic succession is the succession in truth of the whole community, not just of individual bishops, arguing strongly for this as the ecclesiological context within which (in a quotation from an Orthodox–Roman Catholic statement of 1982) 'the episcopate appears as a central point of the apostolic succession'.[25] The statement is carefully nuanced: it leaves space for those who would identify other 'key points' in the apostolic succession (such as fidelity to Scripture, preaching of the Gospel, or engagement in mission) and for those times when succession in episcopacy has been broken. The stress on the whole Church as the bearer of apostolicity, and so of apostolic ministry (not *necessarily* in unbroken historic succes-

---

22   For Anglicans, it is 'a congregation of faithful men, in the which the pure Word of God is preached, and the Sacraments be duly ministered according to Christ's ordinance' (*The Book of Common Prayer*, 1662, Article of Religion XIX). For Lutherans, it is 'The assembly of all believers among whom the Gospel is preached in its purity and the holy sacraments are administered according to the Gospel' (Article VII of the Augsburg Confession, T. G. Tappert ed., *The Book of Concord*, Philadelphia: Fortress Press, 1959, p. 32).

23   *The Porvoo Common Statement*, paras. 17, 21.

24   *A Commentary on 'Concordat of Agreement'*, p. 16.

25   *Apostolicity and Succession*, House of Bishops' Occasional Paper (London: General Synod of the Church of England, 1994), p. 23.

sion) as a dimension of *koinonia*, is now leading to a significant shift in experience for many communities of Christians. It is fundamental to the report of the Anglican–Methodist International Commission, entitled *Sharing in The Apostolic Communion*.[26] Their practical proposals for 'growth into fuller communion', including (in an echo of 'The Meissen Common Statement') 'eucharistic communion going beyond mutual hospitality' and (by the participation of a bishop of 'the historical episcopate' in all future ministerial ordinations) mutual recognition of ministries, would not have been possible without a new consensus as to how the churches could understand their nature and mission in the light of a theology of *koinonia*.

In the bilateral and internal dialogues with which Anglicans have been involved there has been significant advance in two phases. The first phase has seen an acceptance of an integrated theology of communion which has brought new and inclusive insights into the catholicity of the Church. The second phase has seen a subtle shift to an emphasis on apostolicity as the diachronic dimension of communion. The combination of the two has for Anglicans facilitated growth and diversification in communion, a touch of spring in the search for 'visible unity'.

ROMAN CATHOLICS AND COMMUNION

We turn now to some of the main Roman Catholic sources and dialogues. For Roman Catholics, the Second Vatican Council, which met from 1962 to 1965, has been the dominating event in the twentieth-century life of the Church. In retrospect, it is clear that theologians like de Lubac, Congar, and Hamer,[27] digging deep in patristic sources of the East and the West, prepared the way for a complete renewal of the Church's self-understanding. In key Council documents of Vatican 2, like

---

[26] London: Anglican Consultative Council; Lake Junaluska, NC: World Methodist Council, 1996.

[27] Amongst the most important texts in English are: Y. Congar, *Divided Christendom* (London: Geoffrey Bless, 1939), *Dialogue Between Christians* (London: Geoffrey Chapman, 1966), especially pp. 208–13, *Diversity and Communion* (London: SCM, 1984); H. de Lubac, *Catholicism* (London: Burns and Oates, 1962); J. Hamer, *The Church is a Communion* (London: Geoffrey Chapman, 1964).

Lumen Gentium (the Dogmatic Constitution on the Church), *Unitatis Redintegratio* (the Decree on Ecumenism), and *Gaudium et Spes* (the Pastoral Constitution on the Church in the Modern World), the Church is presented in an inclusive sense as 'universal sacrament of salvation', 'people of God', and 'a communion of life, love and truth'.[28] More than that, the Church is seen as yearning to address itself to the deepest needs of 'the whole human family'.[29] It was, however, also possible to argue from the Council documents, especially from *Lumen Gentium*, for an ecclesiology that stressed hierarchy and jurisdiction in the service of the communion of the Roman Catholic Church.[30] The tension between these two ecclesiological approaches remains unresolved throughout the Documents of Vatican 2 and subsequent debates.[31]

When the Latin American Bishops met in conference at Medellin in 1968, they handled the ecclesiology of communion with increasing confidence, taking it in new directions of sharp relevance to their polarised and politicised situation. They affirmed the importance for every Christian of belonging to a 'base community', a group where there could be 'personal

---

[28] For detailed study of *Lumen Gentium*, which I have not entered into here, G. Philips, *L'Église et son mystère au IIe Concile du Vatican, histoire, texte et commentaire de la constitution* Lumen Gentium (2 vols., Paris: Desclée) is fundamental. W. Kasper discusses 'The Church as Communion: Reflections on the Guiding Ecclesiological Idea of the Second Vatican Council' in *Theology and Church* (London: SCM, 1989), pp. 148–65. Jean Rigal, in *L'Ecclésiologie de Communion* (Paris: Cerf, 1997), pp. 59–81 discusses communion as 'the central and fundamental concept of Vatican 2'.

[29] *LG* 1, 8ff, 48; *UR* 3, 13; *GS* 2, 42, 45.

[30] *LG* 18, 22, 27; 'Preliminary Explanatory Note' (*Nota praevia explicativa*), where 'hierarchical communion' is discussed. On the last, see J. Grootaers ed., *Primauté et Collegialité, le Dossier de G. Philips sur le* Nota Praevia (Leuven: Leuven University Press, 1986).

[31] See A. Acerbi, *Due Ecclesiologie, Ecclesiologia Giuridica ed Ecclesiologia di Comunione nella* '*Lumen Gentium*' (Bologna: Edizioni Dehoniane, 1975). J.-M. R. Tillard commends Acerbi's analysis, arguing that though the 'ecclesiology of *communion*' prevailed at the Council, 'many layers of the other ecclesiology remained in place', and that there was 'a distinct jarring produced by the clumsy lack of co-ordination between the ecclesiologies' ('The Church of God is a Communion', *One in Christ* 17 (1981), 117). A particular focus of discussion has been the new *Code of Canon Law* (London: Collins, 1983). See the analysis by E. Corecco 'Aspects of the Reception of Vatican II in the Code of Canon Law' in G. Alberigo, J.-P. Jossua and J. A. Komonchak eds., *The Reception of Vatican II* (Washington, DC: Catholic University of America Press, 1987), especially pp. 273–88, 293–6. This is a confused debate as protagonists on both sides claim, with justification, to be working within 'an ecclesiology of communion'.

fraternal contact among its members'.[32] Ten years later, at
Puebla (1978), the same conference of bishops used communion
and participation as the central theme for an extended study of
evangelisation. This was summed up in a working document
produced before the meeting:

We speak of *communion* with God, in faith, in prayer, in sacramental
life, . . . a communion that is the root and driving force of evangelisation . . . We speak of *participation* in the Church, in all its levels and
tasks; a participation in society and its different sectors; in the nations
of Latin America; . . . in an attitude of continuous dialogue.[33]

Evangelisation is presented as 'a summons to participate in
the communion of the Trinity', and the bishops stress that 'the
communion that is to be fashioned between human beings must
manifest itself in every aspect of life, including economic, social,
and political life'.[34] 'Communion' is used throughout the
Puebla text to mean at one and the same time participation in
the life of the Trinity, participation in the Church, and participation in the political process where Christians work in solidarity with the poor for social justice.[35]

The Final Report of the Extraordinary Synod of Bishops,
which met seven years later in Rome in 1985, was a less radical
but still more authoritative document, which looked backwards
twenty years to the Second Vatican Council and forwards
towards further progress in implementing the decisions of the
Council within the life of the Church. Unresolved tensions over
ecclesiology were evident in one of the questions put to the
episcopal conferences beforehand:

Has the double aspect of the mystery of the Church been rightly
understood and translated into real life – that is, the Church as
communion, and the Church as hierarchical institution?[36]

---

[32] Second General Conference of Latin American Bishops, *The Church in the Present-Day
Transformation of Latin America in the light of the Council, Conclusions* (second edition,
Washington DC: USCC, 1973), p. 201.

[33] Third General Conference of Latin American Bishops, *Puebla, Evangelisation at Present
and in the Future of Latin America, Conclusions* (Slough: St Paul Publications, 1980), p. 28.

[34] *Ibid.*, paras. 218, 212, 215.

[35] See Kilian McDonnell, 'Vatican 2, Puebla, Synod: *Koinonia*/Communion as an
Integral Ecclesiology', *Journal of Ecumenical Studies* 25:3 (Summer 1988), 414.

[36] P. Hebblethwaite, *Synod Extraordinary* (London: Darton, Longman and Todd, 1986),
p. 31.

The point was further emphasised in a key speech by Cardinal Danneels, which, because of his role as *Relator* with responsibility for presenting the preliminary reports to the Synod and co-ordinating drafting for the Final Report, was itself a first draft of the Synod Report. Danneels pinpointed ecclesiology as 'the heart of the crisis', and criticised 'a tendency to oppose the Church as institution to the Church as mystery, the people of God vs. the hierarchy'. Problems that needed to be resolved included 'the relationship between the universal Church and the particular churches; the promotion of collegiality; the theological status of the episcopal conferences; . . . relations with the Roman Curia'.[37] In each of these cases, a carefully articulated 'ecclesiology of communion' offered a way through. In its report, the Synod reaffirmed that the hierarchical and institutional dimensions of the Church's life, which had been so strongly and defensively stressed through the nineteenth century, had indeed been set in a new (or, strictly, renewed) context by the Council:

We are all called, through faith and the sacraments, to live, fully, communion with God. Inasmuch as she is communion with the living God, Father, Son and Holy Spirit, the Church is, in Christ, the 'mystery' of the love of God present in the history of mankind . . . The structures and relations within the Church must express this communion.[38]

The Report of the Synod is a robust restatement of the ecclesiology of communion, a restatement, however, that resolves none of the tensions between differing interpretations of the meaning and requirements of communion for the life of the Church. For one influential commentator the appeal to 'communion' was to be related not to the facing of hard questions, but to their avoidance: 'In the Final Report, invocations of "communion" and "collegial spirit" have triumphed over *frank admission of serious problems of structure and relations in the Church today.*'[39]

---

[37] *Ibid.*, p. 114.
[38] 'The Message of the Synod to the People of God', *Synod Report* (London: CTS, 1986).
[39] J. Komonchak, 'The Theological Debate' in G. Alberigo and J. Provost eds., 'Synod 1985 – An Evaluation', *Concilium*, December 1986, p. 59 (original emphasis). For a

One of the key recommendations of the Synod was to call for a catechism in which 'the manner of doctrinal presentation should be biblical and liturgical'. The Catechism of the Catholic Church, written in response to this request, was published in 1992. It follows the pattern of the Catechism of the Council of Trent and the catechisms of Reformers such as Luther and Calvin, structuring its teaching around the creeds, the sacraments, the commandments, and the Lord's Prayer. These 'pillars' give structure and clarity to what the Pope calls in his introduction 'a sure norm for teaching the faith and thus a valid and legitimate instrument for ecclesial communion'.[40] Though it resolves none of the tensions in interpreting and applying a 'theology of communion' within the Catholic Church, the Catechism marks a further significant step in demonstrating the biblical, patristic, and liturgical formation of a theology of communion, which is intended to shape the Christian practice of the whole Church. It affirms clearly that, 'Human beings are made to live in communion with God';[41] and that the Church exists to promote and sustain this communion. We do not have to follow in detail the Catechism's extended account of Church life and teaching in the service of 'communion with God'. As a complement to themes we have already discussed, we should, however, note the integral link with the tradition of Catholic social ethics. The important section on 'The Human Community' focuses Catholic social and ethical teaching on the human need for community: 'The human person needs to live in society. It is not a matter of adding an optional extra, but a need of human nature.'[42] Human beings need to be converted to social living, to 'the common good', to an acceptance of the exercise of authority, and so, ultimately, to the recognition of divine authority. Within the Church such a conversion is presupposed by a theology of communion (which is why the *structural articulation of divine authority* is a major issue within a

more positive assessment, see the article 'Final Report of the Last Synod' by J.-M. R. Tillard (pp. 64–77).

[40] *Catechism of the Catholic Church* (London: Geoffrey Chapman, 1994), Apostolic Constitution '*Fidei Depositum*', p. 5.

[41] *Catechism*, para. 45 (translation amended).

[42] *Ibid.*, para. 1879 (translation amended).

theology of communion). The Catechism, which is presented as 'an organic unity', has at its centre communion with God and community among human beings. The vision is one of unity and of harmony. On specific matters, however, like that of the relation between the Pope and the rest of the college of bishops, tensions remain.[43] What has been established by the Synod and the Catechism, once more, is that within an agreed framework of the ecclesiology of communion there has to be room for a variety of interpretations – which are bound at times to come into conflict. The Catechism teaches a participatory eccle-siology of communion, compatible with both the understanding of the Church as a 'communion of communions' and the hierarchical and centralist interpretations of ecclesial commu-nion which have often characterised Vatican policy during the pontificate of John Paul II.

Another form of the same debate takes place between those who stress the priority of the realisation of the Church of God in the local community and those who stress the priority of 'the universal Church' over particular, local churches. Behind such disagreement lies the difference between platonist and aristotelian ecclesiologies, the first deriving particulars from universals, the second universals from particulars (a difference that should be illuminated by the following two chapters). A Church which understands itself to be a 'communion of communions' will live in the tension, and at times the conflict, between the two. The problems of Anglicans, struggling with the issue of a lack of power at 'the centre', are the mirror image of the problems of Roman Catholics, struggling to recover from the exaggerations of nineteenth-century ultra-montanism. The 'Letter from the Congregation of the Doc-trine of the Faith to the Bishops of the Catholic Church on Some Aspects of the Church Understood as Communion', published, like the Catechism, in 1992, takes a platonist position when it affirms that the universal Church is 'not the result of the communion of the churches, but, in its essential mystery, . . . a reality *ontologically and temporally* prior to every

---

[43] See J.-M. R. Tillard in M. J. Walsh ed., *Commentary on the Catechism of the Catholic Church* (London: Geoffrey Chapman, 1994), p. 192.

individual particular church'.[44] This position, espoused by
Cardinal Ratzinger,[45] has been strongly criticised by J.-M. R.
Tillard[46] and J. D. Zizioulas,[47] who see in it a distortion of the
patristic theology of ecclesial communion and the danger that
the authority of the local church of Rome, or, still worse, the
Vatican, will be identified with the supposed authority of an
'ontologically prior' universal Church. Hence the importance
in an ecclesiology of the Church as a 'communion of communions' of the *reception* of authoritative teaching as the ultimate
test of its fidelity to apostolic truth. The debate about the
relation between the universal Church, the local churches,
and the exercise of authority within an ecclesiology of communion exposes some vital questions of ecclesial identity.[48] It is
not surprising, though it may certainly be dangerous, that a
magisterial organ (the Vatican, the Congregation for the
Doctrine of the Faith), given executive responsibility, and the
need at times to speak and act for 'the Church', should argue
theologically in a way that favours strong central authority,
nor is it surprising that those who fear the practical and

---

[44] Congregation for the Doctrine of the Faith, 'Letter to the Bishops of the Catholic
Church on Some Aspects of the Church Understood as Communion', 1992, para. 9.

[45] See Cardinal Joseph Ratzinger, 'Anglican–Catholic Dialogue: Its Problems and
Hopes', *Insight* 1:3 (March 1983), 5.

[46] On this precise issue Tillard remains conspicuously silent in his major study *L'Église
locale* (Paris: Cerf, 1995).

[47] John D. Zizioulas, *Being as Communion* (London: Darton, Longman and Todd, 1985),
p. 258: 'If the locality of the Church is not to be absorbed and in fact negated by the
element of universality, the utmost care must be taken so that the structures of
ministries which are aimed at facilitating communion among the local Churches do
not become a superstructure over the local Church . . . All structures aiming at
facilitating the universality of the Church create a *network of communion of Churches, not
a new form of Church.*'

[48] See the carefully crafted paragraphs in *The Church: Local and Universal*, one of two
studies commissioned and received by the Joint Working Group between the Roman
Catholic Church and the World Council of Churches, Faith and Order Paper 150
(Geneva: WCC, 1990), section II.3 (21–4), where it is argued that an eschatological
and pneumatological (one might say, properly Trinitarian) approach to this question
will give exclusive priority neither to the local nor to the universal Church but will
suggest a 'simultaneity of both'. A similar line is taken in the Report of the Third
Phase of the Lutheran/Roman Catholic International Dialogue, 'Church and
Justification: Understanding the Church in the Light of the Doctrine of Justification',
PCPCU Information Service 86 (1994), 148, para. 102: 'We may speak of a reciprocity in
the relations between the local and the universal church.'

ecumenical implications of such an approach should resist this line of argument equally strongly.

The generalised use of a theology of communion or *koinonia* as a framework for mutual rapprochement has been highly significant in a number of bilateral dialogues involving the Roman Catholic Church. Here we take the example of two major dialogues: with the Lutherans and the Orthodox.[49] Some, but not all, of the issues that are raised begin to have a familiar ring.

A third phase of the Roman Catholic–Lutheran international dialogue,[50] begun in 1986, led to the publication of the highly significant report, 'Church and Justification: Understanding the Church in the Light of the Doctrine of Justification'.[51] The Church is discussed as 'God's Pilgrim People', as 'Body of Christ', and as 'Temple of the Holy Spirit' but the central conception of the Church, to which a major section of the report is devoted, is as '*Koinonia/Communio* founded in the Trinity'.[52] This section opens by bringing all these notions together:

Participation in the communion of the three divine persons is constitutive for the being and the life of the Church as expressed in the three New Testament descriptions of it as 'people of God', 'body of Christ' and 'temple of the Holy Spirit'.

[49] Other Roman Catholic bilateral dialogues which have set out a communion ecclesiology include that with the Pentecostals ('Perspectives on Koinonia', *PCPCU Information Service* 75 (1990), 179–91) and that with the Disciples of Christ ('The Church as Communion in Christ', *PCPCU Information Service* 84 (1993), 162–9).

[50] A Lutheran–Roman Catholic Study Commission first met in 1967 and in 1972 produced a very general report on 'The Gospel and the Church', which called for 'occasional acts of intercommunion', a recommendation from which four of the Roman Catholic participants dissented. Other reports followed: on the eucharist (1978), for the anniversary of the Augsburg Confession (1980), on ministry (1981), and for the anniversary of the birth of Martin Luther (1983). 'Ways to Community' (1980) described both the ecumenical goal and the steps leading up to it in terms of community (*Gemeinschaft*). 'Facing Unity' (1985) contained the highly significant proposal that bishops of the two traditions could share a collegial exercise of oversight, based on a mutual recognition 'that in the other tradition the Church of Jesus Christ is actualized'. Through joint ordinations a common ministry would be created. Though this proposal has not been taken up in Lutheran–Roman Catholic practice, it has borne fruit in the proposed 'Concordat' between the American Episcopal Church and the Evangelical Lutheran Church in America.

[51] *PCPCU Information Service* 86 (1994), 128–81.

[52] *Ibid.*, Section 3.3, 142–4.

The *koinonia/communio* of the Church is expressed through the preaching of the Gospel, through baptism and the celebration of the Lord's Supper. This *koinonia/communio* is an anticipatory reality for it is only on the last day that 'the universal people of God will first gather in its entirety'. So far there is complete agreement between the Roman Catholic and Lutheran positions. Differences emerge in understandings of the local church, and its relation to all the other local churches with which it is in communion. Since 1990, according to its constitution, the Lutheran World Federation has described itself as 'a communion of churches which confess the triune God, agree in the proclamation of the Word of God and are united in pulpit and altar fellowship'. For Roman Catholics, such a definition would not say enough about the present identity of the churches since it omits the 'reciprocal' relation between the local churches and 'the universal Church' for which communion with the local bishop, holding his office in historic succession, and with the Bishop of Rome, is constitutive. The report stresses that this disagreement does not impugn an agreed understanding of the centrality of justification to the identity of the Church. The ultimate measure and criterion of the life of the Church is the Gospel itself – and the Gospel is an invitation into communion. For both Lutherans and Roman Catholics the Church is the *communio sanctorum*, 'the community of those united in faith through the Holy Spirit, the community of "those who are sanctified in Christ Jesus [and] called to be saints"'.[53] What impedes eucharistic sharing is a significant divergence of understanding about the relation between the local church and 'the universal Church', and about the exercise of authority to ensure the continued identity of the Church in unity and truth.

The report concludes by setting out Lutheran and Catholic views on unresolved issues, including that of 'The Church and the Kingdom of God'. In setting the ecclesiology of communion alongside an ecclesiology of the Church as sign and instrument of the coming of the kingdom of God, the Lutheran rejection of the Church as a 'Platonic republic' is specifically noted.[54] The

[53] *Ibid.*, p. 178, para. 293.
[54] *Ibid.*, p. 179, para. 301 (*'civitas platonica'*; cf. 'Apology of the Augsburg Confession

important point being made here is that it is not the structures of the Church as instruments of communion but the *quality* of communion they support that is a sign of the coming of the kingdom of God. The disagreement is over the necessity of structures such as episcopacy and the jurisdiction of the Bishop of Rome for the promotion and safeguarding of this communion in the truth of the Gospel. Even if such disagreement is not in and of itself a sufficient cause for continuing breach in communion, the problem – which once more springs from the general difference between a platonist and an aristotelian approach to ecclesiology – is that it interlocks with a range of other issues. Given a breach in communion, it is hard to discern at what point there would be sufficient mutual understanding of the place and function of specific Church structures for eucharistic communion to be restored.

The dialogue with the Orthodox has, like that with the Lutherans, made explicit a high level of agreement about life in communion within the local church. The first of the agreed statements, published in 1982 and significantly entitled 'The Mystery of the Church and of the Eucharist in the Light of the Mystery of the Holy Trinity' is a concise statement of eucharistic ecclesiology. The Church is described as 'the sacrament of the Trinitarian *koinonia*, the "dwelling of God with men" '.[55] Its 'mystery' is the mystery of the divine life, its being the being of the New Jerusalem:

There is a 'Jerusalem from on high' which 'comes down from God', a communion which is at the foundation of the community itself. The Church comes into being by a free gift, that of the new creation.

Such newness is seen when the whole community is gathered for the eucharist: this is 'the real newness of the Trinitarian *koinonia* communicated to men in the Church through the eucharist'. The community is one in faith: there is a united

---

vii.20, T. G. Tappert ed., *The Book of Concord*, p. 171). There is an irony in the use of this term to describe the visible Church, since 'Plato's republic' was his vision for an ideal society, one he thought never to have existed historically. Plato himself does not discuss the consequences of any attempt to equate an actual, historical society with his ideal republic, or to realise his ideal republic on earth.

[55] See P. McPartlan ed., *One in 2000?* (Slough: St Pauls, 1995), pp. 41ff.

response to the proclamation of the Word, the community together recites the creed, which is a summary of the apostolic tradition to which the bishop bears witness 'in virtue of his succession'. Within the assembly the bishop has a special place 'at the service of the initiatives of the Spirit so that nothing may prevent them from contributing to building up *koinonia*'. The local church must be seen in the context of that wider communion which it realises in one place:

Like the community of the apostles gathered around Christ, each eucharistic assembly is truly the holy Church of God, the Body of Christ, in communion with the first community of the disciples and with all those [communities] throughout the world which celebrate and have celebrated the memorial of the Lord. It is also in communion with the assembly of the saints in heaven, which each celebration evokes.

The integral link between the eucharist, orthodoxy, episcopal ministry, and communion, both within the local church and between the churches, is plain, but the eucharistic blockage remains: Roman Catholics and Orthodox have not shared the eucharist for almost a thousand years. At Valamo in 1988, their common understanding was well put:

Just as the apostles gathered together the first communities by proclaiming Christ, celebrating the Eucharist and leading the baptised towards growing communion with Christ and with each other, so the bishop, established by the same Spirit, continues to preach the same Gospel, to preside at the same Eucharist and to serve the unity and sanctification of the same community. He is thus the icon of Christ the servant among his brethren.[56]

The problem with this apparently calm and ideal view is a serious disjunction between eschatology and history: the history of the relation of eucharistic communities is all too often one of tension, breakdown in relations and conflict. We know too well that from the earliest days of the Church there have been bitter disagreements over who can be included within the eucharistic community and where the authentic eucharistic community may be located. Lying behind such conflicts are not only issues of politics, but also those of translation: questions of hermeneu-

[56] *Ibid.*, p. 79.

tics. For the Church, in the flux of history, and in diverse cultures, simply to repeat the same words and the same actions is not at all necessarily to present 'the same Gospel', 'the same Eucharist' and to be 'the same community'. Theologically, assurance of sameness (of identity) is a matter of the Spirit *and* of ecclesial structures, of experimentation and change as much as of faithful repetition. Ultimately, the question of identity within tradition is a question of *judgement*: we return again by another route to the question of authority and the structures of the Church. Issues of primacy, magisterium, and communion have not yet been addressed in Roman Catholic–Orthodox dialogue. The level of agreement about the actual life of the local church is encouraging, but does not necessarily mean there will yet be convergence between institutions on the ground. Indeed, the need amongst competing human groups to find means of establishing boundaries and of differentiating themselves from one another should never be underestimated as a factor in the sustaining of mutual exclusions. This is where the theology of communion offers real hope: it invites the *building* of communion step-by-step towards the point where the most difficult questions of institutionally embedded disunity may be addressed in a context of trust.

Although the Roman Catholic contribution has been made mainly through bi-lateral dialogues, it has also been made through the work of the Faith and Order Commission of the World Council of Churches and the Joint Working Group between the Roman Catholic Church and the World Council of Churches, whose study document 'The Church: Local and Universal' offers a fine summary of the ecclesiology of *koinonia*.[57]

This document begins by asserting that a proper understanding of *koinonia* enables us to hold 'two dimensions of the Church – its locality and universality – not as separate entities but as two integrated dimensions of one reality'.[58] The theology of *koinonia* illuminates the role of the Church as 'a kind of sacrament or sign and instrument of intimate unity with God and of

---

[57] See note 48.   [58] *Ibid.*, 1.5 (5).

the unity of all humanity (*LG* 1)'. The document shows clearly how important the ecclesiology of communion has been for Roman Catholics in bilateral discussions with representatives of the Anglican, Methodist, Orthodox, and Reformed traditions, and also in the self-understanding of Roman Catholics, the Lutheran World Federation, and of Anglicans. The life of the local church is discussed first in this light. Then the universal Church is presented as ' the communion of all the local churches united in faith and worship throughout the world'. The document concludes with a consideration of 'the structure of communion':

Communion . . . refers to a dynamic, spiritual, objective reality which is embodied in ecclesial structures. The gift of communion from God is not an amorphous reality but an organic unity that requires a canonical form of expression. The purpose of such canonical structuring is to ensure that the local churches (and their members), in communion with each another, can live in harmony and fidelity to 'the faith which has been once and for all entrusted to the saints' (Jude 3).[59]

Though the structures of communion in the various Christian traditions vary, there is a real communion between the churches: 'The barriers of our divisions do not reach to heaven.'

The ecclesiology of communion has not yet brought about for Roman Catholic Christians a growth in shared eucharistic participation with Christians of other traditions. However, the widespread acceptance of a theology of communion, both within the Catholic Church and in other churches, to which this document bears witness, has transformed the experience of Roman Catholics in a variety of ways, from internal reforms such as the use of the vernacular in the liturgy and the growth of lay participation in the decision-making of the church, to ecumenical involvement[60] at every level except full participation in the World Council of Churches. The theological understanding may well be in place for new steps that will draw

---

[59] *Ibid.*, IV.1 (42).
[60] The 1993 Directory for Ecumenism (*Origins* 23, 29 July 1993, 130–60) gives detailed guidelines for Roman Catholic ecumenical involvement. The stated ecclesiological basis (11–17) is an outline of 'The Church as Communion'.

Roman Catholicism, despite setbacks and difficulties, still closer to other Christian traditions, which share so deeply with them a common understanding of the identity and mission of the Church of God. The Papal Encyclical of 1995 *Ut Unum Sint* adopts the approach of an ecclesiology of communion, and an openness about the role of the papacy and its place within such an ecclesiology. The appeal of the Pope, first to the Orthodox, and then to all the churches, has struck a chord in many places:

Could not the real but imperfect communion existing between us persuade church leaders and their theologians to engage with me in a patient and fraternal dialogue on this subject, a dialogue in which, leaving useless controversies behind, we could listen to one another, keeping before us only the will of Christ for his Church and allowing ourselves to be deeply moved by his plea 'that they may all be one . . . so that the world may believe'?[61]

This is a remarkable invitation to address what is now a key area of division between the churches: their articulation as a communion of churches and the place of the Bishop of Rome within that articulation. The basis of the invitation is the convergence of all the churches around an ecclesiology of communion. A positive response, showing that not only the churches in discussion with the Roman Catholic Church, but the Roman Catholic Church itself, are truly open to trans-formation, would be the next step on the journey to visible unity.

THE WORLD COUNCIL OF CHURCHES AND COMMUNION

Bilateral conversations such as those we have considered above have become a major and continuing feature of the ecumenical scene. The Report of the fifth Forum on Bilateral Conversations, held under the auspices of the World Council of Churches, has a theological analysis, which draws attention to the way in which 'the notion of *koinonia* is central in the understanding of the nature of the church in almost all dialogues'.[62] The Report of

---

[61] Encyclical Letter, *Ut Unum Sint* (Vatican Press: 1995), p. 107, para. 96.
[62] G. Gassmann ed., *Fifth Forum on Bilateral Conversations Report* (International Bilateral Dialogues 1965–91), Faith and Order Paper 156 (Geneva: WCC, 1991).

the sixth Forum lists thirty-three such dialogues.[63] Though the dialogues agree that there are a number of visible elements of *koinonia*, such as common confession of faith, baptism, eucharist, ordained ministry, sharing of goods, ecclesial structures, they do not agree on whether all these visible expressions of communion are necessary for the full, visible unity of the Church. They also disagree on the steps forward and the preconditions for eucharistic communion. Nevertheless, *koinonia* is seen as 'the fundamental understanding of the church emerging from the bilateral dialogues' and the hope is expressed that 'within this perspective . . . the outstanding differences are most likely to be resolved'. It is within this perspective also that the World Council of Churches has taken major steps forward in the field of multilateral dialogue.

The WCC has implemented several major, multilateral projects which have deepened the *koinonia* of the churches. The most significant was the process that produced the report *Baptism, Eucharist and Ministry*,[64] which was accepted at the meeting of the Faith and Order Commission in 1982. BEM has been translated into more than thirty languages, and is reckoned to be by far the most successful publication of the WCC.[65] By 1990, responses had been received from 186 churches and collated in a brief report, which concludes with a discussion of the underlying ecclesiological perspectives of the churches' responses. The suggestion is made that *koinonia* be pursued seriously in Faith and Order work towards a convergent vision on ecclesiology, though a caution is added that 'the notion of *koinonia* should not be regarded as the only possible approach'.[66] Nevertheless, the central concept remains 'an ecumenically oriented ecclesiology of *koinonia*', to be supplemented by complementary conceptions and images drawn from different bilateral dialogues, images such as the Church as the gift (*creatura*) of the Word of God, the Church as the mystery or sacrament of

---

[63] G. Gassmann ed., *Sixth Forum on Bilateral Conversations Report* (International Bilateral Dialogues 1992–4), Faith and Order Paper 168 (Geneva: WCC, 1995).

[64] *Baptism, Eucharist and Ministry*, Faith and Order Paper 111 (Geneva: WCC, 1982).

[65] *Baptism, Eucharist and Ministry 1982–1990, Report on the Process and Responses*, Faith and Order Paper 149 (Geneva: WCC, 1990), p. 9.

[66] *Ibid.*, p. 150.

God's love for the world, the Church as the pilgrim people of God, and the Church as the servant and the prophetic sign of God's coming kingdom. These are, however, supportive images: it is the understanding of the Church as *koinonia* which is thought most likely to lead to 'a convergent vision on the nature, unity and mission of the Church'.

In 1982, the Faith and Order Commission instituted another major project of convergence: *Towards a Common Expression of the Apostolic Faith Today.* The aim has been to work for a common understanding of the apostolic faith through an ecumenical explication of the Nicene–Constantinopolitan Creed. A provisional report appeared in 1987, which was then amended in the light of responses received to become the report *Confessing the One Faith* (1990).[67] This provides a benchmark for future ecumenical work: there is now an agreed statement as to what is meant by 'the apostolic faith'. This faith is clearly Trinitarian and ecclesial, as the section on 'The Church and the Trinitarian Communion' makes clear, when it says of the Church:

This community finds its full manifestation wherever people are gathered together by word and sacrament in obedience to the apostolic faith – i.e. in a local church. All local churches and their members should enjoy unity in the same faith and life, reflecting the Trinitarian communion of the Father, Son and Holy Spirit. Each local church is authentically the Church of God, when all it preaches, celebrates and does is in communion with all that the churches in communion with the apostles preached, celebrated and did, and with all that the churches here and now are preaching, celebrating and doing in communion with the apostles and under the apostolic gospel. In this way the universal Church consists in the communion of the local churches.[68]

Ecclesiologically, none of this is surprising. What is striking is that it should be stated in an ecumenical explication of the Nicene–Constantinopolitan Creed – stating with the greatest possible clarity that 'confessing the one faith' is not a matter of believing credal propositions alone, but of sharing in a communion, or life, the authenticity of which is promoted and upheld

---

[67] *Confessing the One Faith*, Faith and Order Paper 153 (Geneva: WCC, 1991).
[68] *Ibid.*, p. 84, para. 226.

by the acceptance of the Creed. The report itself has no section on hermeneutics, but it is clear that the Creed is here explicated within an overarching 'hermeneutic of communion'.

The seventh General Assembly of the WCC in 1991 in Canberra once again took up this theme in its statement, 'The Unity of the Church as Koinonia: Gift and Calling'.[69] The importance of this statement is that it affirms the progress in common understanding already made by placing *koinonia/communio* at the centre of ecumenical discussion. What this means for the life of the Church, both local and universal, is developed further:

The unity of the Church to which we are called is a *koinonia* given and expressed in the common confession of the apostolic faith; a common sacramental life entered by the one baptism and celebrated together in one eucharistic fellowship; a common life in which members and ministries are mutually recognized and reconciled; and a common mission witnessing to the gospel of God's grace to all people and serving the whole of creation. The goal of the search for full communion is realized when all the churches are able to recognize in one another the one, holy, catholic and apostolic Church in its fulness. This full communion will be expressed on the local and universal levels through conciliar forms of life and action. In such communion churches are bound in all aspects of their life together at all levels in confessing the one faith and engaging in worship and witness, deliberation and action.

The statement closes with a call for further progress with the mutual recognition of baptism on the basis of the BEM document, progress on the mutual recognition of apostolic faith on the basis of the Nicene–Constantinopolitan Creed, moves towards mutual recognition of ministries, the offering of eucharistic hospitality wherever possible, and progress in linking the struggle for deeper communion within the Church with that for justice, peace, and the integrity of creation.[70] On the explicit basis of a theology of communion, the Canberra Statement set

---

[69] See G. Gassmann ed., *Documentary History of Faith and Order, 1963–1993*, Faith and Order Paper 159 (Geneva: WCC, 1993), pp. 3–5.

[70] This was followed up at a consultation between representatives from the Justice, Peace and the Integrity of Creation process and the Commission on Faith and Order in 1993. See T. F. Best and W. Granberg-Michaelson eds., *Koinonia and Justice, Peace and Creation: Costly Unity* (Geneva: WCC, 1993).

a programme for the following decade, one which the churches have been following and which has borne conspicuous fruit.

The Canberra Assembly of the World Council of Churches gave a powerful boost to the study of *koinonia/communion* as an ecumenical focus. It was further taken up at the Fifth World Conference on Faith and Order, held at Santiago de Compostela in 1993, where the theme was 'Towards Koinonia in Faith, Life and Witness'.[71] The Faith and Order work of the previous thirty years was reviewed, the biblical basis for an ecclesiology of *koinonia* rehearsed, the strengths and weaknesses of work so far assessed, with major presentations by some of the key theologians in this area: John Zizioulas, Jean Tillard, and Wolfhart Pannenberg. The issue that faced the delegates at Santiago and urgently faces all the participating churches is whether they can find a sufficient basis in their extensive exploration of *koinonia* to make further concrete moves towards one another. In his address, Konrad Raiser, General Secretary of the WCC, looking forward to the eighth assembly of the WCC in 1998, called for 'an act of conversion . . . in the sense of a convergence towards the centre of koinonia'.[72] Similarly, the Pope in *Ut Unum Sint* wrote that 'The Catholic Church must enter into what might be called a "dialogue of conversion", which constitutes the spiritual foundation of ecumenical dialogue.'[73] The extent to which these are convergent appeals remains to be seen.

CONCLUSION: COMMUNION AND THE CHURCHES

The question of *koinonia* is not just the question of the unity or diversity of the Church, but of the unity and diversity of the Church *in truth*. The liturgical expression of such unity is easy to envisage when one has in mind the gathering of the Christian community with the bishop in one place on Sunday for the eucharist. It is important to engage with this eucharistic model of unity, which can be traced back to the letters of Ignatius of

---

[71] See the Official Report, T. F. Best and G. Gassmann eds., *On the Way to Fuller Koinonia*, Faith and Order Paper 166 (Geneva: WCC, 1994).
[72] *Ibid.*, p. 173.   [73] *Ut Unum Sint*, 82.

Antioch and the Johannine Apocalypse, because it has been powerfully deployed in contemporary ecclesiology, particularly in the work of John Zizioulas and Jean Tillard. It needs complementing, however, by a serious engagement with the explosive diversity of worship, teaching, and practice which has been the actual situation of the churches since their emergence. Talk of the 'undivided church' and of the 'great tradition' needs to be complemented by a deep awareness of the competing churches and the tension between traditions. Such is the gap between 'the tranquillity of order' of which Augustine spoke, and our actual experience either within or without the Church, that any notion of order and truth which does not see God's truth-ful order as emergent, provisional, and fragile is likely to lead to an over-confident institutional suppression of questioning and dissent. When we begin to reflect on the ecumenical experience of the Church in this kind of critical light, as I have tried to do in this chapter, it may seem that the practice of *koinonia* raises as many questions as it resolves. Certainly, there can be no easy resolution to the intellectual, spiritual and ethical tension of 'living in *koinonia*'. These are the tensions of legitimate diversity, authentic unity, and creative fidelity to apostolic tradition. Of such tensions there can be no premature resolution, though the eschatological hope of the Church is that the scattered fragments of the Body of Christ are already being gathered into one. Separated churches have to learn what it means to share now, in an alienated world, the *koinonia* that is the life of the Trinity. This is why the ecclesiology of communion is an ecclesiology of adventure and hope, oriented towards visible – that is eucharistic – unity.

In this chapter I have sought to convey the importance of the theme with which we are dealing by considering a range of ecumenical documents which have *koinonia* as a common theme. I have at times made reference to the tension between platonist and aristotelian ecclesiologies. It is necessary now to go far behind the language of contemporary ecumenical discussion to discuss *koinonia* in the experience and writing of Plato and Aristotle, for their influence, often unnoticed and unnamed, pervades the Church's construal of the common life, even today. In the following chapters we shall trace the thread of *koinonia*, both in experience and reflection, from the imaginative world of Plato and Aristotle, through that of Second Temple Judaism and the earliest Christian communities, to that of the Cappadocian Fathers and Augustine. In following this trajectory, we shall seek to gather from the thought and experience of *koinonia* associated, in the broadest sense, with the emergence of specifically Christian communities some pointers for the practice and theology of *koinonia* amongst the churches today.

CHAPTER 3

Plato's vision

There is a well-known passage in Plato's *Gorgias* where Socrates takes issue with Callicles. For Callicles, society is the arena of struggle between individuals; for him 'might is right'.[1] His refusal to recognise the demands of social participation may be a throwback to an older, heroic code of behaviour, but it is more likely to represent the 'new morality' of the Sophists, to which Socrates is deeply opposed. Callicles will admit no link between friendship (*philia*) or communion (*koinonia*) and what he sees as virtue. By contrast, Socrates argues that the man who pursues neither justice nor temperance, and who does not restrain his desires, in effect leads the life of a robber. He can be beloved of neither man nor God, for with him there can be no *koinonia* – no social bond. Socrates goes on:

> Where there is no communion (*koinonia*), there can be no friendship (*philia*). And wise men tell us, Callicles, that heaven and earth and gods and men are held together by communion and friendship, by orderliness, temperance and justice; and that is the reason, my friend, why they call the whole of this world by the name of order (*kosmos*), not of disorder.[2]

For Socrates, the individual is a microcosm and the universe a macrocosm. *Koinonia* is the word he uses to express the bond

---

[1] In *The Politics* (1255a), Aristotle touches on the contemporary debate between power and justice. He notes that the disagreement 'is due to one party identifying justice with goodwill, while the other identifies it with the mere rule of the stronger' (S. Everson ed., Aristotle, *The Politics*, Cambridge: Cambridge University Press, 1988).

[2] *Gorgias* 508a (LCL 166, Cambridge, Mass.: Harvard University Press, 1967). Cf. 487c, where Socrates says ironically, 'I know, Callicles, that four of you have become partners in wisdom (*koinonous sophias*).' At *Symposium* 188c, Eryximachus speaks of 'all sacrifices and ceremonies controlled by divination, namely, all means of communion (*koinonia*) between gods and men' (LCL 166).

which holds all things together, in whatever way, as *kosmos*, as an integrated whole. The problem with Callicles and those like him is that they do not recognise the bond. They refuse *koinonia*.

KOINONIA AND THE LIFE OF THE POLIS

This sense of all things being held together as one whole pervades the work of Plato, who sees all human living through the prism of the Greek *polis*. His dramatic conversations are enlivened by a sense of everyday life in Athens: the baths, the *agora*, the lawcourts, the countryside near the city, the darkness of a prison cell. His writings are peopled with the characters that made up the intellectual, military, and cultured life of Athens in the generation just previous to his own. It is within and from the city that these characters, centred on Socrates, reflect on (and reflect) the human situation. Never does Plato reflect on the individual in isolation, but always on the individual as he (women lived in seclusion and were excluded from citizenship)[3] belongs to a community.

His best-known work, which is rather misleadingly entitled in Latin *Respublica*, is a sustained reflection on the ethical life of the individual and the constitution of the social universe as seen in and through the lens of the *polis* to which he belongs. When Aristotle, Plato's best-known pupil, speaks of man as 'by nature a political animal' (*politikon zoon*)[4] he adds that the man who is by nature, and not just by fortune, without a *polis* is either

---

[3] The attitude of Plato to women has been much discussed. In *The Symposium* the prophetess Diotima has a central role. It is she who, in a reported conversation (201d–212a), teaches Socrates, and so all the diners, about the ascent to absolute beauty. Much has been made of Plato's 'revolutionary' proposal in the *Republic* (456) that women could be amongst the guardians and, if so, would need to be given the education to enable them to fulfil that role. Julia Annas argues trenchantly that this proposal is more to do with 'a huge untapped pool of resources' that could be available to the state than any concern for women's rights, since Plato lacks the fundamental notion of equal human worth and dignity. 'No feminist could be happy with an argument implying that there is nothing wrong with any actual society that oppresses women' (*An Introduction to Plato's Republic*, Oxford: Clarendon Press, 1981, pp. 181–5). In the *Laws* Plato does not modify his position on the general inferiority of women (*Republic* 455d, *Laws* 781b) but he repeats his pragmatic concern for the education of women and their participation in public life, including the holding of public office.

[4] *Politics* 1253a.

worthless or above humanity, like the 'tribeless, lawless, hearth-less' man reviled by Homer.[5] With the thought that full, demo-cratic, participatory membership of a *polis* is constitutive of the fullest human flourishing Plato would have been in profound agreement, not because city life, as so often today, conferred anonymity, but because city life, political life, meant *koinonia*, life in community. When prescribing the number of citizens for his ideal colony, Magnesia, he stipulated that there should be 5,040, both because this is a number divisible by every number up to ten and many beyond that, and because such a number would afford the maximum strength and variety of skills whilst still enabling citizens to be well-known to each other, something he considered of prime importance.[6]

There is about Plato's idealisation of the *polis* a marked strain of nostalgia. For him, the great days of Athenian supremacy had passed, with the general trauma of defeat in the Peloponne-sian War and the personal trauma of the death of Socrates. Plato remained utterly loyal to his memory, though the Socrates of his literary imagination moved further and further towards being a vehicle for the expression of Plato's own philosophy, which was increasingly that of a utopian conservative.

It is in the *Republic*[7] that Plato offers his most searching exploration of the relation between civic life and the place of

---

[5] In the Homeric world the *thes*, the unattached, propertyless labourer who worked for hire, was the lowest of the low. 'A *thes*, not a slave, was the lowest creature on earth that Achilles could think of. The terrible thing about the *thes* was his lack of attachment, his not belonging.' Before the emergence of the *polis*, the centre of belonging was the *oikos*, the authoritarian household. The *oikos* was 'the centre around which life was organized, from which flowed not only the satisfaction of material needs, including security, but ethical norms and values, duties, obligations and responsibilities, social relationships, and relations with the gods' (M. I. Finley, *The World of Odysseus*, second edition, Harmondsworth: Penguin, 1979, p. 57). In chapter 7 below, the importance of the *oikos* and the concept of *oikeiosis* in the emergence of the early churches is discussed.

[6] *Laws* 738. Aristotle's criticises this number, which he finds quite unrealistic: 'The number of 5,000 citizens . . . will require a territory as large as Babylon, or some other huge site, if so many persons are to be supported in idleness, together with their women and attendants, who will be a multitude many times as great. In framing an ideal we may assume what we wish, but we should avoid impossibilities' (*Politics* 1265a).

[7] The translation used here is F. M. Cornford, *The Republic of Plato* (Oxford: Oxford University Press, 1941).

the individual, what it means, to use the term anachronistically, to be a person. Socrates explains (368d) that in order to make comprehension of his discussion easier, he will move from consideration of justice in the life of the city, where the issues are writ large, to that of justice in the life of the individual, where they are harder to see. The move from the social, which means the political, to the individual is likened to a short-sighted person finding it easier to read an inscription written in large letters rather than in small letters. From the analogy, we can see that the priority of the social at first appears purely pragmatic. Socrates' continuing exposition, however, shows in more detail why there is so much to be gained from prior attention to the social. For him, the origin of political life lies in the fact that none of us is self-sufficient so 'we call in one another's help to satisfy our various requirements; and when we have collected a number of helpers and associates (*koinonous*) to live together in one place, we call that settlement a state' (369c). As Aristotle later put it, 'Man is the animal made for community' (*koinonikon zoon*).[8]

'Justice', which is the explicit theme of the *Republic* (the Greek title is '*Concerning Justice*') is, in Plato's view, the highest virtue, both for individuals and the *polis*. It is present where the elements that constitute both *polis* and individual are enabled each to perform their proper function. Each element must be fully participant in the whole and the individual citizen fully participant in the life of the whole community. Within Socrates' ideal *polis* there are three orders: a higher order of guardians (*phulakes*) called rulers (*archontes*), a lower order of guardians called auxiliaries (*epikouroi*), and all the rest, who are in various ways craftsmen (*demiourgoi*). In the composition of each group he imagined, respectively, gold, silver, or iron and brass. A child born to parents of one metal, who is found to have a different metallic make-up, must be moved from them to take its 'proper' place within society. Plato's interest focuses notoriously on the guardians, their education, family life, and civic duties. Their task is to rule the state and to that end they are to live as a self-

---

[8] *Eud. Eth.* 7.10; 1242a 25.

consciously superior caste. None of them may possess private property beyond the barest necessities. They are to have their meals in common, living like soldiers in a camp. They are to have wives and children in common. To the objection that their severe communitarian discipline will make them less than happy, Socrates answers that his prime concern is 'to secure the greatest possible happiness for the community as a whole' (420b). Only so will there be justice.

Within the state there will be justice when each of the orders lives in the proper manner according to its proper virtue. The wisdom of the state will reside in the guardians who have the knowledge and skill to rule wisely. The courage of the state will reside in the strength with which the auxiliaries (soldiers) hold onto the convictions that have been given them by their education. The temperance of the state will reside not just in the moderate and obedient behaviour of the craftsmen but in each order (all are in their own way craftsmen, *demiourgoi* (421c)), so all citizens must exercise self-mastery[9] to promote the harmony of the whole. 'When each order . . . keeps to its own proper business in the commonwealth and does its own work, that is justice and what makes a just society' (434c).

For Plato, 'the best ordered state . . . most nearly resembles a single person'. The way he expresses this is characteristic, for he does not see all parts of the body as of equal importance, though all are interdependent. If someone hurts a finger, 'the whole community (*koinonia*) of those bodily connections which are gathered up in the soul and unified by its ruling element is made aware and it all shares as a whole in the pain of the suffering part' (462d).[10] Thus, the best organised community 'will recognise as a part of itself the individual citizen to whom good or evil happens, and will share as a whole in his joy or

---

[9] Cf. Socrates' admonition to Callicles, enjoining orderliness, temperance, and justice (*Gorgias* 508a) above.

[10] Translation adapted. The metaphor of the *polis* or community as body was common in antiquity (see Margaret M. Mitchell, *Paul and the Rhetoric of Reconciliation*, Tübingen: J. C. B. Mohr, 1991, pp. 157–60). It suggests a strong view of *koinonia* within the body politic. We may notice in this context Paul's extended use of the metaphor in 1 Cor. 12:12–27, and also in Rom. 12:4–5. Of particular relevance is 1 Cor. 12:26: 'If one member suffers, all suffer together; if one member is honoured, all rejoice together.'

sorrow'. This applies to all three orders in society, though the way in which it applies to craftsmen is much less clear than for guardians, who are Plato's primary interest. All have their part to play and all belong to one another, for all are citizens – though equality is a matter of the order to which the individual belongs, not of citizenship in itself.

This corporate understanding of the state, of the orders within the state, and the individual within their order, is integral to the argument of the *Republic*. Having outlined the functioning of his ideal society, Plato turns to the functioning of the individual, never forgetting that the individual is a member of that society. It is argued that we can easily recognise within ourselves basic human desires, which for good reason we resist. Since 'the same thing cannot behave in two opposite ways at the same time', there must be two distinctive elements of the soul, one of irrational appetite (*epithumia*) and the other of rational reflection (*logos*). In addition, Socrates identifies a 'passionate' or 'spirited' element (*thumos*) that makes us feel angry or indignant. This element is quite distinct from 'appetite'. Indeed it may come into conflict with appetite or reason. We may be angry with our own instinctive desires (characteristically, Plato does not discuss how we might be angry with our reason). He argues that the same three elements exist alike in the state and in the individual soul. In the just person, each part of their nature will perform its proper function. It is the function of reason to rule, assisted by the 'spirited' element. Control over the appetites is promoted by the right combination of musical and gymnastic training, a matter Plato discusses in some detail. A person is wise when governed by reason, brave when the spirited part of their nature is subordinated to reason, temperate when all three parts of their nature act in harmony and there is subjection to reason. The just person knows their place within the state and so the harmony within the individual promotes the harmony of the state. 'Justice is produced in the soul, like health in the body, by establishing the elements concerned in their natural relations of control and subordination, whereas injustice is like disease and means that this natural order is inverted' (444d). Belief in a natural order and harmony both within the individual and the state, and in the benign hegemony of reason, is all of a piece with Plato's conviction that in the ideal *polis* the philosopher will be ruler. Given his exploration of the social and cosmic context, such ideal rule could never be heteronomous, but only the bringing to fulfilment in unity of the co-ordinated and harmonious life of the *polis*.

Plato knew perfectly well the difficulty of making political systems reflect in practice 'the trouble-free perfection of theory'.[11] By the time, late in life, when he produced a plan for an imagined Cretan colony in which the entirely foreseeable conflicts of the colonists would be regulated by a body of law, his conservative idealism had become distinctly reactionary. The laws of Magnesia, once established, are, he stipulates, to remain unchanged, except for minor adjustments, as they will be held by the colonists to be of divine origin. Their purpose is to promote the freedom, unity (or harmony) and wisdom of the city. The stability and the supremacy of law is of the highest importance. There is to be a balance of authority and liberty under a benevolent dictatorship 'where supreme power in a man joins hands with wise judgement and self-restraint'.[12] Plato's colony is to be a city where the gods, then the soul, and finally the body, are all held in honour, and the citizens participate together in the happiness of the virtuous life. As in the *Republic*, he advocates community of wives, children, and property, but he acknowledges that this is nowhere likely to be realised and what must be looked for is a practicable second-best. There can be no absolute right over land, which is inalienable and belongs ultimately to the *polis*, but the citizens need a sense of ownership and a moderate profit incentive. His aim is that the citizens should be friends (*philoi*). Thus there is an absolute ban on usury[13] and the unscrupulous accumulation of

---

[11] *Laws* 636a (The translation used, unless otherwise stated, is that of T. J. Saunders, Harmondsworth: Penguin Books, 1970).

[12] *Laws* 712a.

[13] Compare the absolute ban on usury in pre-Reformation Christian teaching as characterised by R. H. Tawney: 'To take usury is contrary to Scripture; it is contrary to Aristotle; it is contrary to nature' (*Religion and the Rise of Capitalism*, Harmondsworth: Penguin Books, 1938, pp. 55 ff).

wealth, just as there should be no extreme poverty. As for the courts, citizens are to feel they have a stake in the system 'because anyone excluded from the right to participate in trying cases feels he has no stake in the community whatever'.[14] Such participation, however, is to be carefully moderated by the superintendence of representative officials, who will try the hardest cases. The political system is intended to be participatory, but not to concede equality of voting power. Plato consistently argues that there are those in the community who have greater wisdom, intellectual ability, or wealth and that they should have responsibilities commensurate with those gifts. Those with humbler gifts equally have their proper, but humbler, role as citizens. A key function for the guardians is to ensure that no citizen is excluded from appropriate participation in the life of the *polis*. To this end, the system of election to the ruling council will 'strike a mean between monarchy and democracy, as a constitutional system always should'.[15]

Such is human nature that the constitution of actual *poleis* will never be perfect. Virtue for citizens is always in process of achievement, always the goal for which models can be held out behind or ahead. In the *Republic*, Plato speaks of a 'pattern set up in heaven' (*en ourano paradeigma*)[16] which can be seen by anyone who wishes. As to its earthly realisation, present or future, he professes ignorance, but for the one captivated by this vision, it is the politics of the heavenly 'republic' alone which engage him. In the *Laws*, Plato's thinking is still governed absolutely by a transcendent ideal, which he sketches in quasi-mythological terms. His Athenian speaks of various prehistoric floods and plagues which wiped out most of the inhabitants of earth, and after which there had to be a fresh start. He speculates about the origin of Athenian political life after one such flood, which left only isolated hill-dwellers.[17] As human interaction revived, 'men's isolation prompted them to cherish

[14] *Laws* 768b.
[15] *Laws* 756e (translation by A. E. Taylor in E. Hamilton and H. Cairns eds., *The Collected Dialogues of Plato*, Bollingen Series LXXI, Princeton: Princeton University Press, 1963, p. 1336).
[16] *Republic* 592b.   [17] *Laws* 678 ff.

(*agapein*) and to love (*philein*) one another'. There were no quarrels over the abundant supply of food and raw materials, no extremes of poverty and wealth, no war, and from such wellbeing there came a community of citizens who co-existed harmoniously, and in their simplicity unquestioningly believed the teaching they had received about the gods. They were better in character, braver, more self-controlled, and in every way more just than their successors.

This sketch of an ideal primitive community is filled out in the *Timaeus* and *Critias*, where mythology and history once more blend. Plato describes a prehistoric struggle, nine thousand years ago, between a flourishing Athenian community and the invading kingdom of Atlantis. In one terrible night 'of violent earthquakes and floods', the fighting men of Athens were swallowed by the earth and the whole of Atlantis by the sea. Prior to that both *poleis* had enjoyed a golden age. In Athens all had lived the life which Plato depicted in the *Republic* as the ideal. Rulers and auxiliaries shared within their order a simple common life (*hapanta panton koina*).[18] The soil had been fertile so that agriculture flourished as did the crafts within the city. The name of Athens was supreme in Greece for virtue of every kind. Similarly blessed was the life of Atlantis, but the divine element in the makeup of the Atlanteans became corrupted. When love of the common good cooled, the Atlanteans remained aware that in their profound moral collapse the prelude to physical disaster had taken place.

For Plato, then, the ideal *polis* is one where every citizen can be confident of their full participation in the manner appropriate to their gifts and standing. It is a community dedicated to virtue, and therefore one that values education, piety, and good order. Though there may have been such a community in the past and though it may exist 'in heaven', the task on earth now, within the flow of time, is to move towards the realisation of that *koinonia* which is recognisable, in ideal form, outside time. This brings us to a second dimension of *koinonia* or participation for Plato: *koinonia* in a 'higher realm'.

---

[18] Compare Acts 4:32, '*en autois panta koina*' ('They had all things in common').

KOINONIA WITH AND IN A HIGHER REALM

For Plato, this world is a world of change which is contingent upon a 'higher realm' of unchanging and eternal being, the existence of which we can know by induction and the truth of which we can know by direct, intellectual apprehension. As he wrote in the *Timaeus*, 'if this world is beautiful and the maker is good, it is clear that he was looking to the eternal . . . and, since these things are so, the world must of necessity be a copy (*eikon*) of something'.[19] The world we encounter by means of our senses is the deceptive world of shadows and reflections, but if we are guided by reason we will rise above these distractions to an unclouded apprehension of reality.

Plato's approach to the world of transcendent reality is both inductive and intuitive. This seems to have been his own development of the position of Socrates, who in the early dialogues constantly pushes his interlocutors to consider the difficulties raised by their unquestioning use of key moral terms. Thus, in the *Euthyphro*, Socrates exposes the overconfidence of a young man who is prepared publicly to accuse his father of murder. Socrates' examination reveals that the young man who thinks he has acted in such a principled fashion cannot actually say what he means by calling an action pious (*hosios*) or impious. How is it, asks Socrates in the *Laches*, that a general who would confidently identify a courageous deed gets tied up in knots when asked to say what he means by 'courage'? Where Socrates characteristically brought his interlocutors to an acknowledgement of their own state of puzzlement and indecision (*aporia*), Plato developed a positive metaphysic whose starting point is the manifest presence (*parousia*) in the world of recognisable but ultimately indefinable qualities like holiness and courage. In answer to the problem exposed by Socrates, Plato came to teach that in an ideal world there existed real universals.

Such a universal, usually called a 'Form' (*eidos*) or an 'Idea' (*idea*), could never be perceived by means of the human senses, but Plato thought the existence of Forms would be evident to

[19] *Timaeus* 29b.

anyone who puzzles over the consistency of properties we see in objects, or the consistency of qualities we see in actions. How is it that when we see two similar objects we recognise their 'likeness'? How is it that when we see a series of good actions, we recognise that they all have 'goodness'? For Plato, there are not properties or qualities which simply inhere in objects or actions in the world. That which inheres in the object is the 'presence' of the 'Form'. Developing the thought of Socrates, whose interest in universals was linguistic rather than metaphysical, Plato posited a distinction or separation (*chorismos*) between 'Form' and 'presence' in the world.[20] A crucial question, then, for Plato is the *relation* between 'Form' and 'presence'. From the variety of language employed[21] it is clear that this relation between object or quality and Form – for which one key term is *koinonia* – remained for Plato a central area of *aporia*, of difficulty, which he never to his own satisfaction resolved.[22] Once more, and in a different dimension, *koinonia* was for Plato simply a given, a transcendental condition of there being a world at all, which was crucial to his metaphysical understanding, but *what koinonia is he could not say.*

It is in the *Phaedo*[23] that Plato's metaphysical structure is first presented with some systematic clarity. The *Phaedo* is an early dialogue, set in Socrates' prison cell. The philosophical discussion is overshadowed by an acute awareness amongst all the participants (including the reader) that Socrates is shortly to die. The animated talk among friends is far more than a pleasant way of whiling away some hours until Socrates must

---

[20] W. D. Ross argues that in the early dialogues, written while Plato was dominated by the influence of Socrates, there is no trace of 'transcendentalism', for Socrates was interested only in ascertaining what it was that was common to all just acts, to all beautiful objects, and the like; but as Plato's mind matured he moved gradually towards a transcendental view of the Ideas as entities existing in their own right, only imperfectly mirrored in sensible things and human actions. It is of the later Plato that Aristotle spoke when he criticised the 'separation' (*chorismos*) Plato posited between Ideas and sensible things' (*Plato's Doctrine of Ideas*, Oxford: Clarendon Press, 1951, p. 233).

[21] See Ross, *Plato's Doctrine of Ideas*, pp. 228–30.

[22] See H.-G. Gadamer, *The Idea of the Good in Platonic–Aristotelian Philosophy* (New Haven: Yale University Press, 1986), pp. 10–12.

[23] For study of the *Phaedo*, I am indebted to the translation and commentary by R. Hackforth (Cambridge: Cambridge University Press, 1955).

drink the poison. For Socrates, life, which is characterised by philosophical reflection, is a 'preparation for death'. Faced with death, which he sees as release, he seeks to liberate his friends from their irrational grief. This he does by demonstrating the pre-existence and the post-existence of the soul. The accounts of the destiny of the soul given in the dialogue are far from consistent, but the broad outlines are clear. The soul comes from a 'higher' transcendent world, is 'imprisoned' in the body, from the fetters of which it can find freedom through ascetic practice and philosophical reflection, and at death it returns to the world from which it came. The soul is not a 'Form' but it is a 'visitor' in this world from the higher realm of Forms, and the presence of souls in the world suggests that humans are denizens of two worlds. Hence the human capacity to rise above distraction in this world to a world of transcendent reality.

This is why, for Plato, knowledge is essentially 'remembering' (*anamnesis*). The soul 'remembers what it learnt in the transcendent world'. In the *Meno*, by dint of careful questioning, a slave is brought to 'remember' the truths of geometry which, it is suggested, he could not possibly have learnt by other means and did not even know that he 'knew'. The key point about such 'remembering' is that it is participatory. We are able to 'learn' and enunciate both mathematical and moral truth because the learning of such truth is essentially re-cognition. This is why, when Socrates the master dies, his pupils are not left without recourse. They will not simply recall what he has said to them (Plato's writings at this stage seem to be based upon remembered sayings and incidents but already to be developing more systematically Socrates' quizzical and potentially anarchic wisdom), but, by dint of their participation in the same cosmos of reality, truth, and wisdom, taking Socrates as a guide, they will develop their own philosophical understanding. To read one of the Socratic dialogues is actually to participate in this activity.[24]

Plato's epistemology cannot, then, be seen in isolation from the metaphysic in which it is so deeply embedded. Already in

---

[24] Cf. Gadamer, *The Idea of the Good*, p. 6.

the *Phaedo*, the outlines of Plato's integrated philosophy of *koinonia* – in this context best translated *participation* – are clear: objects and people in the world *participate* in 'Forms'; the soul *participates* in the 'world' of Forms; to 'know' is to *participate* in that transcendent world; philosophy exists as the love and fostering of such *participation*. Cornford brings out the way in which Plato's account of knowing is embedded in his metaphysical understanding when he shows how for Plato 'anamnesis, the separate existence of the soul before birth and the separation of Forms from sensible things, all stand or fall together'.[25]

In the *Republic*, discussion of the just society turns upon understanding and apprehension of the Good.[26] At a crucial point in his exposition of the education that befits a philosophic ruler, Socrates pauses to draw his famous analogy between the Good and the Sun. This analogy turns on his notion of perception: just as the eye truly perceives an object when it is lit up by light from the sun, so the mind truly perceives the object of knowledge, truly *knows* when that object is 'irradiated by truth and reality'.[27] The source of such 'irradiation' is Goodness itself, the Idea[28] or Form of the Good. From the Idea of the Good, good objects in the world derive 'their very being and reality'.

Plato's account offers a theory of perception and misperception. This he develops by means of Socrates' well-known analogy of the Divided Line.[29] The line of which Socrates speaks is best thought of as vertical. It is divided into two

---

[25] F. M. Cornford, *Plato and Parmenides* (London: Kegan Paul, Trench, Trubner, 1939), p. 75.

[26] See, for example, the discussion in Gadamer, 'The *Polis* and the knowledge of the Good', *The Idea of the Good*, pp. 63–103.

[27] F. M. Cornford, *The Republic of Plato*, p. 219.

[28] H.-G. Gadamer argues that 'The Idea of the Good' is better than 'The Form of the Good' because Plato uses only *idea*, never *eidos*, with relation to 'The Good' (*The Idea of the Good*, p. 27). The Idea of the Good is *beyond* being (*epekeina tes ousias*, *Republic* 509b). The realm of Forms is a *topos huperouranios* (*Phaedrus* 247c), like Augustine's 'heaven of heavens'.

[29] Amongst the extensive literature on this passage, I am indebted to two seminal articles in particular: J. E. Raven, 'Sun, Divided Line, and Cave', *The Classical Quarterly* NS 3 (1953), 22–32; John Ferguson, 'Sun, Line, and Cave Again', *The Classical Quarterly* NS 13 (1963), 188–93. See also Cornford, *The Republic of Plato*, pp. 221–6. W. K. C. Guthrie has a characteristically clear discussion in *A History of Greek Philosophy*, vol. 4 (Cambridge: Cambridge University Press, 1975), pp. 506–21.

sections such that the top is longer than the bottom. Each section is divided in the same proportion as the whole line, so there are two unequal parts above the division and two unequal parts below it. The upper section of the whole line represents the intelligible world (the world of Forms) and the cognition of that world which is available to us; the lower represents the world of appearance and the cognition we have of that. Beginning at the bottom, Socrates speaks first of our knowledge of images of visible things: this he calls 'imagining' (*eikasia*). Above that is the perception of visible things: this he calls 'belief' (*pistis*). Passing from the world of appearances to the intelligible world, the knowledge of mathematical objects is called 'thinking' (*dianoia*). In the higher segment of the intelligible world, knowledge of Forms is called 'intelligence' (*noesis*) or 'knowledge' (*episteme*). Plato assigns to each 'state of mind' a degree of clarity and certainty corresponding to the measure in which their objects possess 'reality and truth'.[30]

This scheme he illustrates in his myth of the cave. He describes an underground cave where men have been chained since their childhood. These men have been made to face a wall, unable to turn. Behind them, at the mouth of the cave, there burns a fire, and between them and the fire there is a low wall behind which people carry aloft objects that include images of men and of animals. The shadow of these objects is thrown onto the cave wall in front of the prisoners, who, hearing the voices of those who pass to and fro, take the shadows of figures of men and of animals to be the 'real' objects.

Socrates, who describes this scene, suggests that one of the prisoners is freed, then compelled to face and move towards the fire. Initially, the prisoner would be pained even by the brightness of the fire and try to turn back to the comfort of the shadows. If he were dragged from the cave into the light, he would at first be dazzled by its brightness. Gradually, he would be able to look at shadows, then reflections in water, and then at 'real' objects in this 'upper' world. If he were to look at the sky,

[30] Cornford, *The Republic of Plato*, p. 221.

initially it would be only at night, at the gentler light of the stars and moon. Finally, however, he would be able to look directly at the sun. If he were then able to return to the cave after his experiences of the light, he would be unable to see in the darkness. Those still chained there would be aware that he blundered around and would conclude that his journey to the upper world had ruined his sight. If he attempted to free them and take them to that world, they would resist and, given the chance, kill him.

In the myth of the cave, Plato has turned his analytical description of human cognition into a narrative. The stages of the narrative – vision of shadows of images; vision of images; vision of 'real' objects in the 'upper' world; vision of transcendent bodies (stars, moon, sun) – correspond exactly to the divisions on the divided line. In both the analysis and the narrative it is easy to see that Plato is presenting us with a hierarchy of cognition, up which we pass as our knowing is purified, and this was how his thought was used in later mystical writing.[31] While we exist in this delusive world of appearance, we must struggle not to be enmeshed and dominated by it. While we stay at the level of perception of objects in and for themselves, we remain at the level of 'appearance'; when we 'see' that they are imbued with 'truth and reality' by virtue of their participation in transcendent Forms, that perception is a perception of the truth and reality of the intelligible world. This account of cognition, in which ontology, epistemology, and ethics are all brought together, and in which cognition is understood as a mode of participation, of *koinonia*, was subsumed in the dominant and developing pattern of Christian sacramental thought and even today continues to provide its fundamental pattern.

In the *Sophist*, Plato's stranger raises the problem of one object that has a number of qualities, and so partakes of a number of Forms. The relation of the Forms with each other is then discussed, because it is the task of the philosopher to know what kinds of combination are possible between different

---

[31] See A. Louth, *The Origins of the Christian Mystical Tradition* (Oxford: Clarendon Press, 1981), pp. 3–17, *passim*.

Forms.[32] The exercise of such discernment is what Plato means by 'the science of dialectic', which is the study not of propositions about the world, but the way reality actually is. 'Dialectic is not Formal Logic, but the study of the structure of reality – in fact Ontology, for the Forms are the realities.'[33] Even though *koinonia* and its cognates is used in both contexts, there is for Plato an important difference between the *koinonia* when an object 'partakes' of a 'Form' and the *koinonia* between Forms.[34] The first is not reciprocal: 'Forms do not partake of things.' The second is reciprocal: 'In speaking of Forms "participation" is synonymous with "blending" or "combination" and is a symmetrical relation.' In Plato's use of *koinonia* for the relation between Forms, we can see the beginnings of a metaphysical understanding, which was taken up and reworked by Christian thinkers, who drew on it to speak of relation within God – which is the fundamental insight of the Christian doctrine of the Trinity.

The nearest thing in Plato to a summary of his cosmology is the *Timaeus*, a late dialogue, and much the most important of Plato's writings for the development of later, especially medieval, Christian theology, where it exercised a decisive influence on Christian cosmology.[35] Here the Theory of Forms is recapitulated, but in the wider context of an account of the origin of the *kosmos* in which there is a central role for the '*demiourgos*' or craftsman who shapes the *kosmos* according to the pre-existent Forms in a receptacle we may think of as space. The *Timaeus* again makes clear Plato's highly integrated sense of reality. The visible cosmos that human beings inhabit is by no means the whole of reality. It is, as we have seen, a copy of a transcendent and pre-existent world. Time is for Plato 'the moving image of eternity'[36] and this physical world in its entirety is for him the changing image of the unchangeable. What gives access to

[32] *Sophist* 253d. Cf. F. M.Cornford, *Plato's Theory of Knowledge, The Theaetetus and the Sophist of Plato translated with a running commentary* (London: Routledge and Kegan Paul, 1935), p. 263.
[33] Cornford, *Plato's Theory of Knowledge*, p. 266.   [34] *Ibid.*, p. 297.
[35] R. Klibansky, *The Continuity of the Platonic Tradition during the Middle Ages* (London: Warburg Institute, 1939).
[36] *Timaeus* 37.

eternal and unchanging reality is reason, whether reason be exercised mathematically, logically, or morally. In each case the phenomena with which reason has to deal can provide for the reasoning mind access to eternal and unchanging truth.

Plato's whole philosophy turns upon his belief that we have, through the exercise of the mind, access to truth. This access is possible only because the objects within our *kosmos* and the active mind both participate in the 'higher world of Forms'. There have been major scholarly debates about the nature of this participation. Ross divides the words that Plato uses for this relation into those such as *metechein, koinonein*, and *parousia* that stress the immanence of the Forms and those such as *paradeigma, eikon*, and *mimesis* that imply or suggest their transcendence.[37] He finds a development towards the language of transcendence as Plato moves beyond his early writing in which he was dependent on Socrates' concern for the use of words and the induction of universals from linguistic usage. However, the picture is by no means clear and, from the variety of terms he uses, Ross concludes that Plato 'may even have had an inkling of the fact that the relation is completely unique and indefinable. Both "sharing" and "imitating" are metaphors for it, and the use of two complementary metaphors (expressed by a range of terms) is better than the sole use of either.'[38] This conclusion may be taken as a salutary warning. Overuse of the one English word 'participation' may give to the Platonic system an apparent clarity and systematic rigour which it lacks. There is, nonetheless, throughout Plato's work a consistent engagement with what we might call 'the mystery of coinherence'.[39] For

---

[37] See Ross, *Plato's Theory of Ideas*, especially pp. 228–30.

[38] Ross, *Ibid.*, p. 231.

[39] Ross' 'two complementary metaphors' for the relation between objects and Forms suggest that we should not be surprised to find tension at this point in theologies indebted to platonism. This is particularly relevant for the development of Christology, where in the early centuries a range of 'complementary metaphors' was used to describe the relation of Jesus to the Father. Arius, whose background was that of platonist Alexandria, famously drew on relational metaphors which suggested the subordination of the Son to the Father. (See R. Williams, *Arius*, London: Darton, Longman and Todd, 1987, pp. 109–16.) The Council of Nicea (325 AD) attempted to preclude such subordinationist teaching by a more precise use of the philosophical language of substance (*ousia*), affirming that Jesus Christ was 'of one substance' (*homoousios*) with the Father, but this was later taken, especially within Alexandrian

Plato the relation between object or 'appearance' and Form could be spoken of as *koinonia* – as could the relation between Form and Form – but what that *koinonia* was remained a mystery, which we have here called the mystery of co-inherence. For Plato, it is simply a given about the world that there is a transcendental bond of *koinonia* that embraces all things and all people. Those who do not know this do not know the world.

KOINONIA IN DIALOGUE

We cannot, however, give this bond further consideration until we have looked more closely at Plato's characteristic philosophic method, which is, of course, that of dialogue. In his dramatic dialogues, he is simply showing us what it is to approach truth by thinking, and showing this thinking as a shared, participatory activity, as discussion. To quote R.G. Collingwood, whose hermeneutical approach was deeply influenced by Plato, 'When Plato described thinking as a "dialogue of the soul with itself"', he meant (as we know from his own dialogues) that it was a process of question and answer, and that of these two elements the primacy belongs to the questioning activity, the Socrates within us.'[40]

The activity of dialogue, of course, presupposes *koinonia*. Central here is his notion of the soul as a visitor from a higher world, where it has been in touch with the Forms, the 'memory'

---

thinking, to privilege the divinity of Jesus. Full 'complementarity' was secured at the Council of Chalcedon (451) with the affirmation of a 'two-natures' Christology. In his *Christian Faith* (1821–2), Schleiermacher (a translator of Plato), attempted to express the relation between Jesus and the Father in terms that by-passed 'two-natures' Christology (which he thought nonsensical) by returning to a Christology of 'participation'. Today, when we no longer think readily in terms of divine or human substance (*ousia*) or nature (*phusis*), the development of a Christology which affirms the *participation* of symbol in *symbolizandum*, and which sees in Jesus the representative, or the 'symbol', of God and of true humanity, has rich potential. Paul Tillich called for 'the replacement of the two-nature theory' by 'dynamic-relational concepts', suggesting that 'incarnation' and 'adoption' are complementary and can be used in this way. See, P. Tillich, *Systematic Theology* (combined volume, London: Nisbet, 1968), volume 2, pp. 160–73.

[40] R. G. Collingwood, *An Autobiography* (Oxford: Oxford University Press, 1939), p. 35. See also H.-G. Gadamer, 'The Model of Platonic Dialectic' in *Truth and Method* (second, revised edition, translation revised by J. Weinsheimer and D. G. Marshall, London: Sheed and Ward, 1989, pp. 362–9 (*WM*, pp. 368–75)).

(we might say 'imprint') of which contact it to some extent
retains. What the dialogue does is to draw out that memory as it
is retained by each partner, or better, 'between' the partners.
The memory, and so the understanding, will be fresher and
clearer in one than in another because of that one's greater
continuing participation in the Good and the true. It is never
the case that one partner has all of the truth and that another
partner has none of it. Each, to a greater or lesser degree,
shares in the truth, and on the basis of that sharing, and of the
common use of reason, each can draw the other to a higher
level of understanding, in the process learning, or 'remembering' new things themselves. Though Socrates may be por-
trayed as far advanced, beyond any of his interlocutors, he can
still be discomfited and can be seen learning within the process
of dialogue.

The *Phaedrus*,[41] usually thought to be a dialogue from Plato's
maturity, illustrates well the development of participatory
understanding as the dialogue unfolds. Socrates and Phaedrus
are the two participants, but the words of a third, Lysias, are
reported, so the views of three men are debated. The problem
with which the dialogue is concerned is initially rhetorical:
Lysias has delivered a speech arguing that a young man should
only yield to the sexual advances of one who is not in love with
him. Socrates recognises the emptiness of this, but Phaedrus
persuades him, albeit with some embarrassment, to argue the
same case, which he does to the best of his ability. Checked by
his 'inner voice' (*daimonion*), he makes it clear that he finds this
position blasphemous, and moves beyond the rhetorical to
argue the opposite case. Socrates now adopts the *persona* of
Stesichorus to expound his true views upon the nature of love
and the way in which we should love. The dialogue comes to a
climax with an account of the life of the soul, and the ascent of
the souls of the two lovers to the realm of truth and beauty. The
dialogue then proceeds to questions of method, of rhetoric,

---

[41] R. Hackforth, *Plato's Phaedrus*, translated with an introduction and commentary
(Cambridge: Cambridge University Press, 1952) is invaluable, as is G. R. F. Ferrari,
Listening to the Cicadas, A Study of Plato's Phaedrus (Cambridge: Cambridge University
Press, 1987).

dialectic, and writing. It concludes with a prayer to Pan and the other surrounding gods, to which Phaedrus says, 'Make it a prayer for me too, since friends have all things in common' (279c). The phrase is a well-known Greek tag. *Koinonia* in conversation is thus concluded with *koinonia* in prayer.

Plato's dialogues are always *mises-en-scène*. In the *Phaedrus*, the context is delicately chosen to reflect the movement and subject of the conversation. More than that, the dialogue is itself a participation in the *kosmos* of which this particular grove by a shady riverbank is a delightful microcosm. This is the only dialogue in which Socrates, who never leaves Athens and its talk, seduced by the prospect of conversation with Phaedrus, escapes the city. He is 'led out' to a new and delightful context, a grassy bank beside the Ilissus. Phaedrus is amazed at Socrates' simple pleasure in his surroundings and says, 'Anyone would take you, as you say, for a stranger being shown the country by a guide instead of a native' (230d) – a hint of things to come when Socrates will be a guide to Phaedrus, as he expounds to him the native air of the country beyond the heavens to which his soul belongs. As Socrates warms to his theme (and to the presence of Phaedrus) through the late morning, so the heat of the day builds up. All the time the cool River Ilissus flows by. They are tempted to drowsiness, but refuse the temptation, passing to renewed analysis of dialectic. In the final section of the dialogue, up to the very conclusion, consciousness of earthly, physical surroundings drops away.

Socrates is critical of Lysias' rhetoric, because he writes things in a 'haphazard' fashion. He does not define his subject, his discourse is not constructed like a living creature with a head, body, and feet (264c). Such rhetorical criticism suggests that the structure of the *Phaedrus* itself must be less haphazard than may at first appear. The last third of the dialogue, concerned with dialectic, cannot be seen as a prolonged after-thought, an appendage to the increasingly passionate account of love. For Socrates, there is no anticlimax in moving from discussion of what it means to give oneself in love to discussion of how to do philosophy. The seeker after truth will be both '*paiderastes*' ('lover of a youth') and '*erastes logou*' ('lover of discourse'). This is clear from the structure of the dialogue: Phaedrus and Socrates meet; Phaedrus reads an artless speech in which it is argued that a lover should yield only to one who is not in love with him; Socrates argues the same thing with better rhetoric; Socrates is checked by divine influence, comes to himself, and then argues the opposite *ex animo*; there is a brief interlude; Socrates then expounds to an utterly compliant Phaedrus the nature of dialectic, and the reader is left to conclude that in the future Phaedrus, now chastened and transformed by his encounter with Socrates, will no longer borrow written words to argue a case he does not believe, but since the words of Socrates have been written on his soul, will struggle to find 'living words' that will lead himself and others on in the ascent to beauty and truth.

There are hints of Plato's understanding of the 'Socratic method' at various points in the dialogues. In the *Phaedo* (89d) Socrates warns against becoming *misologoi* (haters of discussion, or argument). Those who now care only to overcome their opponents by force of argument are profoundly lacking in health. The function of argument is to elicit the truth, and argument that loses concern for truth only produces *misologoi*. What people in this sad condition do not see is that it is not the process of argument which is unhealthy, but the souls of those who deploy it amorally. We must strive to see that our souls are healthy, and then we shall deploy argument in a sound or healthy manner.

Socrates' own role in the deployment of sound argument is discussed briefly in the *Theaetetus*, one of the later dialogues in which discussion about the nature of discussion becomes much more prominent. For Plato, this may well have represented an 'ascent' to a 'higher' form of discourse, more abstracted from human discourse. It has been well said that in these late dialogues, 'the bones show more clearly through the skin'.[42] As Plato's writing becomes more theoretical, it becomes less clear that his understanding of dialectic or mathematics is at root participatory, and easier to develop out of his philosophy a logic

---

[42] Cornford, *Plato's Theory of Knowledge*, p. viii.

detached from its human context. In the *Theaetetus* (161a)
Socrates commends Theodorus because he is *philologos* ('a lover
of argument'). What Theodorus does not understand is the role
that Socrates plays in the development of arguments. He thinks
that Socrates can produce arguments out of his bag at will.
Socrates explains that he is not able to do that because the
arguments do not come from him, but from the person with
whom he is talking. He, the son of a midwife, is like a midwife
who draws the argument from another. Like the midwife, who
is past the age of childbearing, he himself cannot give birth to
wisdom; he can only bring it forth from others. Typically,
Socrates makes the process sound one-sided, overemphasising
the wisdom to be drawn from the other and discounting his
own. In arch self-deprecation, he counteracts the radical misunderstanding of his own position, which sees him as the
dispenser of wisdom or, worse still, of clever arguments.

The distinction is made clear by an analogy in the *Laws*,
where the Athenian contrasts the practice of the slave doctor
who has learnt some medicine by watching his master and
picking up experience along the way with the practice of the
free doctor who understands the nature (*phusis*) of the situation.
The slave doctor prescribes a remedy 'as if he had precise
knowledge, and with the self-confidence of a dictator' (720c).
The free doctor, however, takes an ordered case-history which
exposes the 'nature' of the situation, 'sharing' or 'communicating' (*koinoumenos*) with the patient and his friends. During this
process of dialogue, he both learns and teaches and his prescription is given only with the patient's consent. He seeks to lead
(*agein*) the patient back to health. Restoration to health is an
exercise which depends on the *koinonia* between doctor and
patient.

This remarkable medical vignette, like so many of the dialogues themselves, is an extended metaphor for the work in which
the philosopher engages. Talk which takes place in the service
of wisdom, virtue and truth is inalienably a co-operative,
participatory activity in which each participant, however dis-
crepant their understanding, their intellectual or spiritual
health, has some contribution to make from their own soul's

inchoate knowledge of the truth. True dialogue involves both speaking and listening (the free doctor listens), it involves participants who are together engaged with the struggle for health or virtue (the free doctor treats free patients) though there must be a place for the recognition of the level of technical skill brought by a skilled person to the dialogue. The deployment of words, argument, or rhetoric in the service of truth can never be detached from its human, and therefore moral (which means social and political) and metaphysical context. What Plato offers through the depiction of Socrates as an *erastes logou* is a model of the philosopher as one who functions in *koinonia*, though *koinonia* achieved through a willingness constantly to challenge any premature or uncritical form of agreement. The *koinonia*, the partnership in dialogue, that Plato commends through the figure of Socrates, is one that depends upon engagement with the subject in hand. Clever rhetoric simply obscures the issue. The issue is the emergence of truth through the deployment of argument in dialogue. Not rhetorical cleverness, which can argue anything, but commitment to virtue, and to the dialogue as a means to the disclosure of truth, is the means of deepening *koinonia* that Plato commends.

CONCLUSION: PLATO'S VISION OF *KOINONIA*

Through his dialogues, Plato gives a remarkably coherent exposition of the *koinonia* in which humanity is embedded, and on which being recognisably human depends. More than this, there is a sense of there being one *kosmos* in which each individual has their proper place. The primary physical realisation of *kosmos* is the *polis*, so the individual's identity is determined by their *koinonia* within the political community, or, by contrast, their exclusion from political society. There is a systematic and dynamic unity in Plato's presuppositions about political and metaphysical *koinonia*, the unity of the *kosmos*, and his own commitment to the method of dialogue in the apprehension of truth.

Here we have the lineaments of a number of later Christian

developments, which are all developments in the theology of *koinonia*: the Church understood as the Christian analogue to the *polis* (a '*civitas platonica*'); the Christian vision of the transcendent City of God; the metaphysic of ascent which provides the framework and sometimes the very phraseology for the development of Christian mystical, incarnational, and sacramental teaching; and the stress on dialogue that promotes the development of dialectic as a method of intellectual, and specifically theological, enquiry.[43]

For Plato, *koinonia*, whether experienced in common membership of the polity of Athens, through the experience of virtue and the Good, or in the engagement of conversation and intellectual enquiry, is constitutive of what it is to be human. This platonic vision was taken up and massively reinforced by later Christian teaching. However, Plato's vision has its dangers. Some of these we shall see as we consider the critique of his brilliant pupil Aristotle.

---

[43] One classic study of Platonic influence on later Christian theology is E. von Ivanka, *Plato Christianus* (Einsiedeln: Johannes Verlag, 1990).

CHAPTER 4

Aristotle's revisionism

CRITIQUE OF PLATO

The platonic vision of 'two worlds' and the ascetic path from one to the other was the overarching framework for much of early Christian thought. Christianity began as a messianic movement amongst Jews, but rapidly took root amongst the Greeks and other peoples who inhabited the cosmopolitan cities of the Hellenistic world. It began as a way of living, with a spirituality and teaching that was cultivated through the common life of little ecclesial cells. It survived through institutionalisation, as it developed a recognised ministry, church organisation, and an ordered body of teaching. The Greek thought-world in which it flourished was formed in the platonic mould, and proved remarkably hospitable to this dynamic new movement. Plato's vision of a just and ordered society in which each takes their place, from the 'philosopher-king' to the humblest craftsman, has continued to captivate the Christian imagination, both as a vision of the church in the world and as a vision of the heavenly City of God.

The story of the emergence of the modern world at the time of the scientific revolution and the Enlightenment, of the rejection of 'medievalism' and the rise of secularism, can readily be told as the story of the long demise of platonism. This is how it is put by Nietzsche, the most articulate and prophetic modern critic of platonism. In the *Twilight of the Idols*,[1] he has a brief

---

[1] F. Nietzsche, *Twilight of the Idols and The Anti-Christ* (Harmondsworth: Penguin Books, 1968), pp. 40–1.

section entitled 'How the "Real World" at last Became a Myth'. He outlines six steps:

(1) 'The real world, attainable to the wise, the pious, the virtuous man – he dwells in it, *he is it*.' Plato is identified with this view.

(2) 'The real world, unattainable for the moment, but promised to the wise, the pious, the virtuous man.' The idea, he says, 'becomes Christian'.

(3) 'The real world, unattainable, undemonstrable, cannot be promised, but even when merely thought of [is] a consolation, a duty, an imperative.' The idea, he says, has become 'pale, northerly, Königsbergian', that is to say Kantian.

(4) 'The real world' is now 'unattainable? – Unattained, at any rate. And if unattained, also *unknown*. Consequently also no consolation, no redemption, no duty.' This is called 'the cockcrow of positivism'.

(5) The 'real world' is now 'an idea grown useless, superfluous, *consequently* a refuted idea: let us abolish it!' Now 'Plato blushes for shame; all free spirits run riot.'

(6) 'We have abolished the real world: what world is left? the apparent world perhaps?. . . But no! *with the real world we have also abolished the apparent world!*' 'Mid-day', says Nietzsche, '. . . end of the longest error; zenith of mankind; INCIPIT ZARATHUSTRA.'

Nietzsche believed that it was time to construct a 'new world': the world of Zarathustra. He offered not so much a critique as a brilliant short history of the demise of platonism. This is the story behind the bursting of his madman into the town-square with the news that 'God is dead.' Nietzsche is the prophet who has seen this, and felt the terror when the 'real world' of platonist Christianity is at last pronounced dead. He proclaims the death of the world of 'being', which, despite the abuses it engendered, was also a world of security, and the coming of a time in which all is 'becoming'. What Nietzsche, the prophet of post-modernism, saw was the completion of a process that had begun with Aristotle, for it was Aristotle, Plato's pupil, still working within a platonist framework, who first insisted in response to Plato that philosophical attention should be focused more critically and more systematically on *this* world. Later Christian spirituality, of course, following Plato's tendency to see this world as but a pale reflection of one that is 'higher', was often to pull sharply in the other direction.

Nietzsche hails – in trepidation – the evaporation of Plato's 'real world'. The most impassioned and influential modern critic of Plato's teaching about *this* world has been Karl Popper in *The Open Society and its Enemies*.[2] Popper has described how he began to write his volume entitled 'The Spell of Plato' on the day in March 1938 when he heard that the Germans had occupied his native Austria. In his autobiography, he called the writing of this and *The Poverty of Historicism* his 'war effort',[3] something that needs to be remembered in reading so passionate a book. For Popper, Plato is the enemy of all that is to be valued most highly in the open society – principally the right to criticise. Thus, he writes on Plato's ethical teaching:

We must . . . realize that those who . . . exalt Plato's reputation as a teacher of morals and announce to the world that his ethics is the nearest approach to Christianity before Christ, are preparing the way for totalitarianism and especially for a totalitarian, anti-Christian interpretation of Christianity. And this is a dangerous thing, for there have been times when Christianity was dominated by totalitarian ideas. There was an Inquisition; and, in another form, it may come again.[4]

Popper puts his finger on a vitally important truth about Plato's social vision. It is elitist, and with that, it has all the potential to be repressive. It offers a certain kind of freedom for some (the guardians), provided they are prepared to pay the communitarian cost of a highly politicised education, deprivation of private goods, lack of freedom in sexual relations, and communal child-rearing; for women, for slaves, and for metics ('resident aliens', of which Aristotle was one) it offers no freedom at all. Plato's attitude to art, which he sees as prone to

[2] K. R. Popper, *The Open Society and its Enemies*, 2 vols. (London: Routledge and Kegan Paul, 1945).
[3] K. R. Popper, *Unended Quest, An Intellectual Autobiography* (Glasgow: Fontana, 1976), p. 115.
[4] Popper, *The Open Society*, vol. I, p. 104.

mislead by its production of delusive representation in a world of delusion, is, of course, highly censorious:

We must not only compel our poets, on pain of expulsion, to make their poetry the express image of noble character; we must also supervise craftsmen of every kind and forbid them to leave the stamp of baseness, licence, meanness, unseemliness, on painting and sculpture, or building, or any other work of their hands; and anyone who cannot obey shall not practise his art in our commonwealth.[5]

The real purpose of art is to edify, and, if it does not edify, the artist is to be expelled. Plato believed we could *know* we are in touch with the good, the true, and the beautiful, and wanted vigorously to ensure that art serves the purpose of putting others similarly in touch. In the twentieth century above all, we have had such terrible experiences of propagandist uses of art and of institutionalised violence on the grounds that the state knows or will prescribe what is good for people, that Plato's naive confidence in the civic purpose of art, and his preparedness to support this with censorship and expulsion, causes a deep frisson. Artists hold before us the possibility of alternatives. In Plato's vision of the work of the artist, there is no place for such dangerous play. Popper, who is in his own way equally solemn, sees a direct line from moral and political certitude to repression. We have to face the fact, he maintains, that 'our dream of heaven cannot be realized on earth'.[6] We have to come down to earth and live with the reality of conflict that marks every human society:

There can be no human society without conflict: such a society would be a society not of friends but of ants. Even if it were attainable, there are human values of the greatest importance which would be destroyed by its attainment, and which therefore should prevent us from attempting to bring it about.[7]

Popper's recipe for avoiding chaos is the use of the critical method, the exercise of what he calls 'critical rationalism', the slow work of corrective critical thinking to eliminate error in what we say and believe. For him this is far from a prescription

---

[5] F. M. Cornford, *The Republic of Plato* (London: Oxford University Press, 1941), p. 90.
[6] Popper, *The Open Society*, vol. 1, p. 200.
[7] Popper, *Unended Quest*, p. 116.

for a moral free-for-all, but it is a specific against moral hubris. He is keen to stress that one of the main arguments of *The Open Society* is directed *against moral relativism*: 'The fact that moral values or principles may clash does not invalidate them.'[8] It is Aristotle, rather than Plato, who gives an account of how that might be the case.

ARISTOTLE ON VIRTUE AND FRIENDSHIP

Aristotle was Plato's pupil for twenty years, during which time he thoroughly imbibed his master's philosophy. On Plato's death, he moved away from Athens. In the next twelve years, he engaged in research on marine biology and became tutor to the young Alexander, son of Philip of Macedon. He then returned to Athens, where he founded his own philosophical school, the Lyceum, teaching there for a further twelve years until shortly before his death in 322 BCE.

Aristotle retains in his thought some of the central platonic emphases, but thoroughly transmuted. Both Plato and Aristotle have transcendent notions of the soul, of the intellect, and of virtue, and for both the demands of the state transcend the wants of the individual. The cast of Aristotle's mind is, however, as different from that of Plato as that of Plato from Socrates. Where Aristotle is 'a middle-class professional man, a husband and a father, scientific observer and practical administrator', Plato is 'the Athenian aristocrat, mystic, ascetic, puritan'. The political thought of Aristotle is marked by such non-Platonic features as, 'the value of family life, the pursuit of health and happiness . . . , the importance and value of property, respect for public opinion . . . above all, his sense of the possible, his conviction that one half at least of politics is making the best of what you have'.[9]

Plato is by far the easier for us to read because of the element of drama in his dialogues. The dialogues that Aristotle is said to

---

[8] *Ibid.* This is also a major theme in the work of Isaiah Berlin. See, for example, *Four Essays on Liberty* (Oxford: Oxford University Press, 1969), pp. 167–72.

[9] T. A. Sinclair, *A History of Greek Political Thought* (London: Routledge, Kegan Paul, 1951), pp. 210–11.

have written have been lost. Most of the texts we have seem to be lecture notes, which can be extremely hard going. There is no element of characterisation, of narrative, or of dialectic to enliven them. Plato draws us into his dialogues and his vision of two worlds; Aristotle directs his gaze at this world and encourages us to do the same. He is the supreme collector, classifier, and analyst. Like Plato, he is interested in ethics, politics, law, mathematics, metaphysics, and aesthetics, but Aristotle approaches each field with the mind of a scientist, endlessly curious to collect and classify information about plants, animals, the weather, the heavens, constitutions, virtues, and vices. As he classifies, he asks the questions of a natural philosopher, working by observation and induction, believing that knowledge is bred by generalisation out of perception. 'No one can learn or understand anything', he says, 'in the absence of sense.'[10] It is from his observation of the world that he is drawn into questions of logic, ontology, and theology, relentlessly pursuing his desire 'to know'. His map of human knowing is divided into three: the practical, the productive, and the theoretical. The practical includes ethics and politics, inexact sciences concerned with what is morally right and what is just, conceptions 'which involve much difference of opinion and uncertainty';[11] the productive includes art, rhetoric, farming and engineering, all forms of 'making' or *poiesis*; the theoretical includes mathematics, natural science, and theology. Theology is 'first science' because it has 'to consider being *qua* being – both what it is and the attributes which belong to it *qua* being'.[12]

Like Plato, Aristotle believes that there is an order in the

---

[10] *On the Soul* III.8; 432a 6. (Unless otherwise stated, I have used the translation and reference in J. Barnes ed., *The Complete Works of Aristotle*, 2 volumes, Bollingen Series LXXI.2, Princeton: Princeton University Press, 1984.) Aristotle's practice of observation and induction was uneven. Martha Craven Nussbaum comments: 'Had he devoted to the psychology of women, or even to their physiology (about which he makes many ludicrous and easily corrigible errors) even a fraction of the sustained care that he devoted to the lives and bodies of shellfish, the method would have been better served' (*The Fragility of Goodness*, Cambridge: Cambridge University Press, 1986, p. 371).

[11] See *Nic. Eth.* 1.3; 1094b 15–16 (LCL translation).

[12] *Metaphysics* VI.1; 1026a 31.

world which is there to be discovered and analysed. He shares with Plato the sense that all things are held together as one whole or *kosmos*, but is highly critical of Plato's theory of Forms, by participation in which the world as we know it is constituted, and plays down his teaching that we should direct the soul's gaze through or even away from particulars in this world to contemplate universals in a higher world of abstraction, known to us by intellectual intuition. For Plato, there is an ontological separation of 'two worlds' the interpenetration of which he describes with words such as *koinonia* and *methexis*. We have seen that he moved in his life towards a greater emphasis upon the transcendence, towards the separation rather than the close co-inherence of the two worlds. Aristotle thinks much more in terms of two levels of knowledge about this one world. He does not, however, reject there being a transcendent dimension to the act of knowing. He retains an ontological differentiation between intellect and objects in the world, and between divine being and beings. To this extent, Aristotle was working with the presuppositions he had inherited from his teacher and his thinking was conditioned by his formation in Plato's Academy. He has, however, a much wider horizon than Plato and is able to set his thought in some sort of comparative context. In this sense, he is the father of modern anthropological and socio-logical approaches to knowledge, for he recognises that our understanding of political life and of virtue is related to our experiences of community. For Aristotle, it is within the life of a particular community or communities – Athens is of course his model – that virtue, which is the moral *telos* of human beings, is learnt and cultivated.

For Aristotle 'man' (*anthropos*) is 'the animal with a tendency to community' (*koinonikon zoon*).[13] Before coming to his explora-tion of forms of human community in the *Politics*, Aristotle explored the moral life of the human in community. In the

---

[13] *Eud. Eth.* VII.10; 1242a 25 (translation adapted). This whole paragraph (1242a 20–1242b 2) contains an important discussion of justice related to 'man' (*anthropos*) as the animal who is not only 'political' (*politikos*), but 'household-maintaining' (*oikono-mikos*) and 'with a tendency to live in community' (*koinonikos*). For discussion of 'Aristotle on Justice', see A. MacIntyre, *Whose Justice? Which Rationality?* (London: Duckworth, 1988), pp. 103–23.

Eudemian and the *Nicomachean Ethics*,[14] he discusses the place of virtue and friendship in the life of the individual – who is a good citizen of the *polis*. His method is the reverse of Plato. Where, in the *Republic*, Plato looks at justice in the *polis* so he can show how the individual fits into this, Aristotle looks at justice in the life of the individual to show how the virtuous individual thrives in the life of the *polis*. However, though he is prepared to concentrate his attention on the individual, he still recognises that the study of the individual is an abstraction from those social milieux (friendships, the life of the household or the *polis*) which are natural for human beings.

Central to Aristotle's enquiry is his conception of moral virtue as a mean between two extremes. This is one of the points where he most clearly differentiates himself from Plato. For him, moral virtue is not a participation in some transcendent Form but a balance, a refined and disciplined skill which is learned in the actual exercise of virtue. Aristotle talks of learning by doing: human beings 'become builders by building, and lyre-players by playing the lyre; so too we become just by doing just acts, temperate by doing temperate acts, brave by doing brave acts'.[15] Virtues such as courage (*andreia*), temperance (*sophrosune*), or generosity (*eleutheriotes*) are thus states of character, developed dispositions to behave according to the mean between excess and deficiency. The virtuous person will look for that mean and live according to it, something that comes with commitment, education, and practice.

Aristotle's account of the moral virtues culminates in a discussion of justice found in both the *Eudemian* and the *Nicomachean Ethics*. Typically, he begins from the widespread recognition of justice as 'that moral disposition which makes people

[14] The *Nicomachean Ethics* may be taken to be the authoritative statement of Aristotle's mature ethical thought. *Pace* A. Kenny (*The Aristotelian Ethics*, Oxford: Clarendon Press, 1978), the *Eudemian Ethics* are usually thought to represent a less mature earlier draft and the *Magna Moralia* a later summary by another hand. D. S. Hutchinson reflects this scholarly consensus in his chapter on Aristotle's 'Ethics' in J. Barnes ed., *The Cambridge Companion to Aristotle* (Cambridge: Cambridge University Press, 1995), pp. 197–8.

[15] *Nic. Eth.* II.1; 1103a 33ff. Compare the notion of a 'practice', developed by Alasdair MacIntyre from his discussion of 'Aristotle's Account of the Virtues' in *After Virtue*, second edition (London: Duckworth, 1985), pp. 146–64, 187–94.

disposed to do what is just and makes them act justly and wish for what is just',[16] but he deepens his analysis by observing the variety of ways in which the term 'justice' is actually used. 'Justice', he says, 'sums up' all the virtues: in this 'perfect virtue' all the others are included. Where the virtues he has hitherto discussed characterise the virtuous *individual*, justice includes care for the other person. More than other virtues, it is a term of *relation*.

For Aristotle there is a proper order within the *polis*, which is both universal (masters are superior to slaves; men to women and children; humans to animals) and, in its specific expression, a matter of law and constitution (the variety of which he examines in the *Politics*). Justice consists in the maintenance of due order, which is a matter of proportion (*analogia*). For example, the tariff of punishments for various crimes established by law must be proportionate to their seriousness and, in trading, the relative value of goods should be recognised by proportionate payment. Where this happens there is *koinonia*; without the establishment of justice (proportion) in such key areas of political life there can be no *koinonia*. Justice, then, is the maintenance of a social equilibrium, which the just person discerns and actively supports. Hence the important public role of the *dikast* (the judge or jury-man – potentially any citizen) who must be 'justice personified'. The key presupposition throughout Aristotle's discussion, not only of justice but of all the virtues, is that these can only be practised where there is some underlying bond of association – where there is *koinonia*.[17]

From his discussion of justice, Aristotle moves on to discussion of friendship (*philia*), which is a distinctive and elevated form of *koinonia*. Friendship both implies virtue and is necessary for living the good life. Perfect friendship is friendship between those who are alike in virtue. Bad men will be friends solely for pleasure or to use one another; good men will be friends through the strength of their mutual commitment (*koinonia*), for 'friendship depends on *koinonia*' ('*en koinonia gar he*

[16] *Nic. Eth.* v.1 10; 1129a 9 (translation adapted).
[17] *Nic. Eth.* v.5; 1133b 7ff; v.6; 1133a 27.

philia).[18] Aristotle lists various examples of common enterprises that draw people together. Sailors go on a voyage
together to make money; soldiers share together in warfare in
the hope of plunder or victory; religious guilds and social
clubs bring people together for pleasure. Each enterprise in its
own way generates *koinonia* within the life of the *polis*. In these
situations, friendship springs up, but it is often inferior friendship. For there to be the highest friendship, it must be between
equals. The political context radically affects the quality of the
friendship: 'While in tyrannies friendship and justice hardly
exist, in democracies they exist more fully; for where the
citizens are equal they have much in common.'[19] 'Friendship
is a partnership (*koinonia*).'[20] *Koinonia* between virtuous friends
is an end in itself just as virtue is an end in itself. Such *koinonia*,
quite simply, opens the way to happiness (*eudaimonia*).

ANTHROPOLOGY AND POLITICAL PARTICIPATION

For Aristotle, the *polis* is the supreme *koinonia*, which aims at the
highest good. He begins his *Politics*:

Every state is a community (*koinonia*) of some kind, and every *koinonia*
is established with a view to some good; for everyone always acts in
order to obtain that which they think good. But if all communities aim
at some good, that which is the highest of all, and which embraces all
the rest, aims at good in a greater degree than any other, and at the
highest good, and that is the community entitled the state, the political
koinonia.[21]

For Aristotle the state has a moral identity, since it aims at the
good, an aim which ensures human flourishing in the highest
degree. It is composed of various smaller units of community in
which humans are also to flourish in ways appropriate to that
level of community. In saying this, he is simply applying the
same method of scientific investigation, with the same presuppositions, that he has throughout his work: 'As in other depart-

---

[18] *Nic. Eth.* VIII.9; 1159b 32; *Nic. Eth.* VIII.8–12 (1159b–1162a) is a key section for
    Aristotle's understanding of *koinonia*.
[19] *Nic. Eth.* VIII.11; 1161b 9–10.   [20] *Nic. Eth.* IX.12; 1171b 32.
[21] *Politics* I.1; 1252a 1–5 (translation adapted).

ments of science, so in politics, the compound should always be resolved into the simple elements or least parts of the whole. We must therefore look at the elements of which the state is composed.'[22]

Aristotle's basic element is the household, which is composed of two *koinoniai*: that of the male and the female for reproduction, and that of the master and slave for economic security, or, in the case of the poor, that with their animals who do the slave-like work.[23] Out of several households is made the village, which arises as a form of extended family under one ruler. However, 'When several villages are united in a single complete community, large enough to be nearly or quite self-sufficing, the state comes into existence, originating in the bare needs of life, and continuing in existence for the sake of the good life.'[24] Aristotle goes on to make clear his presupposition: that the nature (*phusis*) of anything, be it man, horse, or household, becomes apparent as it fulfils its *telos*, or purpose.[25] The nature of man (*anthropos*) is that of a 'political animal' (*politikon zoon*). Man's *telos* is therefore to flourish as a political animal, to 'live well' in the community of the *polis* (which is why when Aristotle discusses 'living well' in the *Ethics* what he proposes is not an individualist ethic but an ethic which culminates in an exposition of friendship).[26] Distinctive of human beings is the use of language (a social skill), together with the perception of good and bad, right and wrong, and other moral qualities. Sharing in these qualities (*touton koinonia*) is constitutive of all human

---

[22] *Politics* I.1; 1252a 19–21.

[23] In the *Politics* (e.g. 1.5; 1260a 40) Aristotle appears to contradict what he says in *Eud. Eth.* VII.9, where he claims that between 'soul and body, artisan and tool, and master and slave' there can be no *koinonia*. His basic point is that where one party uses the other purely *as instrument* there can be no *koinonia* – no association. In the *Nic. Eth.* (VIII.xi; 1160b 31f.) he clarifies his position: 'Where there is nothing common to ruler and ruled, there is not friendship either . . . e.g. between craftsman and tool, soul and body, master and slave . . . *Qua* slave then, one cannot be friends with him. But *qua* man one can . . . There can also be friendship with him in so far as he is a man.'

[24] *Politics* I.2; 1252b 28–31.

[25] This he has already discussed in his *Physics*. See S. Everson's introduction to *The Politics* (Cambridge: Cambridge University Press, 1988), pp. xix–xxi.

[26] In *Politics* 1263a Aristotle discusses the difficulty for human beings of living together in community: 'In general to live together and to share (*koinonein*) all our human affairs is difficult . . . Community of property therefore involves these and similar difficulties' (LCL translation).

relations in the household and in the *polis*. Aristotle finds priority in the city-state over the household and the individual, for these are parts of the whole, and what are the parts without the whole? (This is the way he looks at it: the whole has the priority; it is more than the mere sum of its parts. The parts look towards the 'achieving' of the whole; we might say towards 'catholicity'.) By nature humans search out *koinonia*, and the *koinonia* in which humans find the greatest fulfilment is that of the *polis*.

The account that Aristotle gives of humans as animals fulfilled in sociality has been of the greatest importance in the development of a theological understanding of catholicism, not only as a formal principle but as a *dynamic* towards integration and towards unity. Aristotle's point is not merely that individuals flourish in association, but that there is a *dynamic*, constitutive of humanity, by which humans are driven to associate, and only when the highest form of association (the *polis*) is achieved is the *telos* of humans achieved, and it then becomes evident what it is to be the human being (we might say 'person') that was hitherto in the making. It is in that form of *koinonia* which we call the *polis* that we finally see what sort of animal the human being is. This is as far as Aristotle normally takes it. He asks few questions about the association of cities.[27] Perhaps because he saw Philip of Macedon and his son Alexander suppressing local forms of association by conquest, he was broadly content to accept the co-existence of independent city-states, amongst which Athens, despite its imperial past, was only one.

Aristotle sets out in the *Politics* to consider what is the best form of *politeia*, or community. *Politeia* is a difficult word to translate because it encompasses both a city's way of life and its polity, or constitution. Aristotle, ever the biologist, calls it 'the life (*bios*) of the city'. Several times, almost as a refrain in the *Politics*,[28] he repeats that the *politeia* is a *koinonia*; in other words, the constitution, the political life of a city, is one of the forms of

---

[27] *Politics* VII.7; 1327b 30–2 is an exception: 'If [the Hellenic race] could be formed into one state (*politeia*), [it] would be able to rule the world.'

[28] *Politics* II.1; 1260b 39; III.3; 1276b 1; III.4; 1276b 30.

koinonia – in fact, for humans, the most developed form of participation in a common life. What ensures the continuity of the state as identifiably the same state is identity of *politeia*, of constitution and life. Though he doesn't say it in so many words, we would not be forcing Aristotle's meaning if we said that what constitutes the identity of the state is identity of *koinonia*. Where there is identity of political institutions, we can take it that there is this identity of *koinonia*, stability of political life. Aristotle's concern was to identify the best form of political life, that which was most likely to promote human flourishing. Typically, he collected 158 constitutions currently in use, before examining and classifying them like a natural scientist. In doing so, he was also assembling material for a critique of Plato's *Republic* and his *Laws*, with both of which he entered into sustained debate.[29]

Aristotle was suspicious of any attempt to realise Plato's programme, because 'all the constitutions which now exist are faulty', so a realistic aim was not to try to write the perfect constitution but to identify from constitutions currently in use criteria by which one might discern one which functions as well as possible. In a pregnant comment, clearly aimed at Plato, he asserts that there can be too much unity in a state, because a state must be *diverse* (*plethos*).[30] It must not be composed of men who are identical. His realism as to how people function in the world leads him to reject Plato's community of wives and children and to defend private property: 'It is clearly better that property should be private, but the use of it common.'[31] Aristotle argues vigorously for unity, just as Plato does, but not for uniformity: 'The state is a plurality (*plethos*) which should be united and made into a community by education (by *paideia*).'[32] He criticises Plato for a lack of confidence in the power of education, of philosophy, custom and law, to bring about the sharing of property in the service of the community.

Participation as a citizen in the life of a *polis* is a natural requisite for the fullest human flourishing. It is not that humans ought for pragmatic reasons to participate in the life of the *polis*

[29] *Politics* II.1; 1261a ff.   [30] *Politics* II.2; 1261a 18–19.
[31] *Politics* II.5; 1263a 38.   [32] *Politics* II.2; 1263b 36–7.

but that the *telos* of human nature is fulfilled when they do so. The man who is excluded from the life of the *polis* is 'like the "tribeless, lawless, hearthless" one' denounced by Homer.[33] Aristotle compares him to an isolated draughts-piece. It is only as a citizen of a *polis* that man can achieve *eudaimonia*, happiness or flourishing, and it is this which shows him to be a political animal: he is naturally disposed to live in *koinonia*, and the best form of *koinonia* to fulfil his nature is that of the *polis*.

Aristotle is an advocate of active citizenship. Citizens must be participant in the civic community, sharing in ruling and being ruled, in the judicial process and political debate. Typically, he is not prescriptive about how exactly this will work out. His concern for the *polis* as a moral entity devoted to the *telos* of living well is paramount. The state itself is an association that has a clear goal, and the best citizens are those who make that goal their own as they work for the common good. Having made clear how he understands participative citizenship, Aristotle goes on to explore the forms of government within which these aims may be pursued. He recognises that there are many forms of constitution, but he concentrates on two broad types: democracy and oligarchy (together with kingship). The key to a stable, efficient and harmonious political community is the role played by the middle class. Whatever form democracy or oligarchy may take, it is vital that the middle class be large and that they be included in the exercise of power. This power is exercised in three ways (though the actual means of its exercise may vary greatly): first, in the legislature; second, in the executive; third, in the judiciary.[34] Aristotle looks for a stable balance between these three, for he sees the cause of revolutions in any disproportionate increase in power on the part of one element or one class in the state. Stability (equilibrium) of the constitution is key. 'Disproportion destroys a state', for it leads to revolution.[35]

Aristotle brings his *Politics* to a close with a sketch of the state which functions as it should, and of the education within it. His definition of the state is 'a community (*koinonia*) of equals,

---

[33] *Politics* I.2; 1253b 4.   [34] *Politics* IV.14; 1297b 35ff.   [35] *Politics* V.9; 1309b 24.

aiming at the best life possible'.[36] It must have only the number of citizens that 'can be taken in at a single view' and for it to thrive all must participate in the common life according to their gifts and abilities. What is vital is to understand the nature of happiness (*eudaimonia*) which is found in the realisation and perfect exercise of virtue. It is by education that the city will promote virtue in its citizens, for we must not 'suppose that anyone of the citizens belongs to himself, for they all belong to the state, and are each of them a part of the state, and the care of each part is inseparable from the care of the whole'.[37] Citizens have a duty towards the state as well as rights within it.

Aristotle's conception of *koinonia* is foundational to his notion of the *polis*. For Plato, the city-state is bound together by the common participation of its virtuous citizens in the Idea of the Good. Aristotle thinks of the unity of the state in a much more distributed way. He is not interested in finding the perfect constitution. He is interested in how actual constitutions work, how *koinonia* is best realised in actual instances of *politeia*. One of his most distinctive contributions from our point of view is to offer a vision of a network of *koinoniai* from the intimate familial bond between a man and a woman, or a master and a slave, or a poor person and their animal, through that of the village to that of the *polis*. This characteristically Aristotelian notion of the 'community of communities' as opposed to the monolithic community of Plato, which realises on earth an ideal hitherto known only in the heavens or in some mythical, aboriginal time, has been of vital importance both politically and ecclesiologically. For example, the two come together in the ever-fresh work of J. N. Figgis, who writes:

What we actually see in the world is not on the one hand the State, and on the other a mass of unrelated individuals; but a vast complex of gathered unions, in which alone we find individuals, families, clubs, trades unions, colleges, professions, and so forth; and further, that there are exercised functions within these groups which are of the nature of government, including its three aspects, legislative, execu-

---

[36] *Politics* VII.8; 1328a 36.   [37] *Politics* VIII.1; 1337a 27–31.

tive, and judicial; though of course, only with reference to their own members.[38]

Figgis numbers Aristotle among the theorists of the unitary state, and in this I think he is wrong. In one of his sharpest formulations, Aristotle wrote, 'It is true that unity is to some extent necessary, alike in a household and in a *polis*; but total unity is not.'[39] Bernard Crick is more perceptive when he praises 'the great Aristotle' for 'recognising the political rela- tionship as one that harmonizes and tries to elevate those differences of opinion and interest which naturally exist within any known State'. The great sin of totalitarian doctrine is 'its hatred of diversifying groups and institutions. The great virtue of Aristotle', says Crick, 'is his understanding of the pluralistic nature of authority and the importance of group diversity.'[40] There are important limits, though, to Aristotle's recognition of diversity within the life of the *polis*. He stopped well short of embracing conflict as a positive dynamic within the *koinonia* of the *polis*. In this, he failed to recognise what MacIntyre has called 'a Sophoclean insight': that it is 'through conflict and sometimes only through conflict . . . we learn what our ends and purposes are'.[41]

ANTHROPOLOGY AND 'THE DESIRE TO KNOW'

'All men desire by nature to know',[42] says Aristotle. To know is more than to classify. It is mentally to relate objects in the world

---

[38] J. N. Figgis, *Churches in the Modern State* (London: Longmans, 1913), p. 70. Figgis' notion of the state as a *communitas communitarum*, which owes much to the hierarchy of *koinoniai* in Book 1 of Aristotle's *Politics*, is discussed critically in D. Runciman, *Pluralism and the Personality of the State* (Cambridge: Cambridge University Press, 1997), pp. 124–49.

[39] *Politics* II.5; 1263a 31–2 (translated by E. Barker, *The Politics of Aristotle*, Oxford: Clarendon Press, 1948).

[40] B. Crick, *In Defence of Politics*, fourth edition (London: Penguin, 1993), pp. 47–53. See also the perceptive discussion, contrasting the attitudes of Plato and Aristotle towards conflict, in Nussbaum, *The Fragility of Goodness*, pp. 352–3.

[41] A. MacIntyre, *After Virtue*, p. 164. Martha Nussbaum frequently stresses the import- ance of the tragedians for Athenian moral and political understanding: 'We are asked [in *Antigone*] to see that a conflict-free life would be lacking in value and beauty next to a life in which it is possible for conflict to arise . . . that, as Heraclitus put it, justice really *is* strife' (*The Fragility of Goodness*, p. 81).

[42] *Met.* 1.1; 980b 22.

in such a way that we can address questions of causality, classification, and teleology. It is to address ourselves not to a static world, but to a world of change, and not to a world made up solely of objects, but to one of which human thought, consciousness, and the relations between humans are constitutive. Aristotle's critique of knowledge begins from a strong critique of Plato. He rejects – or radically modifies – Plato's theory of Forms as an explanation for the world being as he finds it to be.

Plato's theory of Forms was discussed in the previous chapter. We saw how Plato uses a number of different terms to speak of the relation between Form and object in the world: some, like *koinonia, methexis*, and *parousia* emphasise the immanence, the presence of the Form in the particular object, and some like *paradeigma, mimesis*, and *eikon* emphasise the transcendence of the Form over the particular. There was a shift towards an emphasis on transcendence as Plato got older. This was, of course, the time when Aristotle studied with Plato at the Academy, coming to the conclusion that the theory of Forms as Plato presented it was unworkable. His rejection of the theory struck at the heart of his teacher's understanding of the relation, the *koinonia*, between this world and the higher realm of the Forms, leaving it depleted in imaginative detail, but creating a philosophical framework that was much strengthened as a basis for the scientific engagement of later Christian theology with this world. In his critique of the separate and independent existence of Plato's Forms, Aristotle struck at Plato's ontology, his cosmology, at his understanding of politics and ethics. Aristotle gave his own and very different account of transcendence which was vital to his understanding of this world. No less than Plato's is his an integrated vision of participation, but he does not posit a higher world to account for the contingency of this one.

Aristotle criticises Plato's theory because it can be used to prove too little or too much. He finds the basic argument for an other and higher realm of Forms flawed. The commonly used argument, which Plato accepted, goes that for any class of objects, such as 'table', there is that which all the particular instances have in common, but which is identical with none of them. That which is abstracted from the particulars, and eternal, is taken to be the 'Form' (or *Idea*) of the Table. Aristotle accepts the notion of 'form' but argues that this falls far short of a proof that the 'form' as such 'exists': that it is 'a real object with a separate and independent existence'.[43] He is critical, firstly, of the way in which Forms are derived, arguing that according to Plato's logic where there is negative predication there ought to be negative Forms such as 'not-table', which he found nonsensical, as he did the possibility of Forms of perishable things, and so of things that have perished, or of Forms of relative terms, such as largeness. A second line of criticism strikes at the heart of the theory. He argued repeatedly that, 'All the difficulties in the theory of Forms arise from their separation (*chorismos*).'[44] It is on the basis of his sharp understanding of their *separation* that Aristotle maintains Plato's Forms cannot cause motion in objects; they cannot give being (*ousia*) to objects; they cannot make objects intelligible.[45] If this is correct, it explains Aristotle's suspicion of the language of pattern and participatory sharing, including *koinonia*, when talking of the relation between Forms and particular objects, for there is strictly no *thing* there for the particular object to have *koinonia* with:

Other things are not in any accepted sense *derived* from the Forms. To say that the Forms are patterns (*paradeigmata*), and that other things participate (*metechein*) in them, is to use empty phrases and poetical metaphors.[46]

To talk in this way is *kenologein*, to speak empty words.

Aristotle further criticised Plato's theory because it provides no solution to the problems of change and coming-to-be. Since

---

[43] See G. E. R. Lloyd, *Aristotle: The Growth and Structure of his Thought* (Cambridge: Cambridge University Press, 1968), p. 44.

[44] J. D. Mabbott, 'Aristotle and the *Chorismos* of Plato', *Classical Quarterly* 20 (1926), 72. This classic article is still remarkably useful. In his 'Introduction to the Study of Plato' in R. Kraut ed., *The Cambridge Companion to Plato* (Cambridge: Cambridge University Press, 1992), p. 8, Kraut discusses Plato's positing of 'a separate realm of abstract objects called "Forms"'. For recent discussion, see G. Fine 'Separation' in *Oxford Studies in Ancient Philosophy* 2 (1984), pp. 31–87 and G. Vlastos, *Socrates, Ironist and Moral Philosopher* (Cambridge: Cambridge University Press, 1991), pp. 256–65.

[45] Mabbott, 'Aristotle and the *Chorismos* of Plato', 73.

[46] *Met.* 1.9; 991a 21f (LCL translation) also XIII.5; 1079b 25f.

Plato's Forms cannot cause movement or change, Aristotle can see no reason to appeal to their existence in explaining why particular objects in the world are as they are. It just doesn't help, in seeking to grasp the causes of things about us, to add to, and possibly double, their number.[47] The platonic Forms belonged to a higher world of unchanging being, to which Plato wanted to draw philosophical attention. Aristotle's interest was the investigation of form (and matter) in the changing world of nature.

Nevertheless, Aristotle remains something of a dualist. For him, man's investigative ability comes from the application of intellect. Human beings are distinguished from the other animals by possessing the power of intellect (*nous*), which he at various times speaks of as 'divine' or directly moved by God.[48] More than that, he says that each of us actually *is*, more than anything else, intellect, and that this is the 'authoritative (*kurion*) and better part' of us. The 'best and pleasantest' life is the life lived according to the intellect.[49] This life alone comes from outside the world, and is divine. 'Bodily activity has no connection at all [has no *koinonia*] with reason.'[50] The happiness (*eudaimonia*) that belongs to the intellect is separate, 'a thing apart' (*kechorismene*).[51] Thought, then, can exist apart from the body, but in the conditions of this world it must take place in bodies. In his treatise *On the Soul*, Aristotle describes 'active thought' as 'separable, impassible, unmixed'.[52] He speaks of 'active thought' in terms similar to those he uses for the Unmoved Mover of the *Metaphysics*, which is a substance 'eternal and unmovable and separate from sensible things . . . without parts, indivisible . . . impassive, unalterable'.[53] Just as the Unmoved Mover unceasingly engenders motion without being itself moved, so 'active thought' enters into objects in the world to possess them without itself becoming enmeshed in or

[47] *Met.* 1.9; 989b 30–990b 8.
[48] *Gen. An.* ii.3; 736b 28; *Nic. Eth.* x.7; 1177b 30–2; cf. *Eud. Eth.* viii.2; 1248a 26–9.
[49] *Nic. Eth.* x.7; 1178a 2, 7–8.
[50] *Gen. An.* ii.3; 736b 28 cf. *Eud. Eth.* vii.ix; 1241b 18, where there is said to be no *koinonia* between soul *(psuche)* and body *(soma)*. Compare note 23 above.
[51] *Nic. Eth.* x.7; 1178a 22.   [52] *De An.* iii.5; 430a. 17–19.
[53] *Met.* xii.7; 1073a 4–12.

truly part of the world. This is not, however, true of all thought, for Aristotle also refers briefly to 'passive thought'. This is the thought engendered by the impressions that objects in the world make on our senses. Unlike 'active thought', such 'passive thought' is 'perishable'.[54]

There is, then, a tension in what he has to say: he is clear that thought as such is separated from bodily activity, yet in the conditions of this world it must find bodily expression, and to this extent is interwoven with the life of this world. His use of 'active thought', which stands free of bodily involvement, and 'passive thought', which is involved in and contingent upon the world, resolves nothing, but is a way of living with that tension. Since the 'active reason' is eternal and impassible and the 'passive reason' is perishable, this does seem to indicate a belief on Aristotle's part that individuals are not simply conditioned in their thinking by the world about them but that they have a share in, participate in, or are related to 'active reason', though somehow the 'active reason' remains untouched by the vicissitudes of life in the world. In this sense, Aristotle retained something of Plato's structure of transcendence, for both believed the intellect gives access to such a reality, but Plato considered this reality a hyper-physical realm of Forms, the highest point of which is the Form of the Good, whilst Aristotle, who was no less firm in presenting such a reality, presented it much more in terms of abstraction and concentration of essence, which comes to a focus in his highly abstract account of divinity.

For Aristotle, the highest activity of God (the 'Unmoved Mover') and of humans is contemplation (*theoria*). In the world, perception involves the apprehension of sensible objects by the 'passive intellect', which is a kind of uniting. For the God, above and beyond the world, there can only be 'thinking about thinking', which again is a kind of uniting at the level of thought. Both Plato and Aristotle see intellectual union with God as human beatitude. In Plato, this is to be achieved by the ascetic intellectual path he outlines in the *Symposium*, the *Phae-*

---

[54] *De An.* III.5; 430a 25.

drus, and *Letter VII*, which is later developed in neo-Platonism (Plotinus) and in the writings of pseudo-Dionysius as a mysticism of love.[55] In Aristotle, the suggestion of unity by the way of purified desire is also present. In discussing the origin of motion, he argues that what initiates movement is actually desire (*eros*). By giving cause to be desired, to be loved or longed for, the Unmoved Mover initiates motion in the universe.[56] Where Aristotle is prepared to grant transcendence, as he does with thought, he is also prepared to suggest that the link between immanence and transcendence is one of longing or love.

Aristotle's 'Unmoved Mover' is a transcendent intellectual *substance* in which intellect and the impulse to motion come together. This transcendent, unitary reality (in which there is no relation, and which has no capacity for relation) is accessible to those who are not enmeshed in human relationships: it is accessible to the intellect in contemplation, and is (perhaps surprisingly) the object of human desire. Aristotle keeps his account of the life of contemplative fulfilment quite separate from his account of 'life in accordance with the other kind of excellence', that is life according to the moral virtue which binds together the good citizens of the *polis*. This he sees as purely 'human', unlike the excellence of the life of the intellect which is, as we have seen, 'a thing apart'.[57] Whatever link exists in Aristotle's mind between the two forms of excellence is never satisfactorily explored.[58] *Koinonia* in the 'human' virtues is the

---

[55] See A. Louth, *Origins of the Christian Mystical Tradition from Plato to Denys* (Oxford: Clarendon Press, 1981).

[56] *Met.* xii.7; 1072b 4; cf. Lloyd, *Aristotle*, pp. 142–4. Dante's 'love that moves the sun and the other stars' (*Paradiso* xxxii.145) is based upon this passage of the *Metaphysics*.

[57] *Nic. Eth.* x.7–8; 1177b 27–1178a 22 cf. *Eud. Eth.* vii.15; 1249b 13ff: 'What choice, then, or possession of the natural goods – whether bodily goods, wealth, friends, or other things – will most produce the contemplation of god, that choice or possession is best.'

[58] Stephen Clark, reviewing A. Kenny's *The Aristotelian Ethics* (Oxford: Clarendon Press, 1978) in *Philosophical Quarterly* 29 (1979), stresses this point: 'To be sure, Aristotle gives no clear account in the *Eudemian Ethics* or in the *Nicomachean Ethics* of the ways in which ethical virtue conduces to the contemplation of the Divine, nor those in which such contemplation conduces to ethical virtue' (p. 358). See also the discussion by J. L. Ackrill, 'Aristotle on Eudaimonia', in A. O. Rorty ed., *Essays on Aristotle's Ethics* (Berkeley: University of California Press, 1980), especially pp. 32–3.

telos of political life; participation in the life of the intellect (*nous*) is the highest goal of human life in general (a goal which could only ever be attained by the few). In the end, Aristotle sustains a form of Plato's dualism: he fails to unite virtue and knowledge. For them to be united, he would require both a different anthropology and a different theology.

CONCLUSION: 'THE MASTER OF THOSE WHO KNOW'?

We have been studying Aristotle's 'revisionism', a title intended both to convey that Aristotle retains a critical indebtedness to Plato, and that he is a visionary thinker in his own right. His vision of the world is conditioned by his energetic collection of information, his observation and his analytic ability. It is this remarkable blend of gifts that enables him to 'know' and to record so much.

Aristotle suggests ten *categories* of predicate that can be attached to the object in answer to the question, 'What am I looking at?'[59] When Aristotle offers such 'categories' in his analysis of the kinds of things you can say, it is the individual object he has in mind. It has been suggested that Aristotle imagined a man standing before him in the Lyceum and then rehearsed the kinds of questions which might be put or answered about him.[60] He 'categorises' the sorts of things we say about an *individual* to chart the place that individual occupies in the world. When Aristotle goes on, in amplification of his first question (which is simply, 'What?' i.e. 'What *sort* of thing are we talking about? What *is* it?') to talk of 'primary substance',

---

[59] Aristotle's list is very compressed, but it includes: '*What* (that is, the object's substance; for example, 'man' or 'horse'); *how large* (that is, its size; for example, 'four foot', 'five foot'); *what sort of thing* (that is, its quality; for example, 'white'); *related to what* (for example, 'double', 'half', 'larger'); *where* (for example, 'in the Lyceum'); *when* (for example, 'yesterday', 'last year'); *in what attitude* (that is, posture; for example, 'lying', 'sitting'); *how circumstanced* (that is, 'state' or 'condition'; for example, 'having shoes on', 'having armour on'); *how active* (that is, *doing what?*, for example, 'cutting' or 'burning'); *how passive* (for example, 'being-cut', or, 'being-burned'). *Categories* IV; 1b 25–2a 5 (LCL translation, adapted). Cf. J. L. Ackrill, *Categories and De Interpretatione*, translated with notes (Oxford: Clarendon Press, 1974).
[60] T. Gomperz, *Greek Thinkers, a History of Greek Philosophy*, 4 vols., volume 4 (London: John Murray, 1912), p. 39.

he is talking about the 'substance' of the individual. Later, however, he talks about 'secondary substance', which is the 'substance' of the species which makes that individual what it is.[61] When we identify individuals as members of a species, we posit a relation between them which can be categorised as one of 'substance' and this relation for Aristotle transcends what Mackinnon calls 'the nuclear or pivotal realisation of being'.[62] For Aristotle, the universal is regarded as wholly immanent in individual things, in a series of particulars. The problem of their relation then becomes not one of their participation in some common transcendent Form, which is other than the particulars, but their 'substantial' relation to each other, something which Aristotle never satisfactorily explains.

The question as to what a relation *is* becomes more pressing if we consider human relating. How would Aristotle 'categorise' the *relation* between a son and a father, which is determinative for the identity of each as an individual? Is this a purely formal relation – that, logically, the son cannot be a 'son' without there being a father, and vice-versa, or could there be some 'substance' to the relation which makes *the relation itself* something like 'a realisation of being'?[63] Aristotle's extended treatment of 'justice' and 'friendship' in the *Eudemian* and *Nicomachean Ethics* suggests this might be the case. However, there is a gap here, for Aristotle's philosophy never satisfactorily brings together his natural scientific investigations, based on observation of 'primary substance' (individuals), and his discussion of the various types of *koinonia*, where human bondedness in relationship is what he has in view. Though Aristotle acknowledges, say, the diversity of the

---

[61] See *Categories* v; 2a 11f.

[62] D. M. Mackinnon, ' "Substance" in Christology – a "Cross-Bench" View' in S. W. Sykes and J. P. Clayton eds., *Christ, Faith and History* (Cambridge: Cambridge University Press, 1972), p. 281.

[63] The fourth-century theological debate about *the relation* between God the Father and God the Son took place using Aristotelian terminology (*homoousios* and *homoiousios*) which in effect *compared* the individuality of Father and Son. Such terminology precluded dynamic expression of their *relational unity* precisely because, whereas Aristotle analysed what can be said about individuals minutely, he offered no similarly acute way of categorising *relationships*. See Mackinnon, ' "Substance" in Christology', p. 289.

polis as a 'multitude' (*plethos*), he appears never to ask of human relating, 'What *is* it', at any level other than the functional, which for him, of course, involves the teleological. He merely records that this is how human beings function in the world, so 'good' human relations are the prerequisite of 'good' human functioning. What he offers in his *Ethics*, for instance, is a superb characterisation of friendship, which links it cogently with other forms of virtue, and shows how the friendship of those who seek the good is in itself the highest moral good for human beings. Nevertheless, his account of friendship always remains that of the association of two individuals; friendship *itself* is, for Aristotle, literally inconceivable, as are other forms of *koinonia*.

Brilliant though he was at observing the world, shrewd and balanced in his judgements, Aristotle was a relatively poor observer of his own species. He has virtually nothing to say about the conflicts which are constitutive of human existence, about the narrative and dramatic texture of human *koinonia*. He could talk superbly about friendship in general, but he was much less good at talking about the particularities of human loving, particularities for which the natural vehicle is some form of narrative. Dante called him, 'The Master of those who know'.[64] Reading his work, one feels he knew so much, and analysed so brilliantly, yet the analysis we have curiously circumvents the constituent mystery of human existence, the distinctive, particular, and manifold ways in which human beings experience *koinonia*. More than that, he fails to resolve the tension between the knowledge we acquire precisely because we love and the theoretical knowledge for which he considers love must be left behind. Aristotle holds out a twofold hope: that human beings may find fulfilment (*eudaimonia*) in society (in *koinonia*), and that, leaving society behind, human beings may find a higher fulfilment in contemplation of the divine (*theoria*). Neither in Aristotle, nor in his teacher Plato, do these divergent paths come together. For that, there would have to be a new type of knowledge, one in which love and intel-

---

[64] '*Il maestro di color che sanno*', *Inferno* IV 131.

lectual knowledge (as two forms of *koinonia*) are truly integrated. That would require a theological transformation, nothing less than a new and transformative vision of God, such as was later claimed by the Christian Church.

CHAPTER 5

Covenant and community

GREEK AND JEW IN THE *POLIS*

One enduring legacy of Hellenistic colonisation and conquest in the ancient world was the Greek *polis*. For more than five hundred years in many of the great cities of the Ancient Near East the language and culture of the educated was Greek. The *poleis* which flourished from Macedonia to India, and from Anatolia to Egypt, whether independent or under imperial rule, were, however, vastly different to the Athens about which Plato and Aristotle wrote.

The Athens of Plato was a small and tight-knit society in which it was considered important that all the citizens knew one another. It was held together by a common history, common religious traditions, and a common *politeia* or constitution. For both Plato and Aristotle the experience of political *koinonia*, of citizenship, was a metaphor for their understanding of what it is to be human. The man who is without a *polis*, said Aristotle, must be super-human or sub-human.[1] He cannot be of the same species as normal human beings.

The Hellenistic *polis* of the centuries after Alexander was by no means the old Greek *polis* writ large.[2] It was essentially *cosmopolitan*, a meeting-place of peoples, cultures, and religions, often with a shadowy common culture but little sense that citizenship was for all and the ideals of citizenship in all. Under

---

[1] *Politics* I.2; 1253a 2.
[2] Victor Ehrenberg traces the continuity and the contrast between the Hellenic State and the Hellenistic State in *The Greek State* (second edition, London: Methuen, 1969). See, especially, pp. 241–51.

the Hellenistic monarchies, there was 'no common citizenship, no term even to describe membership of a kingdom'.[3] The belief-system of Plato's Athens was enacted in the *leitourgia*, the public ceremonial which might be associated with sporting competition or the performance of plays and the recitation of poems, and also in shared or private devotion at times of special significance or in rites of passage. So interwoven was religion with civic life, however, that the two were indistinguishable: there was no word for 'religion' as such.[4] In the Hellenistic *polis*, public religious culture continued to provide a formal backdrop to civic life and particular devotions to local deities were often popular, but increasingly there came a split between public and private piety. The public culture commanded less and less common assent. Often there was no living belief in deity at all, which left space for private and communal experience of the divine that ranged from intense devotion to particular divinities to broad scepticism about all forms of belief. John North writes of the change 'from embedded to differentiated religion'.[5] Gradually, in the Hellenistic *polis* there was a shift from a common religious culture to something more like the religious pluralism we know today, with distinct religious groupings co-existing and in some cases competing. Against this background, the phenomenon of 'conversion' from one clearly defined religious group to another, as later seen in Paul and Augustine, began to make sense.[6] Amongst the most tight-knit of these religious groups were the Jewish communities of the *diaspora*, with their focus in the life of local synagogues.

   It is at this point we turn to Judaism,[7] which is so radically

---

[3] A. H. M. Jones, *The Greek City from Alexander to Justinian* (Oxford: Clarendon Press, 1940), p. 300.

[4] P. Cartledge, *The Greeks* (Oxford: Oxford University Press, 1993), pp. 152–6.

[5] See John North, 'The development of Religious Pluralism' in J. Lieu, J. North, and T. Rajak eds., *The Jews Among Pagans and Christians in the Roman Empire* (London: Routledge, 1992), pp. 177–9.

[6] The classic study is A. D. Nock, *Conversion* (Oxford: Oxford University Press, 1933). See also, A. D. Nock, *Early Gentile Christianity and its Hellenistic Background* (Harper Torchbooks Edition, New York: Harper and Row, 1964).

[7] The lengthy article on *koinonia* in the influential *Dictionnaire de Spiritualité* (17 vols., Paris: Beauchesne, 1937–75, vol. 8, cols. 1743–69) is divided into five parts: Plato and Aristotle; New Testament; Fathers of the Church; ancient monasticism; and Christian life today. The Greek linguistic thread is followed exclusively and Hebrew sources to a

different from Greek religion in origin and world-view, but which, like the mystery religions of Mithras and Isis, the philosophies of Epicurus and the Stoa, and the mystic remnants of platonism, found a place in the hospitable Hellenistic *polis*. In turning to the Judaism of this period, we shall be exploring the sense in which the key to the world-view of ancient (as of modern) Judaism is *covenant*[8] and how this makes for an experience of the world radically different from that of the Greeks, for it is an experience determined by the conviction that there is but one God who relates to the one people he has chosen, who forms community in a way that is distinctive and unique. What is both at the centre and at the horizon of Jewish consciousness is relation: the individual's relation to God and to God's people at the centre, and the unbroken covenantal relation of the whole people to God at the boundary of all specifically Jewish experience. The synagogue-communities, both in Israel and in the *diaspora*, played a vital part in sustaining this awareness of covenant. The extent to which such covenantal awareness could be taken into the cosmopolitan life of the Hellenistic *polis* was a question that faced the Jews of the *diaspora* in all the great cities like Rome, Ephesus, or Alexandria. The question that troubled these Jews was that of the part they, as a covenant-people, could play within a Hellenised common culture which permitted diversity, but eroded exclusivism.

David Hartman stresses, 'The covenant is not a purely legal obligation; it is a total relationship. The logic of a legal system

large extent bypassed. This gives the erroneous impression that Christian theology of *koinonia* has its roots largely in Greek thought. Though there is no precisely equivalent Hebrew word, the use of *koinonia* and its cognates in the New Testament and subsequent Christian theology is at every point deeply indebted to Jewish experience, especially experience of covenant.

[8] This theme has been developed by D. Hartman, *A Living Covenant* (London: Collier Macmillan, 1985). It is taken up appreciatively in S. David Breslauer, *Covenant and Community in Modern Judaism* (New York: Greenwood Press, 1989), where Hartman is criticised for drawing on the covenants with Noah, Abraham and that of Sinai in his exploration of 'covenantal anthropology', but omitting that with David. For Alan Segal, despite the variety of groups and sects within the Judaism of the Second Temple period (Pharisees, Sadducees, Essenes etc.), 'covenant' was the 'root metaphor' underlying all Hebrew society. See Alan F. Segal, *Rebecca's Children* (Cambridge, Mass.: Harvard University Press, 1986), p. 4. E. W. Nicholson provides a searching analysis of the meaning of 'covenant' in *God and his People* (Oxford, Clarendon, 1986), especially pp. 83–117 ('Covenant as a Theological Idea').

cannot do justice to the relational framework of the covenant
built upon the metaphors of God as lover and teacher.'[9] A
covenantal 'life-world' is one in which the experience of covenant-relation is a dimension of all social action and interpretation. Covenant-relation is thus an assumed dimension of
meaning in everyday life, and since the assumption is of the
presence of God in all human activity and the presence of all
human activity to God, the deepest consciousness of humanity
remains a consciousness of *being-in-relation*. Given the metaphysical background of the Greeks, in a general Hellenistic context
the word *koinonia* and its cognates could only carry a much less
specific sense of relatedness. For the Jew, it is the covenant that
gives shape and form and historical specificity to the perennial
sense of *being-in-relation* with God and with God's people. It is
striking that there is no precise equivalence between any
Hebrew word or concept and '*koinonia*'. Closest to '*koinonia*' is
'*yahath*',[10] which came to mean 'community' both in the sense
of 'togetherness' and, for the Qumran community, in the sense
of 'congregation'. This bond of association, based in the sense
of being the covenant people of God, and realised afresh every
time the people gathered together, transcended the loose bonds
of association within the Hellenistic *polis*, where it was assumed
that a variety of metaphysical outlooks could comfortably
coexist.

For the Jew of the *diaspora*, the *synagogue* (a Greek term), both
as building and as community,[11] was an essential instrument of

---

[9] Hartman, *A Living Covenant*, p. 14.

[10] H.-J. Fabry (*TDOT*, vol. 6, pp. 40–8) shows that the noun *yahath* is rare in the
Hebrew Scriptures, but the most common LXX translations for the noun and adverb
of the same root is *epi to auto* ('together', 'as a whole', 'in the same place'), followed by
hama ('together', particularly in a spatial sense). We may compare the stress in J. D.
Zizioulas, *Being as Communion* (London: Darton, Longman and Todd, 1985; see
pp. 196, 206, 231, 256) on the eucharistic gathering of the local church, meeting *epi to
auto*. In the Qumran literature the noun *yahath* is prominent. Fabry speaks of it
becoming 'absolutised as the central ecclesiological concept at Qumran'. The
parallel with *koinonia*, used in and, later, of the earliest Christian communities, is very
close. See also J.-M. R. Tillard, *L'Église locale* (Paris: Cerf, 1995), pp. 62–3.

[11] For the 'important ambiguity' in the use of synagogue both to mean 'a building' and
'the particular community, viewed as an association, *conventus*, or *synodos*', see
T. Rajak, 'The Jewish Community and its Boundaries' in *The Jews among Pagans and
Christians*, p. 11.

cultural and religious transmission in the time after the Babylonian exile. In large cities, including Jerusalem, Alexandria, and Rome, there might be several.[12] These were places where the community gathered for the reading and teaching of the Scriptures, and for prayer. In cities where the Jews were a minority the synagogue was an important focus for the community: meetings might be held there, there are records of meals being taken, and the distribution of alms to the needy would be organised from the synagogue. James Burtchaell (who emphasises that *synagoge* refers primarily to an organised community and only secondarily to a building where the community assembles) sums up the complex symbolic role of common life within the synagogue in the following way: 'What I refer to as a synagogal way of life was so integrated, so omnicompetent, so communitarian that our distinctions between public and private, or between sacred and secular, or between the person and the community. . . would be largely inapplicable.'[13] It was in the synagogue that membership of the people of God, the people of the covenant, was realised at the local level.

JEWISH COVENANT-BELIEF AT THE TIME OF THE SECOND TEMPLE

For the Jews of the Second Temple period, as much as any other, consciousness of *election* was constitutive of their lifeworld.[14] They believed themselves to have been constituted 'a people' by the God who, centuries before, chose Abraham and his descendants to be, in a distinctive way, his own. This was a consciousness both of themselves as *chosen*, and of God as the one who had chosen them. Their response was to be one of

[12] E. Schürer, new English edition revised and edited by G. Vermes, F. Millar and M. Black, *The History of the Jewish People in the Age of Jesus Christ*, vol. 2 (Edinburgh: T. and T. Clark, 1979), p. 445. For a general account of 'Jewish Community and Greek City', see V. Tcherikover, *Hellenistic Civilisation and the Jews* (Philadelphia: Jewish Publication Society of America, 1966), pp. 296–332.

[13] J. T. Burtchaell, *From Synagogue to Church* (Cambridge: Cambridge University Press, 1992), p. 206.

[14] D. Novak's well-documented study, *The Election of Israel, The Idea of a Chosen People* (Cambridge; Cambridge University Press, 1995) explores this theme from the beginnings of Jewish tradition to the present day.

absolute obedience. There could be no idolatry, no compromise with the covenant demand of an exclusive monotheism. The God who chooses, and who demands obedience, the notion of a covenant people, and that of a promised land, can all be seen in the narrative of the promise to Abraham:

When Abram was ninety-nine years old the Lord appeared to Abram, and said to him, 'I am God Almighty; walk before me, and be blameless. And I will make my covenant between me and you, and will multiply you exceedingly.' Then Abram fell on his face; and God said to him, 'Behold my covenant is with you, and you shall be the father of a multitude of nations . . . and I will establish my covenant between me and you and your descendants after you throughout their generations for an everlasting covenant, to be God to you and to your descendants after you. And I will give to you, and to your descendants after you, the land of your sojournings, all the land of Canaan, for an everlasting possession; and I will be their God.' (Gen. 17:1–8)

Here, in outline, is the shape of later Judaism: God's call of Abram, and promise of many descendants who will be in the same relation to him as Abram himself; the promise of the land of Canaan, possession of which is thus a sign of election and covenant; and the command to walk before the Lord and 'be blameless'. To be in the land, to be walking according to the law of the Lord, to be a child of Abraham, was to be within the covenant, chosen, in relation with God and with other similarly chosen descendants of Abraham.

All-important within the covenant-life was (and is) the place of Torah.[15] The basis for this within Scripture is the narrative of the theophany and the giving of the law at Sinai (Exod. 19–23), which is followed by a passage Nicholson calls 'self-evidently the covenant text par excellence':[16]

Moses came and told the people all the words of the Lord and all the ordinances; and all the people answered with one voice, and said, 'All the words which the Lord has spoken we will do.' And Moses wrote all the words of the Lord. And he rose early in the morning, and built an altar at the foot of the mountain, and twelve pillars, according to the

---

[15] For Jacob Neusner, 'To be a Jew . . . may be reduced to the single, pervasive symbol of Judaism: Torah.' *Torah through the Ages, a Short History of Judaism* (London: SCM, 1990), p. 11.

[16] Nicholson, *God and his People*, p. 164.

twelve tribes of Israel. And he sent young men of the tribes of Israel, who offered burnt offerings and sacrificed peace offerings of oxen to the Lord. And Moses took half of the blood and put it in basins, and half of the blood he threw against the altar. Then he took the book of the covenant, and read it in the hearing of the people; and they said, 'All that the Lord has spoken we will do, and we will be obedient.' And Moses took the blood and threw it upon the people, and said, 'Behold the blood of the covenant which the Lord has made with you in accordance with all these words.' (Exod. 24:3–8)

Nicholson argues that those over whom the blood of Yahweh's sacrifices is cast are thereby consecrated as Yahweh's holy people; they now belong peculiarly to him and have been solemnly commissioned in his service.[17] What is made plain here is the people's response to the giving of the law: 'All the words that the Lord has spoken we will do.' In this context, the words the Lord has spoken are set out in the ten commandments and Book of the Covenant (Exod. 20:22–23:33), the whole being elaborated in Deuteronomy which has been called 'the classic statement of Israel's covenant theology'.[18] Those who belonged to the covenant-people were thus faced with a choice, the choice of obedience to the law and blessing, or disobedience to the law and cursing, and with that cursing loss of the land:

I call heaven and earth to witness against you this day, that I have set before you life and death, blessing and curse; therefore choose life, that you and your descendants may live, loving the Lord your God, obeying his voice, and cleaving to him; for that means life to you and length of days, that you may dwell in the land which the Lord swore to your fathers, to Abraham, to Isaac, and to Jacob, to give them. (Deut. 30:19–20)

This is the choice that is enacted in the making of the covenant at Shechem, where Joshua rehearses before the assembled people all that God has done for them in bringing them into the land, challenging them to be faithful to God by keeping the law within the land which they now possess, as a condition of the covenant to which they now pledge themselves (Joshua 24:1–28).

[17] *Ibid.*, p. 172.
[18] J. D. G. Dunn, *The Partings of the Ways* (London: SCM; Philadelphia: Trinity Press International, 1991), p. 24.

Torah (as the covenant-gift of God) is indisputably the back-drop to the life-world of Judaism, whether ancient or modern, but in the Second Temple period certain distinct markers of law-keeping acquired prominence as signs of law-keeping, and so as vital to Jewish identity. Under the pressure of the Maccabean revolt against the Hellenising influence of Antiochus Epiphanes in the second century BCE, these markers in particular indicated the *distinction* between Jews and Hellenised Gentiles. They were emphasised as the marks of those who truly kept the covenant. The first was *circumcision.* 1 Maccabees records how Antiochus Epiphanes began to reign in Jerusalem in 175 BCE:

In those days lawless men came forth from Israel, and misled many, saying, 'Let us go and make a covenant with the Gentiles round about us, for since we have separated from them many evils have come upon us.' This proposal pleased them, and some of the people eagerly went to the king. He authorized them to observe the ordinances of the Gentiles. So they built a gymnasium in Jerusalem, according to the Gentile custom, and removed the marks of circumcision, and aban-doned the holy covenant. They joined with the Gentiles and sold themselves to do evil. (1 Macc. 1:11–15)

In the revolt that followed circumcision was a central issue: one of the first acts of Mattathias and his friends who led the revolt was forcibly to circumcise all the uncircumcised boys they found within the borders of Israel (1 Macc. 2:46). The Book of Jubilees, which dates from the same period, is equally firm that 'My covenant will be in your flesh as an eternal pact.'[19] The reinforcement of the law about circumcision is uncompromising:

Anyone who is born, the flesh of whose private parts has not been circumcised by the eighth day does not belong to the people of the pact which the Lord made with Abraham but to the people (meant for) destruction. Moreover, there is no sign on him that he belongs to the Lord, but (he is meant) for destruction, for being destroyed from the earth, and for being uprooted from the earth because he has violated the covenant of the Lord our God. (15:26)

A second marker of the covenant, which also took on a new

---

[19] *The Book of Jubilees*, translated by James C. Vanderkam, *Corpus Scriptorum Christianorum Orientalium, Scriptores Aethiopici* 88 (Louvain: Peeters, 1989), 15.13. Vanderkam (p. vi) dates The Book of Jubilees between 170 and 150 BCE.

significance in the situation of conflict was *the keeping of the sabbath*. A major issue to be settled early in the revolt was that of fighting on the sabbath day. Though they fought explicitly against the profaning of the sabbath, Mattathias and his friends had to make the painful decision to take up arms if necessary on the sabbath (1 Macc. 2:41). It was a decision taken in extreme circumstances and recognised as such. The obligation on the observant Jew was (and is) to keep the covenant by observing the law, avoiding all profanation of the sabbath. In the Book of Jubilees, which begins and ends by emphasising the importance of sabbath-keeping, at the conclusion of the narrative of the creation the Angel of the presence says of God:

He said to us: 'I will now separate a people for myself from among the nations. They, too, will keep sabbath. I will sanctify the people for myself and will bless them as I sanctified the sabbath day. I will sanctify them for myself; in this way I will bless them. They will become my people and I will become their God.' (2:19)

There is an analogy between the people of God and the sabbath: both have been blessed and sanctified by God for God. Both are to be kept holy.

A third, similar marker was the keeping of food-laws, especially by *refusal to eat pork*. Under Antiochus Epiphanes there were those who 'chose to die rather than to be defiled by food or to profane the holy covenant; and they did die' (1 Macc. 1:63). They are held up as an example of steadfastness to later generations. For those later generations, to compromise on issues for which the martyrs like Eleazer, or the seven brothers and their mother, gave their lives (2 Macc. 6–7) would be to compromise their Jewish identity, their loyalty to the covenant.[20] In the Book of Jubilees there are repeated reminders to observe the food-laws, and not to eat the blood of 'an animal, cattle, or of any bird that flies in the sky' (21:6) 'because the blood is the vital force' (21:18).

At a time of conflict over the identity of the community, with the threat of its dissolution, the symbolic importance of these markers was much increased. For those caught up in this

[20] A point reinforced by Mary Douglas, *Natural Symbols* (Harmondsworth: Penguin, 1973), pp. 60–4.

process, the sense of belonging to Israel became more vivid and more costly, something that was recorded in narratives like those of the Maccabees for future generations. Circumcision marked the male body as that of a member of Israel; the keeping of sabbath marked the cycle of time as that inhabited by Israel; the keeping of food-laws marked every meal as one taken within Israel. In every act of sexual intercourse, in family life and the cycle of worship, in cooking and in social occasions, the symbolism of the covenant was (and is) present. Such symbolism is rooted not only in Scriptural narrative (in time, and in story) as rehearsed at the synagogue but also in place (in the land, and in the Temple).

The Jews inhabited a Temple state or Temple land. The territory of Judea was the amount needed to provide the resources for the Temple cult.[21] The sacrificial cult was sustained by the produce of the land. The round of sacrifice was prescribed precisely in the law. Possession of the land, keeping of the law, and participation in the cult were co-equally expressions of covenant-participation:

> When you come into the land which the Lord your God gives you for an inheritance, and have taken possession of it, and live in it, you shall take some of the first of all the fruit of the ground, which you harvest from your land that the Lord your God gives you, and you shall put it in a basket, and you shall go to the place which the Lord your God will choose, to make his name to dwell there. And you shall go to the priest who is in office at the time, and say to him, 'I declare this day to the Lord your God that I have come into the land which the Lord swore to our fathers to give us.' Then the priest shall take the basket from your hand and set it down before the altar of the Lord your God. (Deut. 26:1–4)

This is the harvest offering of the agriculturalist, which is appropriate for the harvest seasons of the barley harvest, the wheat harvest, and the fruit harvest. These harvest festivals were taken up into the pilgrim feasts, when observant Jews made a special effort to go up to Jerusalem and make the appropriate offerings: the Feast of the Passover, the Feast of Weeks, and the Feast of Tabernacles. The offerings of Israel,

---

[21] Dunn, *The Partings of the Ways*, p. 31.

however, were not only those of the agriculturalist, but also those of the pastoralist. Central to the cult of the Second Temple was the daily offering of animal sacrifice.[22] De Vaux[23] rejects the suggestions that sacrifice was a gift to a malevolent or selfish deity, that it achieved union with the deity by magic, and that it was a meal taken by the god. He isolates three motifs within the one symbolic action of sacrifice. The first could be seen as that of *thanksgiving.* The sacrifice is an irrevocable gift in recognition of God's gifts to the sacrificer. It is the recognition of obligation, and the acceptance of the sacrifice involves God in a renewed commitment to the sacrificer. The model is that of Noah, who was saved by God from the flood:

Then Noah built an altar to the Lord, and took of every clean animal and of every clean bird, and offered burnt offerings on the altar. And when the Lord smelled the pleasing odour, the Lord said in his heart, 'I will never again curse the ground because of man, for the imagination of man's heart is evil from his youth; neither will I ever again destroy every living thing as I have done. While the earth remains, seedtime and harvest, cold and heat, summer and winter, day and night, shall not cease.' (Gen. 8:20–2)

---

[22] Leviticus 1–7 makes detailed prescription for animal sacrifice. Such sacrifice could be of four broad types. With the *holocaust* the man offering the sacrifice, who had to be in a state of ritual purity, laid his hand on the head of the animal, which had to be male and without blemish, to indicate ownership. He himself cut the throat of the victim and brought it to the altar, where the priest poured the blood, which contains the life, around the altar, before the whole animal was cut up and burnt. For the poor, who could only afford a bird, there was a modified ritual. With the *communion-sacrifice* (*shelem*, but usually *shelamim*), the victim was shared between God, the priest, and the sacrificer, together with his family or guests, who ate their portion as something holy. The fat, considered a life-giving part, and therefore for God, was burnt on the altar. A third type of sacrifice was the *expiatory sacrifice*, the 'sacrifice for sin', and a fourth the *sacrifice of reparation*. Both of these applied when the covenant had been broken by sin. The animal prescribed depended upon the significance of the offerer. Most significant was the offering of a bull by the High Priest, especially on the Day of Atonement, for his sin defiled the whole people. With this sacrifice alone, some of the blood was taken into the Temple building and sprinkled against the veil which curtained off the Holy of Holies or, on the Day of Atonement, into the Holy of Holies, to be sprinkled on the 'mercy-seat'. Where the guilt was not that of the priests, they received the meat from the sacrifice; where the guilt was that of the whole community or of the High Priest, the remains of the sacrifice were thrown on the ash-heap. The 'sacrifice of reparation' was only to be offered by a private individual and the blood was never taken into the Holy Place. See, R. de Vaux, *Ancient Israel* (second edition, London: Darton, Longman and Todd, 1965), pp. 415–23.

[23] De Vaux, *Ancient Israel*, pp. 451–4.

This is the immediate preamble to the covenant with Noah.

A second motif within the symbolic transactions of sacrifice is that of *expiation*: the shedding of blood gives the assurance of remission of sins. One aspect is clearly the costliness of the sacrifice, not in terms of money, but in terms of the life that is poured out in the blood and burnt in the fat, but there is something deeper. It is clear that the sacrificer *participates* in the sacrifice in such a way that the sacrificed animal *represents* the one who makes the sacrifice. In the pouring out of the sacrificial blood, there is a recognition that life-blood, with which the life blood of the sinner is associated, is poured out to expiate the sin. The participation of the one who makes the sacrifice 'in' the sacrifice itself is central to the symbolic logic of the expiatory sacrificial act.

Such participation in expiatory sacrifice introduces the third motif: that of *communion*.[24] This applies particularly with 'communion-sacrifices' (*shelamim*). Here the sacrificer, with his family and guests, shares in consuming the victim together with God and the priests. The 'communion-sacrifice' was 'a joyful sacrifice in which the two ideas of a gift and of communion were both included; the offering was made by man, and it achieved its effect in maintaining friendship with God'.[25] Eichrodt discusses the communion mediated by the 'communion sacrifice' at length. He speaks of 'God's declaration that he is prepared to enter into a special relationship with his people and to give them a share in his own life'.[26] De Vaux comments that this kind of sacrifice, which involved the sharing in a common life and the practice of hospitality was regarded as 'the most complete kind of sacrifice'. He makes the link with Paul's asking

[24] W. R. Smith, *Lectures on the Religion of the Semites* (third edition, London: A. and C. Black, 1927) has been hugely influential. His conclusion, 'The one point that comes out clear and strong is that the fundamental idea of ancient sacrifice is sacramental communion, and that all atoning rites are ultimately to be regarded as owing their efficiency to a communication of divine life to the worshippers, and to the establishment or confirmation of a living bond between them and their god' (p. 439), has been criticised as over-simple, but Robertson Smith's emphasis upon sacrifice as fundamentally communion (rather than magic, tribute, or propitiation) has influenced Eichrodt, de Vaux, and many others.

[25] De Vaux, *Ancient Israel*, p. 453.

[26] W. Eichrodt, *Theology of the Old Testament*, vol. 1 (London: SCM, 1961), p. 157.

in the first letter to the Corinthians, 'Consider the practices of Israel; are not those who eat the sacrifices *koinonoi* in the altar?' (1 Cor. 10:18). What we have here at the heart of the cult and the sacrificial economy is one joyful form of sacrificial *koinonia*.

We have considered the common life that was focused on the synagogue, both in the *diaspora* and in Israel, and also the common life as it was focused in the sacrificial system of the Temple at Jerusalem.[27] The Essene community at Qumran provides an alternative, sectarian model of common life, which was also linked with the way of life of those Essenes who lived in the 'towns' or 'camps' as the Damascus Rule puts it.[28] It is clear from the Dead Sea Scrolls that the Essenes saw themselves as the one true Israel, heirs to a special revelation granted to the Teacher of Righteousness, a remnant chosen to be faithful to the covenant. They saw the Temple as profaned by uncleanness and were actively preparing themselves for an armed takeover of the Temple, to be followed by reform of Temple worship and the liturgical calendar. Initiation to the Qumran community was seen as entry into the 'new covenant', the community itself as 'the community of the everlasting covenant', or simply as 'the covenant'. Their earthly liturgy was regarded as a replica of the heavenly liturgy sung by the choirs of angels in the heavenly temple and their role on earth to be a new and purified Israel.[29] This is clear from the blessings that have survived:

Words of blessing. The Master shall bless them that fear [God and do] His will, that keep His commandments, and hold fast to His holy [Covenant], and walk perfectly [in all the ways of] His [truth]; whom He has chosen for an eternal Covenant which shall endure for ever.[30]

What is suggested is that the members of the community

---

[27] A full account of Israelite sacrifice would need to make explicit mention of the Passover-feast, which involved both Temple-sacrifice and a domestic sacrificial meal, but differs in origin and interpretation from other daily or regular forms of sacrifice. For a graphic description, see E. P. Sanders, *Judaism, Practice and Belief 63 BCE–66 CE* (London: SCM; Philadelphia: Trinity Press International, 1992), pp. 132–9.

[28] G. Vermes, *The Dead Sea Scrolls in English*, revised and extended fourth edition (Sheffield: Academic Press, 1994), p. 9.

[29] See C. Rowland, *The Open Heaven* (London: SPCK, 1982), pp. 117–20, where he discusses the link between passages in the Qumran literature that speak of participation in the heavenly world and Jewish apocalyptic literature.

[30] G. Vermes, *The Dead Sea Scrolls in English*, p. 268 (1QSb,1).

both hold fast to the covenant (*bi'berith*) and are a covenant (*li'berith*).[31] This is an idea to which we shall return. Josephus' laudatory account of the Essene community is well known:

> Contemning wealth, they admire a life lived in common. No man is richer than another man because it is a law that each one who enters the sect then surrenders his fortune to the community. All that is owned is owned in common.[32]

The word Philo uses for the common life of the Essenes, which he, like Josephus, greatly admired, is *koinonia*.[33]

A NEW COVENANT; A NEW COVENANT-COMMUNITY?

For the earliest Christians, the focus of interest was not so much the person of Jesus as the initiation of God's reign of peace and righteousness that he had brought about.[34] The gift they believed had been offered to them by God was the gift of participation in the Kingdom of God, the reign of God that had been established definitively through Jesus in the last days of the world. The expectation that this would happen was characteristic of certain eschatological strands in the Jewish belief of his time,[35] and the affirmation that this had indeed come about, as promised by God, was characteristic of the earliest Christian believers. This ties in Christian understanding of the place of Christ very closely with the covenant, since it is covenant-relation that is the assumptive backdrop[36] for early Christian communities rooted in Judaism, and the consciously assumed or

---

[31] E. Lohse, *Die Texte aus Qumran* (second edition, Darmstadt: Wissenschaftliche Buchgesellschaft, 1971, p. 55), translates in the first instance '*und die festhalten an seinem heiligen Bund*' and in the second '*er hat sie erwählt zum ewigen Bund*'. For the second, compare Is. 42:6 (Hebrew).

[32] Cf. H. St. J. Thackeray ed., Josephus, *The Jewish War*, Books I–III, LCL 203 (Cambridge, Mass.: Harvard University Press, 1927), pp. 369–85. See especially II.viii.3 (p. 369), where the similarity with the language of Acts 4:32 is striking.

[33] Philo's account of the Essenes is in *Omn. Prob. Lib.* XII (F. H. Coulson ed., *Philo*, vol. IX, LCL 363, Cambridge, Mass.: 1941, pp. 53–61). See also Hauck (*TWNT* vol. 3), p. 803.

[34] C. Rowland, *Christian Origins* (London: SPCK, 1985), p. 244.

[35] E. P. Sanders, *Jesus and Judaism* (London: SCM, 1985), pp. 123–9.

[36] See H. C. Kee, *Christian Origins in Sociological Perspective* (London: SCM, 1980), pp. 32–4; N. T. Wright, *The New Testament and the People of God*, vol. I (London: SPCK, 1992), pp. 26ff.

learnt backdrop for those of Gentile background who had to learn the importance for their new-found faith of 'the Scriptures' which bore witness to an inheritance of covenantal understanding. Here we need briefly to turn to what is understood by 'the covenant' or 'covenants' as spoken of in the scriptural records of the earliest Christian communities, to trace the link for them between their belief about a new or renewed covenant in Christ and their experience of *koinonia*.

In the Epistle to the Romans, Paul enumerates the spiritual advantages that have been conferred on those he calls 'my brethren, my kinsmen by race'. 'They are Israelites', he says, 'and to them belong the sonship, the glory, the covenants, the giving of the law, the worship, and the promises; to them belong the patriarchs, and of their race, according to the flesh, is the Christ' (Rom. 9:3–5). It may be that Paul originally wrote 'covenant'.[37] If he did, he was doubtless referring to the covenant made at Sinai, as recorded in Exodus. If he wrote 'covenants', he would have been thinking of covenants with Noah, Abraham, and at Sinai,[38] or, as affirmations of the Mosaic covenant, of covenants at Mounts Gerizim and Ebal (Dt. 27:12; Josh. 8:33), and in the plains of Moab (Dt. 29:1). It is more usual in the New Testament to find references to '*the* covenant', by which the covenant at Sinai is meant.

New Testament thinking is, however, also profoundly affected by the notion of a covenant with David. Explicit language about a Davidic covenant is clearest in the psalms:

> Thou hast said, 'I have made a covenant with my chosen one,
> I have sworn to David my servant:
> "I will establish your descendants forever,
> and build your throne for all generations." '   (Ps. 89:3–4)

and

---

37 This view is strongly maintained by E. J. Christiansen, *The Covenant in Judaism and Paul* (Leiden: E. J. Brill, 1995), pp. 220–3.

38 In the *Book of Jubilees* covenant thought is pervasive. The covenants of *Jubilees* are those with Noah, Abraham, Jacob, and (by implication) that of Sinai. Irenaeus, *Adv. Haer.* III.xi.8 (second century CE), talks of four covenants, the first three according to the Latin version being with Adam, Noah, and Moses, and according to the Greek with Noah, Abraham, and Moses. In both versions the fourth covenant is that of the Gospel of Jesus Christ.

> The Lord swore to David a sure oath
>> from which he will not turn back:
> 'One of the sons of your body
>> I will set on your throne.
> If your sons keep my covenant
>> and teach my testimonies which I shall teach them,
> their sons also for ever
>> shall sit upon your throne.'
>
> (Ps. 132:11–12)

Though the term 'covenant' is not used explicitly in 2 Samuel 7, the promise of God here is crucial for the notion of a covenant with David: 'When your days are fulfilled and you lie down with your fathers, I will raise up your offspring after you, who shall come forth from your body, and I will establish his kingdom. He shall build a house for my name, and I will establish the throne of his kingdom for ever. I will be his father, and he shall be my son' (2 Sam. 7:12–14). Hence the significance for the early Christians of establishing a Davidic lineage for Jesus, and of recording Jesus' characteristic use of the language of sonship, especially his speaking of 'Abba' (Father).[39]

When allusion is made to the Davidic covenant, Christian writing is normally in the mode of fulfilment; when allusion is made to the Mosaic covenant, it is often in terms of contrast, renewal, or supercession.[40] In the Epistle to the Hebrews there is an extended discussion of the role of Christ in establishing what is called a 'better' covenant: 'Christ has obtained a ministry which is as much more excellent than the old as the

---

[39] Rowland, *Christian Origins*, p. 178, following G. Vermes, *Jesus the Jew* (second edition, London: SCM, 1983), pp. 192–213.

[40] One complex example is provided by Gal. 4:21–31. Having reflected through chapter 3 on one covenant (the promise made to Abraham), Paul then develops an allegorical understanding of 'two covenants', one represented by Hagar, which is that at Mount Sinai, and related to 'the present Jerusalem' which is in slavery, and one represented by Sarah (who is not named), which is related to 'the Jerusalem above' which is free. J. D. G. Dunn stresses that this is not a matter of 'old' and 'new' covenant: 'Only one covenant is at issue here – the promise to Abraham of seed' (*The Theology of Paul the Apostle*, Grand Rapids: Eerdmans, 1998, p. 146n). Nevertheless, Paul writes (v. 24) of 'two covenants'. J. Louis Martyn, recognising the anomaly, argues that since Paul's opponents are engaging in a law-observant Gentile mission, 'this odious development . . . drives Paul into the holy madness of affirming two covenants' ('The Covenants of Hagar and Sarah' in J. T. Carroll *et al.* eds., *Faith and History, Essays in Honor of Paul W. Meyer*, Atlanta: Scholars Press, 1990, p. 187).

covenant he mediates is better, since it is enacted on better promises' (Hebr. 8:6).[41]

Allusions to a 'new covenant' are prominent and highly significant in early Christian writing. They draw upon the language of Jeremiah, which is also echoed in Ezekiel:

Behold, the days are coming, says the Lord, when I will make a new covenant with the house of Israel and the house of Judah, not like the covenant which I made with their fathers when I took them by the hand to bring them out of the land of Egypt, my covenant which they broke, though I was their husband, says the Lord. But this is the covenant which I will make with the house of Israel after those days, says the Lord: I will put my law within them, and I will write it upon their hearts; and I will be their God, and they shall be my people. And no longer shall each man teach his neighbour and each his brother, saying, 'Know the Lord', for they shall all know me, from the least of them to the greatest, says the Lord; for I will forgive their iniquity, and I will remember their sin no more. (Jer. 31:31–4)

This passage above all was generative for Christian understanding of Jesus and of the significance of his life, his death, and the coming into being of new communities of emergent Christian faith. In the Epistle to the Hebrews, Jesus is spoken of as 'the mediator of a new covenant' (Hebr. 9:15), something that requires the mediator to be in touch with both parties to the agreement (cf. Gal. 3:20). The passage from Jeremiah is twice quoted verbatim in Hebrews, and there is evidence of widespread interest in the promise of a 'new' covenant in the time of Jesus. We have seen how the Essene community described itself as a 'community of the everlasting covenant' (*yahath berith o'lam*).[42] For the earliest Christians, and in all probability for

---

[41] Hebr. 8:6 is the one reference in the New Testament to a 'better' covenant. The more usual term of contrast (following Jeremiah 31:31–4) is 'new' (1 Cor. 11:25; 2 Cor. 3:6; Hebr. 8:8; 8:13; 9:15; 12:24). Also found is 'second' (Hebr. 8:7; 10:9), and, in one case (Hebr. 13:20), 'everlasting'.

[42] M. Hengel, *Judaism and Hellenism* (London: SCM, 1974) p. 244; Vermes, *The Dead Sea Scrolls in English*, pp. 41–6. Throughout the covenantal imagery of the Hebrew Scriptures there is frequent reference to an 'everlasting (or eternal) covenant'. In the Epistle to the Hebrews (13:20) the writer speaks of 'the blood of the eternal covenant' (*haima diathekes aioniou*). This is a clear reference to the LXX version of Zech. 9:11 ('by the blood of your covenant you have set your captives free'). To this the writer of Hebrews has added 'eternal', the most frequently used adjective for the covenant in the LXX.

Jesus himself, the symbolism of his death was the symbolism of atoning sacrifice, which could also be seen as the inauguration of the promised 'new covenant'.

CONCLUSION: JESUS AS THE COVENANT

In the New Testament, as we have seen, Jesus is spoken of and acts as the 'mediator' of the promised and expected 'new covenant'. It is very striking that in the writing of the second-century Christian apologist, Justin Martyr, and particularly in his Dialogue with Trypho the Jew, Jesus (or 'Christ') is himself several times called the 'covenant'.[43] There is the usual quotation from Jeremiah 31:31–2, which is followed by, 'He is the new law, and the new covenant, and the expectation of those who out of every people wait for the good things of God' (11).[44] A little later, he is called, 'Christ, the Son of God, who was proclaimed as about to come to all the world, to be the everlasting law and the everlasting covenant, even as the forementioned prophecies show' (43). It is Justin who brings together two significant terms, writing of 'the calling of the *new* and *eternal* covenant, that is, of Christ' (118). He follows the Epistle of Barnabas (14) in applying Isaiah 42:6–7 directly to Christ: 'I have given you as a covenant to the people, a light to the nations, to open the eyes that are blind, to bring out the prisoners from the dungeon, from the prison those who sit in darkness.'[45] When (12) he quotes Isaiah 55:3 ('I will make an everlasting covenant with you, even the sure mercies of David. Behold I have given Him for a witness to the people'), the import is the same. 'What is the covenant of God?', asks Justin, and immediately answers, 'Is it not Christ?' (122). More than simply being the mediator of a new covenant, Jesus is here seen precisely *as* the new covenant, an hypostatisation which, it could be argued, is no stranger than speaking of him as the

---

[43] Attention is drawn to this by Jean Daniélou, *Théologie du Judeo-Christianisme* (Paris: Desclée, 1958), p. 218.

[44] The translation is that in the ANCF series (Grand Rapids: Eerdmans, reprinted 1981); the text can be found in Migne, *PG* vol. VI.

[45] *Dial. Try.* 122.

Word or the Wisdom of God, but which adds to such notions a representative dimension, whereby Jesus brings together in his person the two parties to the normative covenant (or covenants) of Israel, divine and human. Here is anticipated the shape of orthodox Christology in which the divine and the human are inalienably bound together in covenant relation.[46] The fact that this is seen as taking place 'in Christ' gives to it a corporate dimension which is vital for the emergent self-understanding of the early church. To say that *Christ is the covenant* is to render the relational symbolism of covenant concrete in the existence and fate of Jesus: in his birth, the renewed or new covenant is born, in his generous and inclusive interpretation of the teaching of his predecessors the new covenant speaks, in his death the new covenant is rejected, in his being raised to new life the new covenant is shown to be eternal. To say that *Jesus is the covenant* is to be reminded that throughout the Hebrew (and Christian) Scriptures the covenant-relation is given by God and monitored by God, God is truly bound and made vulnerable by love. There had always been the possibility that God might withdraw, even if only temporarily, to discipline or punish, from this relationship. For Christians, to say that Jesus Christ is the covenant is to close that possibility. It means that God is seen to give of himself decisively, inalienably in relation. In 'Christ the covenant' he not only enters into a bond with his people; he reveals relation (*koinonia*) to be of his essence.[47] In Christ, covenant and community are one.[48]

---

46 Karl Barth uses this idea in *Dogmatics in Outline* (London: SCM, 1982), p. 69: 'Jesus Christ is the reality of the covenant between God and man.'

47 This idea was later extensively explored in debates concerning both Christology and Trinitarian theology. See Zizioulas, *Being as Communion*, pp. 87–9, W. Pannenberg, *Systematic Theology*, volume 1 (Grand Rapids: Eerdmans, 1991), p. 335, where, with respect to 'the mutual relations of Father, Son, and Spirit', he speaks of 'a concept of essence that is not external to the category of relations'; see also p. 367, and vol. 2, p. 85.

48 This point could be expanded by including other collective representations that are taken into Christology. See, for example, W. Zimmerli and J. Jeremias, *The Servant of God* (London: SCM, 1957) on '*pais theou*' in Deutero-Isaiah, where it is argued (p. 53) that, though a messianic interpretation was predominant in Palestinian Judaism, Hellenistic Judaism preferred to see in the '*pais theou*' a collective representation of Israel. For a similar discussion of 'The Son of Man' in Dan. 7:13, see Rowland, *The Open Heaven*, pp. 178–88.

CHAPTER 6

Little communities and the Catholic church

THE COMMUNITY OF JESUS

Shortly after the death of Jesus, the Galilean prophet, little communities which looked to him as a living Lord sprang up in Jerusalem, in Damascus, and other cities of the region. These were initially groups of Jews, who, despite his crucifixion, accepted the messianic status of Jesus and the proclamation of his earliest followers that he had been raised from the dead. From the earliest days of the community in Jerusalem, there were members who were Hellenised Jews and before long, in cities like Antioch, Gentiles were included within the groups of those who began to be known as 'Christians'.

The origins of the form taken by community life in these little groups were complex. Those in the house churches that were 'the basic cells'[1] of the growing movement would have been members of local synagogues[2] and Temple-worshippers. Their practice may well have been indebted to particular groups within Judaism like the Jerusalem *haberoth*: societies of men who banded together in strict keeping of the law, eating meals together in a state of ritual cleanliness.[3] Their practice reflected

[1] J. E. Stambaugh and D. L. Balch, *The New Testament in its Social Environment* (Philadelphia: Westminster Press, 1986), p. 140.
[2] J. T. Burtchaell argues for the continuity in organisation between Hellenistic Jewish synagogues and the early Christian churches in *From Synagogue to Church* (Cambridge: Cambridge University Press, 1992), especially pp. 339–52. He describes how, 'Each community exist(ed) in a network that comprise(d) all others . . . A local community was bound by adhesions in many directions, through correspondence, embassies, hospitality and disaster relief' (pp. 339–40).
[3] *The Jewish Encyclopedia* (New York and London: Funk and Wagnalls, 1906), vol. VI, 121b–124a; J. Jeremias, *Jerusalem in the Time of Jesus* (London: SCM, 1969), pp. 247–52.

the climate of thought in which the Essene movement with its strict community life, both concentrated and extended,[4] also flourished.

The first non-Jewish members of Christian groups would probably have been 'god-fearers', initially attracted to the life and worship of the Jews. In a city like Ephesus, they might have belonged to a whole variety of religious and philosophical sects and societies whose cultic practices and philosophical teaching formed the 'market of possibilities' which in this period increasingly characterised the Hellenism of the *polis*. The picture of life in major Hellenistic cities at this time is one of 'a great deal of mutual awareness, communication and interchange between the different religious groups in the Empire, and even outside it'.[5] Elements from the cult of Isis and other mystery religions, from Cynicism, Epicureanism, Stoicism, and Gnosticism may well have been present in the life of the early Christian communities. Much of early Christian writing is concerned with the discrimination of the truth of the Gospel from the various errors in which members of the emergent churches were seen to be enmeshed.

The seeds of a distinctively *Christian* common life lie in the life and ministry of Jesus, to which the gospels bear witness. The ministry of Jesus was peripatetic, so there was no settled 'community of Jesus' until after his death. There was, however, a group of disciples that he chose to be with him and from an early stage associated with his mission, which was to proclaim the Kingdom of God. When Jesus proclaimed in Galilee the coming of the Kingdom of God, he invited his hearers to accept

The close link made by Jeremias between the *haberim* and the Pharisees is strongly criticised by E. P. Sanders, *Paul and Palestinian Judaism* (London: SCM, 1977), pp. 152–4.

[4] G. Vermes writes of 'a single religious movement with two branches', one branch being the Qumran community and the other the Essenes living in 'towns' or 'camps' (*The Dead Sea Scrolls in English*, fourth and extended edition, Sheffield: Academic Press, 1995), pp. 1–19.

[5] John North, 'The Development of Religious Pluralism' in J. Lieu, J. North, and T. Rajak eds., *The Jews among Pagans and Christians in the Roman Empire* (London: Routledge, 1992), p. 176. Still useful is A. D. Nock, *Early Gentile Christianity and its Hellenistic Background* (Harper Torchbooks Edition, New York: Harper and Row, 1964), pp. 1–23. See also, Wayne A. Meeks, *The Moral World of the First Christians* (London: SPCK, 1987), pp. 97–123 on 'Christian Communities'.

a radically new way of living, one which was open to all who would listen to what he had to proclaim. Jesus was, however, more than merely a herald. With astonishing boldness, both in terms of his self-presentation and his interpretation of the Scriptures, he sought definitively to gather the scattered people of God. Jeremias has argued strongly: 'The *only* significance of the whole of Jesus' activity is to gather the eschatological people of God.'[6] The *twelve* disciples that Jesus chose (later called apostles, because 'sent out' to fulfil the mission of Jesus) were to represent the twelve tribes of a renewed and restored Israel:[7]

And he appointed twelve, whom he also named apostles, to be with him, and to be sent out to proclaim the message, and to have authority to cast out demons. So he appointed the twelve. (Mk 3:14–16)

At the time of Jesus it was believed that there were only two and a half tribes left: Judah, Benjamin, and half Levi. The nine and a half other tribes were thought to have been lost after the fall of the Northern Kingdom in 722 BCE.[8] Jesus' appointment of the Twelve was a sign of the establishment of the renewed and restored people of God. The Twelve were to be sent out 'two by two' to 'the lost sheep of the house of Israel' (Mk 6:7; Matt. 10:6). In this way they shared directly in the ministry of Jesus. So, for example, they shared in his authority over demons and his power to heal (Mk 6:13). Lohfink stresses that the mission of Jesus and the Twelve was to Israel and not to the Gentiles, but that, according to an important strand in the tradition of theology that Jesus had received, Gentiles might achieve salvation through participation in the destiny of a restored Israel:

When the people of God shines as a sign among the nations (cf. Is. 2:1–4), the other nations will learn from God's people; they will come together in Israel in order to participate in Israel and, mediated through Israel, in God's glory. But all this can happen only when Israel really becomes recognisable as a sign of salvation, when God's salvation transforms his people recognisably, tangibly, even visibly.[9]

The choosing of the Twelve by Jesus was the beginning of this

[6] J. Jeremias, *New Testament Theology* (part one, London: SCM, 1971), p. 170.
[7] G. Lohfink, *Jesus and Community* (London: SPCK, 1985). See pp. 9ff.
[8] Jeremias, *Jerusalem in the Time of Jesus*, p. 278.
[9] Lohfink, *Jesus and Community*, p. 28.

transformation. It was the beginning of the establishment of the community of Jesus.

THE MARKAN COMMUNITY

The records we have of the choosing of the Twelve and of the whole ministry of Jesus were passed on, preserved, written down, and edited within particular early Christian communities that saw themselves as a continuation of 'the community of Jesus'. They looked directly, or indirectly, to the Twelve as authoritative founders of their common life. In these earliest Christian communities those who became disciples were being transformed 'recognisably, tangibly, even visibly'. Each such community would have had its distinctive concerns, its unique situation. For them, the accounts of Jesus' relation to those who followed him would have been a model for their own discipleship. They saw themselves as learning from a living Lord, in whatever particular situation they faced. The gospel narratives in their final form, and the traditions that made up those narratives, functioned for their earliest hearers and readers – and, indeed, for their writers – at two levels. They bore witness to the history of Jesus and his first disciples, and they acted as a model for the continuing history of Jesus and his later disciples in the contemporary community. The liturgical reading of the gospel narratives within the earliest Christian communities was in itself an invitation to the members of those communities to see themselves as belonging to the one community of Jesus, constituted of the various little communities of disciples which were emerging as the fruit of the preaching and the living of the Gospel.

In Mark's narrative we can see how the community – both the community that Jesus was gathering about him at the time of his ministry and the later community of faith – is implicitly included at table with Jesus in the house of Levi:

And as he sat at dinner in Levi's house, many tax collectors and sinners were also sitting with Jesus and his disciples – for there were many who followed him. When the scribes of the Pharisees saw that he was eating with sinners and tax collectors, they said to his disciples,

'Why does he eat with sinners and tax collectors?' When Jesus heard this, he said to them, 'Those who are well have no need of a physician, but those who are sick; I have come to call not the righteous but sinners.' (Mk 2:15–17)

A story like this would have reminded the Markan community[10] that they were to remain open to 'tax collectors and sinners' who wanted to join them, just as much as to a 'ruler of the synagogue' like Jairus (Mk 5:22), who is not turned away when he comes to Jesus in need. They are to be warned by the incident when the disciples speak sternly to the people bringing children for Jesus to touch. Jesus is indignant and insists, 'Let the little children come to me; do not stop them; for it is to such as these that the Kingdom of God belongs' (Mk 10:14). In the gospel narrative, Jesus' family come 'to restrain him' (3:21), and he is told that his mother and brothers are outside asking for him. Jesus replies, 'Who are my mother and my brothers?' Then, 'Looking at those who sat around him, he said, "Here are my mother and my brothers! Whoever does the will of God is my brother and sister and mother"' (3:33–5). In this one saying, the Markan community is called to radical discipleship unimpeded by family ties and to recognition of their own community as the family of Jesus, which includes both women (cf. 15:40–1) and men. This is reinforced later in the gospel:

Jesus said, 'Truly I tell you, there is no one who has left house or brothers or sisters or mother or father or children or fields, for my sake and for the sake of the good news, who will not receive an hundredfold now in this age – houses, brothers and sisters, mothers and children, and fields, with persecutions – and in the age to come eternal life.' (Mk 10:30)

---

[10] The phrase 'the Markan community' is used to refer to the community in which the traditions that went to make up Mark's Gospel were preserved, the concerns or needs of which are presumed to be addressed in the writing of the gospel. Raymond Brown discusses the peculiar difficulties in representing the community addressed by Mark 'even to the elementary point of being sure whether Mark was reinforcing that community in beliefs already held or was inculcating beliefs that were absent' (*The Churches the Apostles Left Behind*, London: Geoffrey Chapman, 1984, pp. 28–9). The concern here is more with the *continuity* of the Christian life of the community or communities in which Mark's Gospel was a formative influence, rather than any attempt to identify to what precise circumstances the gospel traditions, as written down, spoke.

Morna Hooker comments, 'If lost human relationships are repaid a hundred times, this is presumably in the fellowship found in the Christian community.'[11] The community must be close-knit, and it must be vigilant. It is warned that it will endure betrayal from within the natural families of its members and it will also have to face universal hatred:

Brother will betray brother to death, and a father his child, and children will rise against their parents and have them put to death; and you will be hated by all because of my name. But the one who endures to the end will be saved. (Mk 13:12–13)

When that end will be Jesus does not say, but the community is to remain faithful.

The privileged role of the Christian community in hearing, though not always understanding or following, the teaching of Jesus is made plain: 'With many such parables he spoke the word to them, as they were able to hear it; he did not speak to them except in parables, but he explained everything in private to his disciples' (Mk 4:33–4). There are important lessons for the community in the inability of the disciples (from whom Jesus is absent, together with Peter, James, and John) to help an epileptic boy. Faced with the failure of the disciples and the need of the father, Jesus teaches, 'All things are possible to him who believes', to which the father gives the model response, 'I believe; help my unbelief' (Mk 9:23–4). The disciples ask Jesus privately why they were not able to cast the unclean spirit out, and again he teaches them: 'This kind can come out only through prayer' (Mk 9:29). At another point the disciples become angry with James and John who have been seeking privileged seats in the Kingdom at the right and left hand of Jesus. Jesus teaches them, and with them the Markan community:

You know that among the Gentiles those whom they recognise as their rulers lord it over them, and their great ones are tyrants over them. But it is not so among you; but whoever wishes to become great among you must be your servant and whoever wishes to be first among you must be slave of all. (Mk 10:42–4)

11 M. D. Hooker, *The Gospel According to Mark*, Black's New Testament Commentaries (London: A. and C. Black, 1991), p. 243.

Morna Hooker writes,

In their weakness and fallibility, the disciples typify ordinary believers – the Church as it was in Mark's day, and as it has been ever since. The mistakes the disciples make serve to underline the kind of community that the Church *should* be.[12]

The Lord's Prayer is not given in Mark, but Jesus teaches:

Whatever you ask in prayer, believe that you have received it, and it will be yours. Whenever you stand praying forgive, if you have anything against anyone; so that your Father in heaven may also forgive you your trespasses. (Mk 11:24–5)

From the way in which, according to the gospel account, Jesus taught his disciples, the Markan community learnt and relearnt that it was to be a forgiving, praying family, with one father, in heaven. In summary, 'Mark's vision for the community is essentially of a community that is like Jesus.'[13]

If the community is like Jesus, it has a God-given mission in the world, which some will welcome but others will violently repudiate. The Markan community seems to be at the interface between the two. In the gospel narrative, we often hear of a wider group ('the multitude', Mk 8:34), who are receptive to the ministry of Jesus. As the narrative was read, the Markan community would perhaps have been encouraged to recognise in their situation a reflection both of 'the great throng' who 'heard [Jesus] gladly' (Mk 12:37) and of themselves as an inner group of disciples. The wider group is several times distinguished from but associated with the tight-knit group of disciples: 'And he called to him the multitude with his disciples, and said to them . . .' (Mk 8:34; cf. Mk 4:10, Mk 9:14–15). It may be that there is reassurance and encouragement here: the community of Jesus will not consist of a tight and exclusive, privileged group (of Jewish Christians). The inner group will all too often get things wrong, and they will continue to be taught by Jesus. There is a multitude beyond – probably a multitude that includes the Gentiles (cf. Mk 7:26) – which welcomes the message of Jesus but needs the specific ministry of those who

---

[12] M. D. Hooker, 'Mark's Vision for the Church' in M. Bockmuehl and Michael B. Thompson, *A Vision for the Church* (Edinburgh: T. and T. Clark, 1997), p. 41.

[13] Hooker, 'Mark's Vision for the Church', p. 35.

have been more closely associated with him. This is illustrated in the story of the feeding of five thousand, and in Jesus' words to his disciples, 'You give them something to eat' (Mk 6:37), before he took the loaves and the fish 'and gave them to the disciples to set before the people' (Mk 6:41). Mark's Gospel offers to the Markan community a picture both of intimate discipleship, with its pitfalls, and of a wider multitude who readily welcome the message of Jesus. The call to the Markan community to be a community of learning and teaching, and a community that shares what it has with a receptive 'multitude', is plain.

It is not necessary here to go into the many arguments about where and when the Gospel of Mark was written. We cannot say with certainty where the church or churches were that we have called 'the Markan community'.[14] The point here is to show how the gospel functioned as a didactic text for a community or communities which saw in it a witness to the life and ministry of Jesus, and so to the source and character of their own life. There was for them a living continuity between the life of the disciples with Jesus and the life of later communities, including their own, that continued to gather about Jesus as the risen Lord and to attract new disciples. Rowan Williams has noted that the gospels contain no record of the event of the resurrection. He argues that the appearances of Jesus to his disciples after the crucifixion are not 'fleeting manifestations of a normally absent being, but events which establish Jesus' *presence*, the interweaving of his life with the life of his community'.[15] The resurrection appearances are thus inseparable from the worship and teaching of historical human communities characterised by the way in which their members relate to one another, according to a pattern exemplified by Jesus. It is in and through the life of the community that the risen Christ is now known. As Nock writes, 'That Jesus was not dead but living, and

---

14 A strong tradition in the early Church, recorded in the *Ecclesiastical History* of Eusebius (iii.39.15), linked the Gospel with Peter's recollections, and with Rome. Howard Kee places it in Southern Syria (*Community of the New Age*, London: SCM, 1977, p. 177). Morna Hooker writes, 'All we can say with certainty . . . is that the Gospel was composed somewhere in the Roman Empire' (Hooker, *The Gospel According to Mark*, p. 8).

15 R. D. Williams, *Resurrection* (London: Darton, Longman and Todd, 1982), p. 101.

living in the movement; that he would come again; that to others also the new revelation must be imparted; these are the things that made the life and thought of the little community.'[16]

THE JERUSALEM COMMUNITY AND THE SPREAD OF *KOINONIA*

The Book of Acts gives a picture of the life of the first such community, in Jerusalem. Here the theological and narrative interest is dominant. Of the accounts of the earliest Christian communities that we shall examine, Luke's picture of the Jerusalem church is the least clearly a reflection of what went on in an actual community. He sets an idealised picture of *koinonia* amongst the first believers within an idealised history of witness to Christ 'in Jerusalem, in all Judea and Samaria, and to the ends of the earth' (Acts 1:8). Luke's narrative highlights the unique place of the eschatological Christian community in Jerusalem, which is formed upon the Day of Pentecost when Peter preaches in the power of the Holy Spirit, newly given to the Twelve. Those who hear him are said to be those 'devout Jews from every nation under heaven living in Jerusalem . . . Parthians, Medes, Elamites, and residents of Mesopotamia, Judea and Cappadocia, Pontus and Asia, Phrygia and Pamphylia, Egypt and the parts of Libya belonging to Cyrene, and visitors from Rome, both Jews and proselytes, Cretans and Arabs' (Acts 2:5). These hear in their own language the message that has been given the Twelve. They are a kind of 'first-fruits' of the *diaspora*, gathered in to Jerusalem, but they are also a pointer to the regions in all the known world into which the Gospel will spread and where new communities will be formed. The first such eschatological community is that in Jerusalem, where, 'They devoted themselves to the apostles' teaching and *koinonia*, to the breaking of bread and the prayers' (Acts 2:42).

There has been a great deal of discussion about the meaning in this context of *koinonia*: whether it refers to the actual community, visible and present in Jerusalem, or to the bond

---

[16] Nock, *Early Gentile Christianity and its Hellenistic Background*, p. 24.

that binds together that community, or both.[17] The use here must be seen in the light of Acts 2:44, and Acts 4:32, where it is said that 'the whole group of those who believed were of one heart and soul, and no one claimed private ownership of any possessions, but everything they owned was in common' (*hapanta koina*).[18] There is a consensus amongst scholars that *koinonia* is not in the New Testament used concretely in such a way as to be a synonym for *ecclesia*, church.[19] An English translation of *koinonia* in this instance might be either 'community' (NIV, 'the community'), with an emphasis on the participative common life, or 'fellowship' (RSV) where fellowship is realised in an actual community. Best of all is 'the common life' (NEB).

The particular 'communion' or 'community' here is one that shares table-fellowship. At this stage in the narrative, there is no difficulty about table-fellowship: those who have been baptised are taken to have been Jews. What is, however, a sustained theme throughout Acts is the way in which the outpouring of the Holy Spirit generates new experience and understanding of

17 In the *Dictionnaire de Spiritualité* (17 vols., Paris: Beauchesne, 1937–95, vol. 8, '*Koinonia*', cols. 1747–50) four main lines of interpretation are suggested: (1) *koinonia* in the sense of 'unanimity' (Seesemann, Hauck); (2) 'the apostles' teaching and *koinonia*', that is to say 'community of faith with the apostles' (strongly rejected by Campbell); (3) table-fellowship, or the *agape* as the second part of a fourfold pattern of worship outlined by the verse (i.e. apostles' teaching, *koinonia* (*agape*), breaking of bread, prayers)(Jeremias); (4) 'community of goods' involving love for the brethren and sharing of material possessions as an expression of that love (Campbell). A fifth, and attractive, possibility would be table-fellowship in general (without the specific presupposition of a fourfold pattern of worship).

18 In the description of community of goods, David Mealand finds both 'the fulfilment of the promise in Deuteronomy' ('There will be no poor among you', Dt. 15:4; cf. Acts 4:34, 'There was not a needy person among them') and the realisation of the Greek ideal of community', with echoes of catchphrases from Aristotle and Plato. ('Community of Goods and Utopian Allusions in Acts II–IV', *Journal of Theological Studies* ns XXVIII (1977), 96–9). Cf. chapter 3, note 18.

19 Following F. J. F. Jackson, K. Lake and H. J. Cadbury eds., *The Beginnings of Christianity*, Part I: *The Acts of the Apostles*, 5 volumes (London: Macmillan, 1920–33), vol. 5, pp. 389–90. F. Poland stresses that though *koinon* and *ta koina* were frequently used of the formally constituted Greek 'club' (Latin, *collegium*) that was increasingly popular in the Hellenistic world, *koinonia* was only ever used, and that much more infrequently, for the less concrete, 'fellowship' or 'association' (*societas*) (*Geschichte des Griechischen Vereinswesens*, Leipzig: Teubner, 1909). However much the early Christian house-meetings might have looked like those of a 'club' from outside, Christians did not speak of themselves in this way.

koinonia. This is central to the narrative of what takes place on the Day of Pentecost in Jerusalem: the Holy Spirit fills the Twelve, and they speak with 'other tongues as the Spirit gave them utterance' (Acts 2:4). Peter is depicted as the one who enunciates the invitation to baptism and receipt of the Holy Spirit to all the Jews of the *diaspora* ('Men of Judea and all who dwell in Jerusalem . . .'). The response is overwhelming:

So those who received his word were baptised, and there were added that day about three thousand souls. And they devoted themselves to the apostles' teaching and *koinonia*, to the breaking of bread and the prayers. And fear came upon every soul; and many wonders and signs were done through the apostles. And all who believed were together (*epi to auto*) and had all things in common (*hapanta koina*) and they sold their possessions and goods and distributed them to all, as any had need. (Acts 2:41–5)

This is the direct result of the outpouring of the Holy Spirit. In the same way, the baptism of Saul is associated with the direct action of the Holy Spirit (Acts 9:17), as is his commission to take the Gospel to the Gentiles (Acts 9:15; 13:2). Peter's understanding of covenant-fidelity to God, of what is *koinos* ('common', 'unhallowed'), and where *koinonia* ('fellowship, probably including table-fellowship')[20] is permitted, is transformed by the direct intervention of the Holy Spirit (Acts 10:9–19): the outpouring of the Spirit on Cornelius confirms that he should be baptised (Acts 10:44–8). When Peter defends his table-fellowship with the uncircumcised to the more conservative believers in Jerusalem, it is in terms of the gift of the Holy Spirit and the specific initiative of Jesus (Acts 11:15–17). His opponents are silenced. Following that, when there is an announcement of

---

[20] P. F. Esler quotes examples from Greek authors of *koinonein* and its cognates used specifically for Jewish *table*-fellowship in *Community and Gospel in Luke–Acts* (Cambridge: Cambridge University Press, 1987), pp. 78–80. I am indebted to Esler's discussion of issues surrounding 'table-fellowship' (pp. 70–109) but surprised that, although he takes 'the legitimation of a sectarian movement' as his central theme, he pays so little attention to the use by the author of Acts of the specific action of the Holy Spirit to legitimate the inclusive practice of the churches (e.g. admission of Gentiles to full membership). See, however, his study 'Glossalalia and the admission of the Gentiles into the Earliest Christian Community' in *The First Christians in their Social Worlds* (London: Routledge, 1994), pp. 37–51, where he discusses glossalalia and legitimation.

the crucial decision of the apostles and elders at Jerusalem, laying down only minimal conditions for the inclusion of Gentiles within the Christian communities established or strengthened by Paul and his fellow workers,[21] it is in terms of what 'has seemed good to the Holy Spirit and to us' (Acts 15:28). Throughout Acts it is made clear that the emergence of Christian *koinonia*, which is strikingly inclusive of Jews and Gentiles, and which is characterised by regular joyful table-fellowship ('breaking of bread'), is the specific result of the action of the Holy Spirit. We might say that where in Acts the Spirit is active, the evident result in human communities is Christian *koinonia*. Thornton puts the emphasis in exactly the right place when he writes in his classic study, *The Common Life in the Body of Christ*, 'The whole of this section of the Acts is occupied with showing that "the *koinonia*" was something altogether new, originated by an act of God.'[22]

Luke is at pains to show that this Spirit-constituted *koinonia* is not confined to one place or time, but goes out from Jerusalem to the communities that have been mentioned in the account of the gift of the Spirit at Pentecost. Though there is, as the narrative progresses, less stress upon sharing of goods, and more upon sharing in the Spirit, Acts shows how Spirit-inspired *koinonia* spreads through Judea and Samaria to Antioch, through Asia Minor and Greece, through Cyprus and Crete, to Rome. The practical demonstration of the spread of *koinonia* beyond Jerusalem is the response of the church in Antioch to the famine in Jerusalem and Judea: 'The disciples determined, every one according to his ability, to send relief to the brethren who lived in Judea' (Acts 11:29). This is simply the extension,

---

21 It is striking that the fourfold prohibition – abstention from 'what has been sacrificed to idols and from blood and from what is strangled and from unchastity' (Acts 15:29 cf. 21) – includes two types of *koinonia* specifically prohibited in 1 Corinthians: *koinonia* with demons by eating sacrificial meat (cf. 1 Cor. 10:20) and *koinonia* with illegitimate sexual partners (cf. 1 Cor. 6:16). Abstention from 'blood and from what is strangled' is commanded of Noah (Gen. 9:4) in the context of God's universal covenant. To consume the blood would be to share in the God-given life, that is to presume to *koinonia* with God. Such an understanding lies behind the remarkable notion of *koinonia* in the blood of Christ and in the body of Christ in 1 Cor. 10:16–17.

22 L. S. Thornton, *The Common Life in the Body of Christ*, third edition (London: Dacre Press, 1950), p. 6.

from church to church, of that initial sharing of common life in Jerusalem by which 'distribution was made to each as any had need' (Acts 4:35).[23]

THE COMMUNITY AT CORINTH

In the little communities of early Christianity something radically new was taking place. Those who belonged to the community of Jesus had found a new way of belonging to the covenant people of God. The new (or renewed) covenant was experienced as a new 'life-world'. Paul wrote to the Christian community at Corinth, 'If anyone is in Christ, there is a new creation: everything old has passed away; see, everything has become new!' (2 Cor. 5:17). To be in this community is, for Paul, to experience this new creation, this new 'life-world'; it is to be 'in Christ', a member of the body of Christ.

In Paul's letters to the Corinthians we come close to the life of one early Christian community.[24] At the time of Paul's lengthy first visit[25] Corinth had been in existence as a Roman colony for a hundred years. It was strategically situated on the main road across the isthmus connecting the Peloponnese to central Greece, with twin harbours on the east (the harbour of Cenchreae) and on the west (the harbour of Lechaeon). Trade had made Corinth wealthy and there were tensions between the

---

[23] What is a puzzle is the almost total lack of reference in Acts (see only Acts 24:17) to the collection that Paul made amongst the (predominantly Gentile) churches of Greece for the poor saints in Jerusalem, which is elsewhere (Rom. 15:26, 2 Cor. 8:4, 2 Cor. 9:13) called a '*koinonia*'. K. F. Nickle writes that Paul's application of *koinonia* to the collection project 'testifies to the deep concern that he felt about the tense and suspicious relationship existing between the two branches of the Church and to his ardent longing that the fissure be eliminated' (*The Collection*, London: SCM, 1966, p. 124).

[24] Influential recent studies include G. Theissen, *The Social Setting of Pauline Christianity* (Edinburgh: T. and T. Clark, 1982) and Wayne A. Meeks, *The First Urban Christians* (New Haven and London: Yale University Press, 1983). Corinth is well described by Meeks, pp. 47–9.

[25] For a well-informed discussion of the date of Paul's founding mission in Corinth, see David G. Horrell, *The Social Ethos of the Corinthian Correspondence, Interests and Ideology from 1 Corinthians to 1 Clement* (Edinburgh: T. and T. Clark, 1996), pp. 73–7. Horrell favours a date between 41 and 44 CE. Many modern scholars accept a date about 50–2 CE, basing this on the mention in Acts 18:2 of Gallio, who is known to have been proconsul of Achaia in 50–1 or 51–2 CE.

wealthy Corinthian Christians (cf. 2 Cor. 8:14) and those who were poorer.[26] Paul warns that their manner of celebrating the Lord's Supper will 'humiliate those who have nothing' (1 Cor. 11:22). According to the account in Acts 18, Paul came to Corinth from Athens, and first made contact with a Jew named Aquila who had lately come from Italy with his wife Priscilla because Claudius had expelled the Jews from Rome. He stayed with them, probably because they also were tentmakers or leatherworkers, and he worked with them. Each sabbath he argued in the synagogue, persuading Jews and Greek proselytes of his message. Silas and Timothy joined him from Macedonia. At some stage in his eighteen-month stay there was a row with the members of the synagogue, and he announced that he would no longer preach to the Jews but would turn to the Gentiles. Amongst the Jewish believers, however, were Aquila and Priscilla, and Crispus, a ruler of the synagogue, who, together with his household and 'many' other Corinthians, had been baptised (Acts 18:8; 1 Cor. 1:14). Paul also specifically mentions some Christians who were probably Gentiles: the household of Stephanas (1 Cor. 1:16, 16:15), the first converts in Achaia, Stephanas himself, Fortunatus and Achaicus (1 Cor. 16:17).

It is not necessary here to go into the extensive debates about the nature of the divisions in the church in Corinth, the persistence of which is attested not only by Paul's Corinthian correspondence but by the letter of Clement of Rome, written shortly before the end of the first century.[27] What is clear is that Paul's continuing concern throughout the Corinthian correspondence is for unity,[28] and his strategy both for reconciliation

---

26 Theissen, *The Social Setting of Pauline Christianity*, pp. 99–110, 145–74.
27 See Horrell, *The Social Ethos of the Corinthian Correspondence*, pp. 244–50.
28 This is stressed by Margaret M. Mitchell in her fine study, *Paul and the Rhetoric of Reconciliation* (Tübingen: J. C. B. Mohr, 1991). She argues that in dealing with factionalism, which is 'the fundamental problem of *practical ecclesiology*', Paul chose to employ Graeco-Roman political terms and concepts for the church and the inter-relationships of its members. In 1 Corinthians Paul presents a viewpoint of the church as '*a real political body*' (p. 300). Mitchell gives examples of the use of *koinonia* in secular sources and appeals for unity in the body politic (see pp. 157–64). Clearly, 'body' imagery is of the greatest importance for Paul's understanding of common life within the local church. John A. T. Robinson put this point extraordinarily strongly:

and the maintenance of unity amongst the Corinthian Christian community includes reflection and teaching on their participation (*koinonia*) in Jesus Christ and in the Holy Spirit. At the beginning of 1 Corinthians he writes, 'God, who has called you into fellowship (*koinonia*) with his Son Jesus Christ our Lord, is faithful' (1 Cor. 1:9, NIV).[29] Paul concludes 2 Corinthians with the well-known words, 'The grace of the Lord Jesus Christ and the love of God and the fellowship (*koinonia*) of the Holy Spirit be with you all' (2 Cor. 13:14).[30] We could compare Philippians 2:1: 'If there is any encouragement in Christ, any incentive of love, any participation (*koinonia*) in the Spirit, any affection and sympathy, complete my joy by being of the same mind, having the same love, being in full accord and of one mind.' What Paul wants for the Christians of Corinth is what Acts 4:32 depicts: unity of heart and mind, which can come only through participation in Christ and in the Spirit.

Central to Paul's strategy for unity in 1 Corinthians, for overcoming the divisions in the community, is his teaching about the body of Christ:

The cup of blessing which we bless, is it not a participation (*koinonia*) in

---

'It is almost impossible to exaggerate the materialism and crudity of Paul's doctrine of the Church as literally now the resurrection *body* of Christ . . . He is not saying anything so weak as that the Church is a society with a common life and governor, but that its unity is that of a single physical entity; disunion is dismemberment' (*The Body*, London: SCM, 1952, p. 51).

[29] None of the commonly available NT translations uses 'participation' here, but J. Y. Campbell argues strongly for it in his classic article 'Koinonia in the New Testament', reprinted in *Three New Testament Studies* (Leiden: E. J. Brill, 1965), pp. 27–8. Campbell's preferred translation would retain what he sees as the 'primary, and only common, meaning' of *koinonia:* 'participation along with others in something'. He is followed by Geoffrey Lampe: 'In the NT . . . [*koinonia*] means participation' ('Authority in the Church', *Theology*, September 1977, 363). For detailed discussion of Pauline texts, see J. Hainz, Koinonia, *'Kirche' als Gemeinschaft bei Paulus* (*Biblische Untersuchungen* 16, Regensburg: Verlag Friedrich Pustet, 1982).

[30] Compare NEB 'fellowship in the Holy Spirit', which avoids any suggestion of 'fellowship with the Holy Spirit'. Campbell argues strongly (p. 27) for 'participation in the Holy Spirit'. In agreement with Campbell is J. D. G. Dunn: 'What is in view is not a physical entity (like a congregation), but the subjective experience of the Spirit as something shared.' Dunn stresses that, 'What keeps believers together for Paul was not simply a common membership of a congregation, but the common experience of the Spirit' (*The Theology of Paul the Apostle*, p. 561). See also Dunn's article, 'Instruments of *Koinonia* in the Early Church', *One in Christ* xxv, 3 (1989), 204–16.

the blood of Christ. The bread which we break, is it not a participation (*koinonia*) in the body of Christ? Because there is one bread, we who are many are one body, for we all partake (*metechomen*) of the one bread. (1 Cor. 10:16–17)[31]

The concern with which Paul introduces this passage is that the Corinthian Christians should 'shun the worship of idols'. He develops this later by talking of those who worship idols as 'partners (*koinonoi*) with demons'. However, his argument is deployed towards the assertion of the unity of the Corinthians as 'one body'. It is by actually sharing in the wine and the bread that those at the eucharist have their part in the *koinonia* ('Is there not a *koinonia* . . . ?', asks Paul). Such participation presents a vital issue of belonging, of exclusion and inclusion: 'You cannot partake (*metechein*) of the table of the Lord and the table of demons'; you must belong to one or the other.[32] One clear sign that you belong to Christ is your 'worthy' (cf. 1 Cor. 11:27ff) sharing (Paul has just (17–22) spoken to them sharply and clearly about their misbehaviour at the Lord's supper) in the bread and the wine through which the community makes the living memorial of Christ's sacrificial death. When you obey

31 These remarkably compressed sentences have given rise to much controversy. The RSV translation quoted in the text suggests a direct link between 'the cup of blessing', 'the bread', and participation (*koinonia*) in the blood and body of Christ, a link which is often taken to be ingestion of the wine and the bread. The Greek is more condensed: '*to poterion tes eulogias ho eulogoumen ouchi koinonia tou haimatos tou Christou estin . . .*' – literally, 'The cup of blessing which (when) we bless, is there not participation in the blood of Christ? . . .' The NEB translation comes closer to this: 'When we bless "the cup of blessing", is it not a means of sharing in the blood of Christ? When we break the bread, is it not a means of sharing in the body of Christ?' 'When we bless . . . When we break . . .' brings out not only the appeal to the moment of blessing and breaking (as the prelude to common drinking and eating), but also the habitual nature of the action. More technically correct than 'a means of sharing', if a phrase needs to be introduced, would be 'a mode of', followed by 'sharing in', avoiding any suggestion of division between the blessing, breaking, and ingestion, all of which make for *koinonia* (both 'vertical' and 'horizontal'). At the root of the problem in translation is the gerund nature of the verbal noun *koinonia*, which embraces the whole field of 'relating'.

32 E. P. Sanders writes, 'Idolatry involves a participatory union which excludes one from union with Christ (10:14–22). Here Paul does not argue *that* one participates in the body and blood of Christ in the Lord's Supper; rather that *since* one does so, one may not participate in the food and drink in which demons share . . . Union with Christ and union with demons are mutually exclusive' (*Paul and Palestinian Judaism*, p. 455). The same would apply to forbidden sexual union (cf. 1 Cor. 5:1ff; 6:15ff). See *Paul and Palestinian Judaism*, p. 456.

Christ by so participating, you show at the same time that you belong to the body of Christ, and you show that the death of Christ (without which there would be no participation in the body) was for all those who, in the limited time before the Lord's coming, accept the invitation to belong:

For I received from the Lord what I also delivered to you, that the Lord Jesus on the night when he was betrayed took bread, and when he had given thanks, he broke it, and said, 'This is my body which is for you. Do this in remembrance of me.' In the same way also the cup, after supper, saying, 'This cup is the new covenant in my blood. Do this, as often as you drink it, in remembrance of me.' For as often as you eat this bread and drink the cup, you proclaim the Lord's death until he comes. (1 Cor. 11:23–6)

Paul wishes to draw the Corinthians into an appreciation of what it is to participate in Christ, and so to see others as members of Christ's body who are co-participants in Christ, and also what it is to participate in the Spirit and to see spiritual gifts as given for the edification of the whole body (1 Cor. 12:4–6).

For Paul there is a complex tissue of participation holding together the Corinthian community, which has been severely strained by the strife among various parties in the church.[33] His concern for unity is grounded in his understanding of the present Lordship of Christ and of the Spirit, of God working in the community. It is in this context that he calls them to love:

Love is patient and kind; love is not jealous or boastful; it is not arrogant or rude. Love does not insist on its own way; it is not irritable

---

[33] In discussing Paul's 'language of belonging', Meeks (*The First Urban Christians*, p. 88) borrows the term *communitas* from the anthropologist Vincent Turner. For Turner, the bonds of *communitas* are 'anti-structural in that they are undifferentiated, equalitarian, direct, nonrational (though not *ir*rational)', whereas 'structure is all that holds people apart, defines their differences, and constrains their actions' (*Dramas, Fields, and Metaphors*, Ithaca: Cornell University Press, 1974, pp. 46–7, cf. pp. 231–98). In the Corinthian correspondence, Paul could be said by his emphasis on the Spirit to uphold ecstatic or eschatological *communitas*, but his concern for order and structure in the community (of which he takes a more positive view than Turner) comes into tension with this. It would, then, be wrong to equate *koinonia* and *communitas*. The *koinonia* of the Corinthians, as it emerges in the Corinthian correspondence, is a structured freedom. For a similar concern, compare the *Nota Praevia Explicativa* to *Lumen Gentium* ('The Constitution on the Church' from *The Documents of Vatican 2*) on 'hierarchical communion'.

or resentful; it does not rejoice at wrong, but rejoices in the right. Love bears all things, believes all things, hopes all things, endures all things. (1 Cor. 13:4–7)[34]

This, we might say, gives 'flesh and blood' to Paul's notion of *koinonia*. This is how the Corinthians are to treat one another as *koinonoi* or *sunkoinonoi* in Christ.

There is, however, another dimension of participation in Christ to which Paul returns several times: participation in his sufferings. This is plain at the beginning of 2 Corinthians:

Blessed be the God and Father of our Lord Jesus Christ, the Father of mercies and God of all comfort, who comforts us in all our affliction, so that we may be able to comfort those who are in any affliction, with the comfort with which we ourselves are comforted by God. For as we share abundantly in Christ's sufferings, so through Christ we share abundantly in comfort too. If we are afflicted, it is for your comfort and salvation; and if we are comforted, it is for your comfort, which you experience when you patiently endure the same sufferings that we suffer. Our hope for you is unshaken; for we know that as you are *koinonoi* in our sufferings, so also in our comfort. (2 Cor. 1:3–7)

What this passage so clearly shows is the interwovenness of suffering and comfort within the Christian community, between the Corinthians and Paul, and between the Christian and Christ. Suffering and comfort are in this context not individualised experience, but dimensions of shared experience. Writing to the Philippians, Paul talks of his longing 'that I may know [Christ] and the power of his resurrection, and the sharing (*koinonia*) of his sufferings, becoming like him in his death, that if possible I may attain the resurrection from the dead' (Phil.

---

34 Theissen attributes to Paul the teaching of 'love-patriarchalism', in assuring members of the Corinthian church from sharply differing social backgrounds that they could be at one with one another, even without the radical sharing depicted in Acts 2:42ff: 'No longer was there a struggle for equal rights but instead a struggle to achieve a pattern of relationships among members of various strata which would be characterised by respect, concern, and a sense of responsibility' (*The Social Setting of Pauline Christianity*, p. 109; cf. pp. 107–10, 139–40, 164). In other words, Theissen argues (cogently) that Paul was seeking to teach the Corinthians the *koinonia* engendered by Jesus Christ and the Spirit which, unlike the *koinonia* that characterises Luke's idealised picture of the initial community in Jerusalem (Acts 2:42–2; 4:32), was not associated with complete sharing of all material assets ('*hapanta koina*'). In the Corinthian correspondence he both accepts a measure of social and economic differentiation in the Christian community and reinforces their fundamental sense of 'belonging' to one another, of incorporation (*koinonia*).

3:10). There is a tissue of shared experience that binds together Christian believers and binds believers to Christ. It is the tissue of *koinonia*.

The same goes for giving and receiving. Paul frequently returned to his concern for the poor saints at Jerusalem and the collection for them. Thus he commended the Philippians for being the only church that participated (*ekoinonesen*) in a pattern of giving and receiving with him after he left Macedonia (Phil. 4:5). Clearly, the Corinthians joined them, for he wrote to the Romans, 'At present . . . I am going to Jerusalem with aid for the saints. For Macedonia and Achaia (the province of which Corinth was the capital) have been pleased to make some contribution (he uses the term *koinonia*) for the poor among the saints in Jerusalem' (Rom. 15:26). Similarly, when he pleads with the Corinthians to be generous, he takes the example of the Macedonians, saying, 'Going to the limits of their resources, as I can testify, and even beyond that limit, they begged us most insistently and on their own initiative, to be allowed to share ('to have a *koinonia*') in this generous service to their fellow-Christians' (2 Cor. 8:3–4, NEB). A little later, he anticipates the generosity of the Corinthians by saying, 'For through the proof which this affords, many will give honour to God when they see how humbly you obey him and how faithfully you confess the gospel of Christ; and will thank him for your liberal contribution (*koinonia*) to their need and to the general good' (2 Cor. 9:13, NEB). Just as the sharing of bread and wine in worship is a *koinonia* in the body and blood of Christ, so here the giving and receiving of money is a *koinonia* between Christians in distant churches. Such practical charity is seen as one expression of the bond that holds them together, of their communion. We need to remember those who travelled between the churches like Paul and his companions, carrying gifts and letters along the Roman roads and over the sea from one church to another. These are the people who, in practical terms, made the *koinonia* between the churches a living reality. When Paul moved on from Corinth, he commended to them Titus who was returning to them with another brother: 'As for Titus he is my partner (*koinonos*) and fellow worker in your service; and as for our brethren, they are messengers of the churches, the glory of Christ' (2 Cor. 8:23). For a moment one glimpses something of the traffic among the churches, something of the activity of those who travelled on Paul's behalf. They were, with him, agents of *koinonia* among and within the little Christian communities that were beginning to emerge in great centres of communication like Antioch, Ephesus, or Corinth.

THE JOHANNINE COMMUNITIES

In turning now to the Johannine writings, we turn to another community or communities whose life has left a distinctive record. Raymond Brown, whose tracing of that record is unparalleled,[35] paints a vivid picture of the variety of teaching and tradition within the early Christian movement, and the pressures on the unity of the churches:

The Christian situation in a large city would have involved a number of house churches where 20 or 30 people met together; and so there is no reason why there could not have been in the one city house churches of different traditions – for example, of the Pauline tradition, of the Johannine tradition, of the Petrine or apostolic tradition, and even of the ultraconservative Jewish-Christian tradition. Even though house churches of one tradition probably had *koinonia* with those of another tradition, Christians may not have transferred easily.[36]

35 See especially R. E. Brown, *The Community of the Beloved Disciple* (London: Geoffrey Chapman, 1979).

36 R. E. Brown, *The Churches the Apostles Left Behind*, p. 23. James Burtchaell describes the background to the diversity of house churches in the diversity of synagogues: 'Jewish communities were accustomed, and even obliged, to tolerate a diversity of doctrinal views. In large cities, such as Alexandria or Jerusalem, there were enough *synagogai* that they could sort themselves out by preference. Pharisees, Sadducees, Zealots, Therapeutae, Essenes and those of any other sect = *hairesis* could congregate with those of their own persuasion' (*From Synagogue to Church*, p. 279). For example, 'The synagogue of the Freedmen' (Acts 6:9) would have been a Greek-speaking synagogue in Jerusalem at which Jews from the *diaspora* gathered. R. J. Banks surmises that the earliest house churches in Corinth (1 Cor. 14:23) came together, but that this did not happen in Rome – hence Paul's greetings to 'all God's saints' (Romans 1:7) and various Christian groups (chapter 16) but not to the 'whole church' (*Paul's Idea of Community: The Early House Churches in their Cultural Setting*, revised edition, Peabody, Mass.: Hendrickson, 1994, pp. 31–6). By the time of 1 Clement (c.96 CE), the cohesion of the church in Rome was probably greater: the letter is written from 'The church of God which sojourns at Rome, to the church of God sojourning at Corinth' (1 Clement 1).

In speaking of house churches 'having *koinonia* with' one another, Brown takes, and even extends, the phraseology of 1 John 1, where the writer speaks of 'having *koinonia* with' the recipients of the letter, of 'having *koinonia* with' God, or with one another, and of *koinonia* with the Father and with his Son Jesus Christ. Brown writes that, 'The Johannine Christians tend to think of themselves as a communion (*koinonia*: 1 John 1:3).'[37] The situation addressed by this and the other two Johannine letters is one of 'broken communion (*koinonia*)',[38] where two or more groups of Johannine Christians, who share the tradition of Johannine Christianity represented by the Fourth Gospel, have split from one another. Brown brings out the implications of this:

For the author of the Epistles 'brethren' were those members of the Johannine community who were in communion (*koinonia*) with him and who accepted his interpretation of the Johannine Gospel; the secessionists had left and were no longer brethren . . . Almost surely the exact same sentiments could be found among the secessionists.[39]

The situation addressed in 1, 2, and 3 John is considerably worse than the situation in Corinth. Here the strategy is not one of working for unity and reconciliation, but one of demarcation and exclusion. The epistolary writer speaks of 'antichrists' and says, 'They went out from us, but they were not of us; for if they had been of us, they would have continued with us' (1 John 2:18–19). The secessionist group, it seems, deny that 'Jesus Christ has come in the flesh.' It is not clear whether the problem with Diotrephes, who does not acknowledge the authority of the writer of 3 John, is the same, but the split is plain: 'He refuses himself to welcome the brethren, and also stops those who want to welcome them and puts them out of the church' (3 John 10).

---

[37] Brown, *The Community of the Beloved Disciple*, p. 60. The use of *koinonia*, both in the Johannine letters and in Brown's writing is never specifically related to sharing in the eucharist, but the implication must be that those who 'have *koinonia* with' one another share in the eucharist, and in that sharing (but not only in that sharing) make explicit their *koinonia* with the Father and with the Son, and their participation in the Spirit (cf. 1 John 3:24).

[38] Brown, *The Community of the Beloved Disciple*, p. 142.

[39] *Ibid.*, p. 132.

Faced with this division in the Johannine community, the writer of 1 John exhorts them:

Let what you heard from the beginning abide in you. If what you heard from the beginning abides in you, then you will abide in the Son and in the Father. And this is what he has promised us, eternal life. (1 John 2:24–5)

The language he uses is reminiscent both of the beginning of the epistle and of the Fourth Gospel. '*Abiding*' is a characteristically Johannine expression. The one who *abides* in Jesus (cf. John 15:4ff) is the one who has *koinonia* with the Father and with his Son Jesus Christ, and also has *koinonia* with the community (1 John 1:3–7). In 1 John, the characteristic early Christian concern for faithful handing on of tradition is used to emphasise certain points against the teaching of anyone (the secessionists) who would deny them: that 'Jesus Christ has come in the flesh', that 'the blood of Jesus Christ . . . cleanses us from all sin', that members of the community must 'keep his commandments', principally to 'love one another':

That which we have seen and heard we proclaim also to you, so that you may have *koinonia* with us; and our *koinonia* is with the Father and with his Son Jesus Christ. And we are writing this that our joy may be complete. This is the message we have heard from him and proclaim to you, that God is light and in him is no darkness at all. If we say we have *koinonia* with him while we walk in darkness, we lie and do not live according to the truth; but if we walk in the light, as he is in the light, we have *koinonia* with one another, and the blood of Jesus his Son cleanses us from all sin. (1 John 1:3–7 cf. 2:24)

The community addressed here functions with the polarities of the Fourth Gospel: light/darkness, life/death. It now has to define and re-establish itself over against the group or groups that have split off from them. In discussing 'the positive functions of heresy', John Gager has shown how conflict serves a group-binding function, how the closer the relationship the more intense the conflict, and how conflict serves to define and strengthen group structures.[40] In his argument he does not particularly have these Johannine communities in mind, but

---

[40] John G. Gager, *Kingdom and Community* (Englewood Cliffs, New Jersey: Prentice-Hall, 1975), pp. 79–87.

they exemplify his thesis precisely. When *koinonia* between communities is severed, the communities that result are likely to define themselves more tightly. The Johannine epistles are written precisely to prevent the recipients seeing themselves as enjoying *koinonia* of the same type as that of the secessionists. If they continue faithful to what they have received, they may be confident of their continuing *koinonia* with the Father, the Son, and with one another – and so with all who receive, without distortion, the authentic tradition of Jesus Christ.

Brown suggests that the epistles were written about ten years after the gospel. He favours a date of about 90 CE for the gospel and 100 CE for the epistles, noting that the letters of Ignatius, to which we shall turn, can be dated about 110 CE. He further suggests that the first epistle might have been written to Johannine Christians in a large metropolitan centre with many house churches, perhaps Ephesus, and then 2 and 3 John might have been addressed to neighbouring provincial towns with Johannine churches. The problem that these Christian churches would have been beginning to face is that of orthodoxy and heresy, a problem that would become ever more pressing as it became clear that there were not just tensions within churches but also between rival groups claiming to be churches and defining themselves over against each other.

We can see the process at a similar stage of development in the Book of Revelation. There is little reason to suppose that the author of Revelation is the same as the author of the epistles of John, since the style of writing is so different, but there may be some links, since the seven churches mentioned are churches of western Asia minor, including Ephesus and some surrounding towns. The seer writes to the seven churches:

I John, your brother, and fellow-sharer (*sunkoinonos*) in Jesus in the tribulation and the kingdom and the patient endurance, was on the island called Patmos on account of the word of God and the testimony of Jesus. (Rev. 1:9)

He is told in a vision to write what he sees in a book and to send it to the seven churches, to Ephesus, Smyrna, Pergamum, Thyatira, Sardis, Philadelphia, and Laodicea. If these were churches where Johannine Christianity was strong, it makes obvious sense for the writer to adopt the *persona* of 'John'. In his vision he sees seven golden lamps or lampstands and in the middle 'one like a son of man'. The majestic vision of Christ is set symbolically amongst the lamps, and there are seven stars representing 'the angels' of the seven churches, that is to say 'the churches seen as spiritual entities'.[41] Each of the churches is distinct, each is to shine as a light in a dark and threatening world. It is clear from the letters to the seven churches that the struggle against heresy and against persecution is formidable. The church of Ephesus is commended for testing 'those who call themselves apostles but are not' and for hating the works of the Nicolaitans; the church of Smyrna is threatened by persecution from the 'synagogue of Satan'; the church of Pergamum has witnessed the death of Antipas 'my witness, my faithful one who was killed among you, where Satan dwells' and some of the church have followed the teaching of the Nicolaitans; the church of Thyatira tolerates a false prophetess who is seducing church members to practise immorality and eat food sacrificed to idols; the church of Sardis has the name of being alive and is, with a few exceptions, dead; the church of Philadelphia has suffered from the pseudo-Jews of 'the synagogue of Satan'; the church of Laodicea is, famously, 'lukewarm'. Each of the churches, then has its problems from within or without, and the Johannine writer acts as a pastor and visionary, urging them to hear what the Spirit is saying to the churches, urging them to remain faithful to Christ. The image of 'one like a son of man' holding in his right hand the 'angels of the seven churches' (Rev. 1:20) is, quite simply, an image of Christ in full glory and power *holding the churches together.*

KOINONIA AND THE CATHOLIC CHURCH

It has been increasingly recognised that the situation of the little Christian communities, the churches, at the end of the first century was a complex one, where the issue of orthodoxy and heresy had not yet emerged with clarity. It is from Eusebius'

---

[41] J. Sweet, *Revelation* (London: SCM, 1979), p. 73.

Church History, written early in the fourth century, that we have inherited the picture of early church history as the spread of apostolic Christianity from Jerusalem through the Empire to the point where apostolic Christianity is recognised as the official imperial religion: the triumph of orthodoxy.[42] In 1934, the theologically driven Eusebian history was challenged by Walter Bauer.[43] Bauer argued that we should beware of Eusebian history as a story told by the winners. Amongst the losers were the earliest believers in Edessa, Antioch, and Alexandria, whose faith was initially formed by teaching that would later be adjudged heretical. Eusebius and others fabricated a history of evangelisation that suppressed the histories of major 'heretical' groups like the followers of Marcion. This re-writing of history was done in the service of the ecclesiastical expansionism of Rome, which became established in Corinth (as 1 Clement shows), but was not widely successful in the East throughout the second century. Bauer writes,

The form of Christian belief and life which was successful was that supported by the strongest organization – the form which was the most uniform and best suited for mass consumption – in spite of the fact that, in my judgement, for a long time after the close of the post-apostolic age the sum total of consciously orthodox and anti-heretical Christians was numerically inferior to that of the 'heretics'.[44]

Catholic Christianity, as the Christianity of 'the one church of dependable orthodoxy'[45] was imposed through the East from the second to the fourth centuries upon Christians with varying conceptions about God, Christ, the Holy Spirit. These Christians of the East had disparate ways of relating Christianity to Judaism, or to the loose-knit philosophical world-views of Gnosticism, together with different types of piety, worship, and styles of life. Bauer taught a whole generation to take seriously the claims of the various 'heretical' groups that they were no less Christian than their critics.

The most comprehensive critique of Bauer's thesis is still that

---

[42] R. L. Wilken, *The Myth of Christian Beginnings* (London: SCM, 1979) is a vigorous critique of the idealised, Eusebian conception of the Church in the apostolic age.

[43] W. Bauer, *Orthodoxy and Heresy in Earliest Christianity*, English translation from second German edition (Philadelphia: Fortress Press, 1971).

[44] *Ibid.*, p. 231.   [45] *Ibid.*, p. 128.

of H.E.W. Turner in *The Pattern of Christian Truth*.[46] Turner accepted that early Christian thought was much more fluid than the picture of a fixed and static norm suggests. He also recognised that the writings of the sub-apostolic period could not be reduced to a 'single common denominator'.[47] He argued that orthodoxy was a 'fruitful fusion of theological traditions' independently incapable of doing justice to the fullness of the truth of Christ. Similarly, Robert Wilken later wrote:

We miss the character of the early Christian movement if we see it primarily as a history of diverging traditions, each with its own logic and internal coherence, existing alongside of one another. A 'center' was being shaped and formed during this period, and it is historically important to understand how and why this sense of communal identity emerged.[48]

Turner writes of the *lex orandi*, which formed 'the instinctive basis for that exercise of Christian common sense which enabled the Church to reject interpretations of her faith and dilutions of her life even before she possessed formal standards of belief'.[49] He concludes,

The most important element in the evolution of Christian orthodoxy is . . . a kind of Christian common sense exercised at all levels within the Christian Church, which is merely another name for the guidance of the Holy Spirit leading the Church into all truth.[50]

Bauer's critics have shown how deeply the detail of his arguments is flawed.[51] His extreme view of diversity in Chris-

---

[46] H. E. W. Turner, *The Pattern of Christian Truth* (London: Mowbray, 1954). Bauer's thesis excited further discussion after the long-awaited English translation of his book was published in 1971. See Thomas A. Robinson, *The Bauer Thesis Examined, The Geography of Heresy in the Early Church* (Lewiston/Quenston: Edwin Mellen Press, 1988); also S. W. Sykes, ' "Orthodoxy" and "Liberalism" ' in David F. Ford and Dennis L. Stamps eds., *Essentials of Christian Community* (Edinburgh: T. and T. Clark, 1996), pp. 78–84.

[47] Turner, *The Pattern of Christian Truth*, p. 10.

[48] R. E. Wilken, 'Diversity and Unity in Early Christianity', *The Second Century* 1 (1981), 109–10.

[49] Turner, *The Pattern of Christian Truth*, p. 28.   [50] *Ibid.*, p. 498.

[51] See Bauer, *Orthodoxy and Heresy*, Appendix 2, 'The Reception of the Book', pp. 286–316. Thomas A. Robinson concludes, 'The Bauer thesis fails at its two most distinctive claims. The heretics were neither early nor were they strong' (*The Bauer Thesis Examined*, p. 199). For further discussion of the reception of Bauer's thesis, see D. J. Harrison, 'The Reception of Walter Bauer's *Orthodoxy and Heresy in Earliest Christianity* During the Last Decade', *Harvard Theological Review* 73 (1980), 289–98.

tian origins is widely rejected, but his critique of the Eusebian story, which depicts the successful advancement of a united, apostolic church, has permanently changed the study of Christian origins. Williams gives a balanced assessment:

It is right to acknowledge, with Bauer, the insuperable problems in supposing there to have been a single, clearly identifiable 'mainstream', and the ease with which the inchoate structures we have observed can be conscripted into the service of authoritarian and centralizing impulses: the raw material for a good deal of the post-Nicene development of 'imperial' orthodoxy is already there before AD 300. But it is equally important to acknowledge . . . that there are features *within* the most basic activity of communicating about Jesus that make for the precarious evolution of a 'normative' Christianity which is still an interwoven plurality of perspectives on what was transacted in Jerusalem.[52]

The question that faces the scholar of the first and second centuries is now sharpened: in what precisely did this 'common sense' of which Turner speaks consist; what was Wilken's 'centre'; how was it that 'the communicating about Jesus' to which Williams refers made for unity amongst the dispersed and diverse communities that constituted the emergent Christian Church? Williams discusses Christian communication in these centuries both in terms of what he calls 'an almost obsessional mutual interest and interchange', pursued through exchange of letters and personal contact amongst significant figures, and in terms of the 'parabolic story' of Jesus whose presence was seen as 'questioning and converting' in ever more diverse cultures and periods.[53] The 'communicating about Jesus' was seen as a communicating *of* Jesus, which was possible because it was a communication in and by the Spirit. Such communication is another way of speaking about the *koinonia* which constitutes the Christian churches. Their 'common sense' is formed by a pattern of living and self-interpretation which focuses on participation in the living presence of Jesus

---

[52] See R. D. Williams, 'Does it make sense to speak of pre-Nicene Orthodoxy?' in R. D. Williams ed., *The Making of Orthodoxy* (Cambridge: Cambridge University Press, 1989), pp. 1–23. Williams' fine essay contains significant comment on the contributions of W. Bauer and H. Chadwick to this discussion.

[53] Williams, 'Does it make sense to speak of pre-Nicene Orthodoxy?', pp. 11, 17.

Christ. He is the 'centre'. What they have together, by the Spirit, is *koinonia* in Christ and with one another.

CONCLUSION

This chapter has been a study in Christian origins. The thread holding it together has been that of *koinonia*. I have tried to sketch the way in which 'little Christian communities' sprang up during the latter part of the first century in some of the great cities of Empire. It was necessary first to suggest something of the life that Jesus shared with his disciples – the community of Jesus. Then we moved to 'the Markan community', which to some extent modelled itself on, and certainly saw itself as in continuity with, that first community of Jesus. The story of the way in which the community of Jesus gave rise to other communities like the later community of Mark, is told in the Acts of the Apostles, which begins with a remarkable account of the Jerusalem community and their *koinonia*, showing how Spirit-inspired 'common life', symbolised in table-fellowship of Jewish and Gentile Christians, together with other forms of sharing, spread through Asia Minor, Greece, and even to Rome. The Corinthian correspondence is a rich source for consideration of the *koinonia* at Corinth, where the key question was that of continued unity within the church. The Johannine epistles raise the question of *koinonia* between Christian groups that are in dispute. It would have been possible to consider the concerns of other Christian communities in the light of other New Testament writing, drawing on material from Matthew, or Philippians, or Hebrews. The examples chosen were sufficient to depict the emergence of a varied but coherent 'common sense' or *koinonia* among the churches. The concern has been to emphasise not so much diversity nor unity, but rather *continuity*, the beginning of the emergence of the Church as a 'communion of communions'.

From the uses of the term *koinonia* within the New Testament, we have seen that it is a complex term that can refer to participation in received tradition, in the Gospel, in the life of a Christian community, in the eucharist, and in suffering. These are all dimensions of this loose-knit sense of unity in Christ within and between communities that Turner and Wilken speak about. What is also clear is that from the beginning there were tensions between those within the *koinonia* over many issues, some of them, like the keeping of the Jewish law, seen as definitive of adherence to or departure from faith. *Koinonia* came to be used as a term of definition. There were those who were to be recognised as within the *koinonia* and those who were not. The boundaries of the local church and the boundaries of the faith were at various times challenged, fought over, redefined, sometimes, as in Paul's rebuke to the Galatians, 'O foolish Galatians. Who has bewitched you?' (Gal. 3:1) in the most acrimonious terms. The opening up of the whole question of orthodoxy and heresy in the first-century Christian movement is part of the background to the debates over re-readings of the scriptural record, over the authority of tradition, and understandings of *koinonia* in the ecumenical movement today.

Radical openness did not last long. If we turn to the letters of Ignatius of Antioch, perhaps written only ten or twenty years after the Fourth Gospel and the Johannine epistles, we see a changing ecclesiastical world. Ignatius is a representative of an Antiochene Christianity[54] in which there are distinct echoes of Pauline tradition and also of the liturgical material in the Book of Revelation. It appears that he was condemned to death in Antioch and sent to Rome for execution. On the long journey from Syria to Rome he wrote to the churches at Tralles, Magnesia, and Ephesus, possibly from Smyrna, and to the church at Rome. From Troas he wrote to the churches of Philadelphia and Smyrna, and sent a personal letter to Polycarp. One major development that has taken place for Ignatius is that the bishop is now seen as the symbolic representative of the whole Christian community. He writes to the Ephesians, 'I have been able to play the host, in God's name, to your whole community in the person of your bishop Onesimus' (Ephes. 1). The authority of the bishop is thus doubly participatory – the bishop participates in the life of the community and in the life

---

[54] See R. E. Brown and J. P. Meier, *Antioch and Rome: New Testament Cradles of Christianity* (London: Geoffrey Chapman, 1983), pp. 73–81.

of Christ. Ignatius writes, 'Jesus Christ, our inseparable life, is the mind of the Father, even as the bishops that are settled in the farthest part of the earth are in the mind of Jesus Christ' (Ephes. 3). The bishop is to be obeyed as though he were Jesus Christ, because he participates with his church in Jesus Christ, who is the Lord of the Church.

Ignatius never uses the term *koinonia*. There is only one use of *koinos*, but it is a significant one. He concludes his letter to the Ephesian church, 'Fare ye well in God the Father and in Jesus Christ our common (*koinos*) hope.' The use is very similar to that at Titus 1:4, 'To Titus, my true child in a common faith' or at Jude 3, 'Beloved, being very eager to write to you of our common salvation . . .' The centre of the Christian faith is that which is shared between Christians (and between Christians and God). Ignatius has a strong sense of this sharing as a property of the local church, which is made evident wherever the church, with its bishop, is gathered.

Wherever the bishop shall appear, there let the people be, just as wherever Jesus may be, there is the catholic church.[55]

Ignatius' use of the word *catholic* here is striking. He probably uses it to mean the *whole* or the *universal* Church. Just as the bishop is at the centre of the local church, so Jesus Christ is the centre of the universal Church. Ignatius does seem to envisage a Church of churches, a communion of communities, held together as one Church in Christ by the Spirit, by participation in a range of common traditions, and by a common hope that the future is already under the lordship of Jesus Christ, who will gather his people from the ends of the earth, so that there will be one people and one Lord. Though he does not use these precise words, it is Ignatius who outlines the place of the one bishop in the local church as a minister of *koinonia* and who also suggests, by the letters he writes to the churches with which he is in touch, the role of the bishop amongst the churches as one which is vital to the structured *koinonia* of the catholic Church.

[55] *Smyrn.* 8.

CHAPTER 7

Cappadocian 'koinonia'

MYSTICAL PARTICIPATION

The *koinonia* of the Christian Church, and of the Christian believer with God through Christ, is described in the New Testament by means of complementary and overlapping metaphors. One approach, which has proved of enormous significance for Eastern Orthodoxy in particular, is that suggested by the single use of *koinonoi* in the Petrine literature, that at 2 Peter 1:3–4:

His divine power has granted to us all things that pertain to life and godliness, through the knowledge of him who called us to his own glory and excellence, by which he has granted to us his precious and very great promises, that through these you may escape from the corruption that is in the world because of passion, and become partakers of the divine nature (*theias koinonoi phuseos*).

There is no other place in the New Testament where the ground and goal of the spiritual life is put quite like this, but the Eastern Christian tradition in particular has made a great deal of 'participation in the divine nature'. A. M. Allchin, an Anglican writer much indebted to Eastern spirituality, sees the teaching of 2 Peter 1:4, though philosophical in expression, as very much in line with that elsewhere in the New Testament: 'Throughout the New Testament a co-inherence of human and divine is implied, a relationship of union and communion which overthrows our customary ways of thinking both of God and humankind, and opens the way towards the wonder of our adoption into the circulation of the divine life.'[1] Vladimir Lossky, discussing this text, stresses the paradoxical nature of this co-inherence. His presupposition is the absolute incommunicability of the divine being, yet the absolute reality of participation in the divine nature. To solve this antinomy, he follows Gregory Palamas in making a distinction between the essence of God, which is 'inaccessible, unknowable and incommunicable' and the energies, 'forces proper to and inseparable from God's essence, in which He goes forth from Himself, manifests, communicates, and gives Himself'. He quotes Gregory Palamas to the effect that, 'The divine and deifying illumination and grace is not the essence but the energy of God.'[2] It is important to take note of this line of thinking not only because it has been so influential in Eastern Christian mystical theology, but also because it is based upon a development by Gregory Palamas of the teaching of the Cappadocian Fathers with their absolute respect for the unknowability of God, and their similar conviction of the absolute reality of mystical knowledge of the Trinity.[3] Like Barth,[4] Rowan Williams criticises the Palamite tradition because it represents a misunderstanding of trinitarian theology. He argues that to make a separation between the *ousia* and the *energeiai* is to make a nonsense of the doctrine of the Trinity, for the point about the doctrine of the Trinity is that the being of God is identified with God's action. The danger to which Williams points is that, 'Once *ousia* has been "concretized" into a core of essential life, it will inevitably take on some associations of superiority or ontological priority.'[5] There is no such core:

---

[1] A. M. Allchin, *Participation in God* (London: Darton, Longman and Todd, 1988), p. 6.

[2] V. Lossky, *The Mystical Theology of the Eastern Church* (Cambridge: James Clarke, 1957), p. 70.

[3] See T. F. Torrance, *The Christian Doctrine of God, One Being, Three Persons* (Edinburgh: T. and T. Clark, 1996), p. 177.

[4] See the discussion in Karl Barth, *Church Dogmatics* II.1, 'The Doctrine of God' (Edinburgh: T. and T. Clark, 1957), pp. 331–2, where Barth writes, 'We not only have to challenge the separation of the attributes from the being of God, but also to note and emphasise . . . that the perfections of God in their multiplicity and variety do not arise simply from His relation to the world, but are those of His own being as He who loves in freedom.'

[5] C. M. LaCugna, *God For Us* (New York: HarperCollins, 1991), pp. 192–3; cf. R. D.

It is evident that knowledge of *any ousia* 'in itself' is quite unthinkable
. . . strictly *inconceivable*: there is nothing to know. What is known is
'substance-in-act', the properties of a thing as affecting the knowing
subject, the *esse*, the actual existent in relation. *Ousia*, to borrow
Heidegger's language, is always *parousia*.[6]

For the Cappadocians, it is not that Father, Son, and Holy
Spirit have a common *ousia* on which one can reflect in isolation
from their actuality in relation: as three hypostases, as Trinity,
they *are* the divine *ousia*. We are not to think of 'God' as in any
way distinct or distinguishable from Father, Son, and Holy
Spirit. To believe in God is to believe in the Trinity. Lossky puts
this sharply when he says, 'Between the Trinity and hell there
lies no other choice.'[7] What the Cappadocians teach about
mystical participation and about the life of the Trinity is
integrally linked. Commenting on 2 Peter 1:4, Lossky stresses
why these must be understood together: 'Trinitarian theology is
a theology of union, a mystical theology which appeals to
experience, and which presupposes a continuous and progressive series of changes in created nature, a more and more
intimate communion of the human person with the Holy
Trinity.'[8] Behind this notion of *progressive* communion lies the
Trinitarian theology of the Cappadocians, for which their
integrated theology of *koinonia* is absolutely central.

THE CAPPADOCIANS: BASIL OF CAESAREA

Cappadocia, like Pontus, is in central Asia Minor, one of those
areas mentioned at the beginning of the Book of Acts. It is likely
that the origins of Christianity in this barren and mountainous
area lay in the flourishing synagogue community.[9] The first
epistle of Peter is addressed 'to the exiles of the dispersion in
Pontus, Galatia, Cappadocia, Asia and Bithynia' (1 Peter 1:1).
Both Basil of Caesarea and Gregory of Nyssa who were

Williams, 'The Philosophical Structures of Palamism', *Eastern Churches Review* 9 (1977),
  27–44.
[6] Williams, 'The Philosophical Structures of Palamism', quoted in C. M. LaCugna, *God
  For Us*, p. 193.
[7] Lossky, *The Mystical Theology of the Eastern Church*, p. 66.   [8] *Ibid.*, p. 67.
[9] A. Meredith, *The Cappadocians* (London: Geoffrey Chapman, 1995), p. 2 (see note).

brothers) write about the third-century missionary work of Gregory Thaumaturgos, to which their grandmother Macrina owed her conversion. Gregory Thaumaturgos was himself deeply influenced by Origen, the greatest product of the great Alexandrian school of philosophy and the finest biblical scholar before Jerome. Alexandria, which was the place where great scholars such as Philo and Clement taught, was noted for a long tradition of platonism. Origen studied and taught there and also at Palestinian Caesarea, where Gregory Thaumaturgos and his brother Athenodore were among his students. In his *Ecclesiastical History*, Eusebius records of the brothers that Origen 'implanted in them a love of true philosophy and induced them to exchange their old enthusiasm for a theological training. Five whole years they spent with him, making such remarkable progress in theology that while still young both were chosen to be bishops of the churches in Pontus.'[10]

Basil and his younger brother Gregory were born some ninety years later, Basil being born about 330. Theirs was a well-established Christian family, of some wealth.[11] Their friend, Gregory of Nazianzen, was also born about 330, the son of the Bishop of Nazianzen. Basil studied in Caesarea, the capital of Cappadocia, in Constantinople, and in Athens, the leading university of the world, where his acquaintance with Gregory from Nazianzen became a deep friendship. Gregory had by then studied in Palestinian Caesarea and Alexandria, both famed for their connection with Origen. Basil returned to Caesarea in Cappadocia, abandoning a career in rhetoric when he was baptised, and set out on a long journey through Egypt, Palestine, Syria, and Mesopotamia, visiting monks and desert hermits. When he returned he founded a coenobitic monastery,[12] where the monks lived in community, calling on his

---

10 Eusebius, *The History of the Church*, translated by G. A. Williamson (Harmondsworth: Penguin, 1965), 6.30.
11 For the life of Basil, see P. Rousseau, *Basil of Caesarea* (Berkeley: University of California Press, 1994); for general introduction to the works of the Cappadocians, F. Young, *From Nicaea to Chalcedon* (London: SCM, 1983) is invaluable.
12 The word *coenobitic* is derived from the Greek *koinos* (common) and *bios* (life, or, way of life).

friend Gregory to join him, something Gregory did with only moderate enthusiasm. Rather than settling into monastic life, Gregory was persuaded to accept ordination and help his father in the running of the diocese of Nazianzen, just as Basil was drawn into helping with the diocese of Caesarea. Basil's younger brother, Gregory, never travelled to the great educational centres of his time and recorded his debt to his elder brother for his education. He too in time was ordained, and became Bishop of Nyssa, as Basil became metropolitan of Cappadocia, and his friend Gregory bishop first of the tiny community at Sasima, before being shot to prominence at Constantinople, but subsequently deposed, returning to Nazianzen. Basil, who was the most forceful of the three, died in 379; Gregory of Nazianzen was prominent at the Council of Constantinople and then, after his deposition, faded into obscurity, dying about 391; Gregory of Nyssa died about 395. All three were fully involved in the acrimonious post-Nicene conflicts and debates over Catholic orthodoxy. Their struggle was both practical and doctrinal: practically to defend and to maintain the *koinonia* amongst those who held to Nicene orthodoxy; doctrinally to defend and to develop that orthodoxy with respect not only to the co-equal Son, but also the co-equal Spirit, in the *koinonia* of the Holy Trinity. In their mystical theology, their understanding of the unity of the Church, of the participation of Christians in the life of the Church and the life of the Trinity, and their understanding of God as Trinity, are all interwoven. It is they who established the fully Trinitarian pattern of later orthodoxy.

For Basil, the members of the monastic community which he established were *koinonikoi* in the tradition of Pachomian monasticism, which was enjoying an explosive growth in Egypt. The origins of Christian monasticism are usually thought to lie in the withdrawal of Antony, sometime about 269, having given away all his possessions, to the desert outside Alexandria. In the life of Antony written by Athanasius, Athanasius described how 'there were monasteries in the mountains and the desert was made a city by monks, who left their own people and registered themselves for citizenship in the heavens'.[13] The emigration of Christians from the city to become monks, described by Athanasius in terms that echo Plato's description of his vision of the perfect Republic, was an idealistic attempt to realise the perfection of Christian life over against the compromise and corruption of the city. Athanasius uses his account of Antony's attempt to take the Gospel with absolute seriousness to illuminate and reinforce his vision of Nicene orthodoxy, stressing Antony's refusal to associate with heretical groups like the Meletians, Manicheans, and Arians.[14] Though Antony gathered about him other hermits like himself, they never lived a common life, as did Pachomius and his disciples, who became the model for the coenobitic life that Basil later shared shared in Cappadocia.

In what is now widely thought to be the earliest life of Pachomius, explicit mention is made of the ideal of Acts 2:42: at an early stage, though the brothers were expected to contribute to the expenses of the common table and of hospitality, Pachomius allowed them to remain self-supporting, 'because he could see that they were not yet ready to bind themselves together in a perfect *koinonia* like that of the believers which Acts describes'.[15] The *Koinonia* is the technical term used in both Coptic and Greek lives of Pachomius to describe not just individual monasteries, of which at the time of his death in about 346 there were ten, nine for men and one for women, with some 3,000 coenobites,[16] but also the way of life in those monasteries. Most commonly, the *Koinonia* is used to describe the whole monastic body, under its Apa Pachomius. Rousseau captures these resonances when he writes, 'The *Koinonia* itself . . . is interpreted as an instrument of salvation in the fullest sense, an image of the saving community God intended his church to be.'[17] He stresses

---

13 R. C. Gregg ed., Athanasius, *The Life of Antony*, CWS (London: SPCK, 1980), pp. 42–3.
14 *The Life of Antony* 68, p. 82; 89, p. 95; 91, p. 97.
15 A. Veilleux ed. and transl., *Pachomian Koinonia*, vol. I, 'The Life of St Pachomius and his Disciples', Cistertian Studies Series 45 (Kalamazoo: Cistertian Publications Inc., 1980), 'The First Sahidic Life of Pachomius', 11, p. 431.
16 W. K. Lowther Clarke, *St Basil the Great, A Study in Monasticism* (Cambridge: Cambridge University Press, 1913), p. 35.
17 P. Rousseau, *Pachomius* (Berkeley: University of California Press, 1985), p. 58.

Pachomius' desire to foster in the monks a readiness to work together and to encourage one another in the spiritual life.[18] This is evident in 'The Instructions of Theodore', the favoured disciple of Pachomius, who emphasises what he calls 'the holy vocation of the *Koinonia*' and the suffering that goes with it: 'Not only we,' he writes, 'but whoever has loved the holy life of the *Koinonia*, has endured the disgrace that was Christ's and put up with sufferings without wavering.'[19] According to the rules of Pachomius, the community of monks is the 'assembly of the saints' who meet under an '*oikiakos*' or housemaster. A passage from the Testament of Horsiesios, another of Pachomius' disciples, sums up the Pachomian ideal of *koinonia*:

The Apostle taught us that our community, the communion by which we are joined to one another, springs from God, when he said, *Do not forget good works and communion, for God takes pleasure in such sacrifices.* We read the same thing in the Acts of the Apostles: *For the multitude of believers had one heart and soul, and no one called anything his own. They held everything in common. And the apostles gave witness to the resurrection of the Lord Jesus with great power.* The psalmist is in agreement with these words when he says, *Behold, how good and how delightful it is for brothers to live together.* And let us who live together in the *Koinonia*, and who are united to one another in mutual charity, so apply ourselves that, just as we deserved fellowship with the holy fathers in this life, we may also be their companions in the life to come.[20]

This was the ideal, practised in a number of houses united in the one *koinonia*, that Basil encountered when he visited the flourishing monasteries of Egypt in 357 and that he sought to transplant to Cappadocia. On his return, he wrote,

I admired their continence in living, and their endurance in toil; I was amazed at their persistence in prayer and at their triumphing over sleep; subdued by no natural necessity, ever keeping their soul's purpose high and free, in hunger, in thirst, in cold, in nakedness, they

---

[18] Rousseau, *Pachomius*, p. 66. In a note on this page Rousseau draws attention to the importance of the notion of 'covenant' (*diatheke*) for the understanding of *koinonia* by Theodore (who was the outstanding disciple of Pachomius). See also 'The First Sahidic Life of Pachomius', 6, 12.

[19] A. Veilleux transl. and ed., *Pachomian Koinonia*, vol. 3, 'Instructions, Letters and other writings of Saint Pachomius and his Disciples' (Kalamazoo: Cistertian Publications, 1982), 'The Instructions of Theodore', 7, p. 97.

[20] *Pachomian Koinonia*, vol. 3, 'The Testament of Horsiesios', 50, pp. 208–9.

never yielded to the body; . . . always, as though living in a flesh that was not theirs, they showed in very deed what it is to sojourn for a while in this life, and what it is to have one's citizenship and home in heaven. And I prayed that I, too, as far as in me lay, might imitate them.[21]

This was Basil's reaction to the monks of the East when he was not yet thirty. On his return from Egypt to Cappadocia, he sought, with Gregory of Nazianzen, to imitate what he had seen, and then to organise the monks of Cappadocia according to this ideal of the common life.[22]

Basil's starting point for life in community is the dual commandment to love God and to love your neighbour. Working out how to do this in community should come naturally to humans who are by nature social animals. 'Who', asks Basil, in a deliberate allusion to Aristotle, 'does not know that man is . . . a living being made for *koinonia* (*koinonikon zoon ho anthropos*)?'[23] This fundamental human need for community was fulfilled prototypically under the impulse of the Spirit in the *koinonia* of the Jerusalem community where all things were held in common and the Christians distributed to each member according to their need, a paradigm to which Basil returns again and again. So, in his Shorter Rules, in answer to the question, 'Is it lawful to have private property in the brotherhood?', he answers:

This is contrary to the testimony in Acts concerning them that believed, where it is written: 'And not one of them said that aught of the things which he possessed was his own.' So that he that says anything is his private property has made himself an alien to the Church of God and to the love of the Lord Who taught us by both word and deed to lay down our life for our friends, to say nothing of external possessions.[24]

21 Letter 223, quoted Lowther Clarke, *St Basil the Great*, p. 25.
22 Rousseau, *Basil of Caesarea* (Berkeley: University of California Press, 1994), pp. 192, 232 argues that Basil's ideals of community life apply not just to monks but to all Christians and that the Long and Short Rules, which are the main texts giving insight into Basil's prescription for community life, are the results of a long process, reaching well beyond Basil's lifetime.
23 Shorter Rules III, from W. K. L. Clarke, *The Ascetic Works of Saint Basil* (London: SPCK, 1925), p. 157; Migne *PG* 31, 917 cf. Aristotle, *Eud. Eth.* VII.10; 1242a 25.
24 Shorter Rules LXXXV, *Ascetic Works*, p. 262; cf. Longer Rules VII, *Ascetic Works*, p. 166.

With this goes the need for superiors who will care for the needs of each monk: 'Among those who distribute the necessities of life within the monastery there should by all means be some in each rank who can imitate those men in the Acts who did what is there said, namely: "Distribution was made to each, according as any one had need." '[25] For Basil, the members of the community belong together as members of one body: 'In the common life, the private gift of each man becomes the common property of his fellows . . . So that of necessity in the common life the working of the Holy Spirit passes over to all the rest at once.'[26] This sharing in the gifts of the Holy Spirit is for Basil characteristic of life lived in Christian community. It is in the Christian community that we learn the way of love. We learn how to wash one another's feet, and we also learn the practice of confession, in a way that is impossible for the solitary eremite. Basil sees the monastic community as a microcosm of the church. Like the Egyptian Pachomian writers, he applies to the monastic community language that is proper to the whole body of the local church, because he sees a sharp-etched realisation of the *koinonia* in the monastic community which exists for the benefit of the wider body which is the church. More than this, the monastery was to be within reach of those who suffered, providing a hospital and schools. Monks were to engage in manual work to support these charitable enterprises and the community itself. The interface between the monastic community and the rest of the church was particularly important: Basil himself was in the end not content with monastic withdrawal. After two such periods, in 370 he re-entered the mainstream of church life, with all its political conflicts, as a powerful and effective Bishop of Caesarea.

In his work as a bishop Basil carried the ideal of the Christian *koinonia* into the mainstream of church life. His letters show his constant struggle to maintain the *koinonia* of which the eucharist is the central sacrament, and to which baptism is the gateway. This *koinonia* is open to all who will receive the teaching of the

---

[25] Longer Rules xxxiv, *Ascetic Works*, p. 200.
[26] Longer Rules vii, *Ascetic Works*, pp. 164–5; Migne *PG* 31, 932; cf. xxix, *Ascetic Works*, p. 191.

Catholic Church, but a clear line is drawn between the *koinonia* of the Catholics, and the *koinonia* in other, non-Catholic groups. Writing to the monk Urbicus, he asks whether 'the brother-hood' are rejecting the teaching of those who have 'perverse opinions' about the incarnation: 'I therefore urge that these errors receive ecclesiastical correction, and that you abstain from communion (*koinonia*) with the heretics.'[27] Writing to Athanasius, he complains that, despite the known heterodox views of Marcellus of Ancyra, the Roman authorities had 'received him into the communion (*koinonia*) of the Church'.[28] Basil denounces this compromising behaviour: Marcellus de-monstrably did not teach the Nicene doctrine professed by 'the whole body', and so he and his disciples should not be received in communion. Time and again, through the corpus of his letters, we find Basil writing in similar vein to strengthen, or to draw limits to, the *koinonia* of the Catholic Church.[29] Thus, his three 'canonical letters' deal with a whole list of disciplinary points and points of teaching, returning repeatedly to the issue as to whether an offender can be received within the *koinonia* of the local church, and specifically received at the eucharist (the '*koinonia tou agathou*', 'communion of the good [gift]').[30]

A letter written to the church at Ancyra, probably after the death of its bishop Athanasius, exemplifies this. Basil laments his loss, and the loss to the church, but then goes on to say:

Yet of a truth the members of the church, united by his leadership as by one soul, and fitted together into close union of feeling and fellowship (*koinonia*), are both preserved and shall ever be preserved by the bond of peace for spiritual communion.[31]

Basil's concern is to see one *koinonia* of such churches, united in the orthodox faith, and in eucharistic worship throughout

---

27 *Letter* 262 (PNCF VIII, p. 301).   28 *Letter* 69 (PNCF VIII, p. 166).

29 See especially the detailed study by R. Pouchet, *Basile le Grand et son Univers d'Amis d'après sa Correspondance, une Stratégie de Communion* (*Studia Ephemeridis 'Augustinianum'* 36, Rome: Institutum Patristicum 'Augustinianum', 1992); also W. Elert, *Eucharist and Church Fellowship in the First Four Centuries* (Saint Louis: Concordia, 1966), especially pp. 149–84.

30 *Letters* 188, 199, 217 (PNCF VIII, pp. 223–8, 236–40, 255–9); see Pouchet, *Basil le Grand*, p. 438, Elert, *Eucharist and Church Fellowship*, pp. 95–6.

31 *Letter* 29 (PNCF VIII, p. 134).

the world. In support of this, the bishops have to work to stay in *koinonia* with one another, and to warn one another against those who do not keep the orthodox faith. In his letters, Basil shows his concern to follow Paul in his care for 'all the churches'. Thus he writes to the bishops of Italy and Gaul:

Our Lord Jesus Christ, Who has deigned to style the universal Church of God His Body, and has made us individually members one of another, has moreover granted to all of us to live in intimate association with one another, as befits the agreement of the members. Wherefore, although we dwell far away from one another, yet, as regards our close conjunction, we are very near.

Having described the extreme difficulties he is experiencing in the Cappadocian churches, he continues:

We stand in the arena to fight for our common heritage, for the treasure of the sound faith, derived from our Fathers . . . The Holy Ghost is regarded not as [complementary to] the Holy Trinity, nor as participating in the divine and blessed Nature, but as in some sort one of the number of created beings, and attached to Father and Son, at mere haphazard and as occasion may require.[32]

Such teaching is to be strenuously resisted. Correct teaching on the divinity of the Holy Spirit, against the *Pneumatomachoi* and others who would not acknowledge the Spirit's full divinity, was for Basil a test of fidelity to the whole teaching of the Catholic Church, and therefore of fitness for sharing in the *koinonia* of the churches.

Thus it was that in 375 Basil wrote his classic treatise *On the Holy Spirit*. He set out to correct the views of his former friend, Eustathius of Sebaste, who was arguing that the Spirit was neither creature not creator, but somewhere in between. Basil's aim was to defend the full deity of the Spirit, and so to defend the trinitarian understanding of God that was to be held throughout the Catholic Church. He argued indirectly, repeating insistently that the Holy Spirit has *koinonia* with the Father and the Son, making it abundantly clear, without once using the controversial Nicene term 'of one substance', that the Holy Spirit is not in any way to be seen as less than either

[32] *Letter* 243 (PNCF VIII, pp. 283–5), translation amended.

Father or Son. Rather, they are bound in co-equal unity, or *koinonia*.

Basil introduces his study of the Spirit by saying he will examine 'what kind of ideas about the Spirit we hold in common, as well as those which we have gathered from the Scriptures, or received from the unwritten tradition (*paradosis*) from the Fathers'.[33] His mode of arguing is itself participatory:[34] he is expounding an understanding in which he participates because it is the common understanding of the Catholic Church. He begins by asking the Holy Spirit to enlighten him in his exposition, and ends by asking the Spirit to enlighten his readers about any points that need further clarification. Throughout, he presupposes that the Spirit 'shines upon those who are cleansed from every spot, and makes them spiritual through fellowship (*koinonia*) with himself'.[35] The main thrust of his argument is in terms of the activity rather than the being of the Spirit:

Through the Holy Spirit comes our restoration to Paradise, our ascension to the Kingdom of Heaven, our adoption as God's sons, our freedom to call God our Father, our becoming partakers (*koinonoi*) of the grace of Christ, being called children of light, sharing in eternal glory, and, in a word, our inheritance of the fullness of blessing, both in this world and the world to come.[36]

However, through the *koinonia* of the Spirit the very being of humans and of angels is transformed. Of the angels he says, 'Holiness is not part of their essence (*ousia*); it is accomplished in them through communion (*koinonia*) with the Spirit.'[37] Communion with the Spirit is communion with the Father and the Son because the Spirit is linked with the Father and the Son by 'communion of nature' (*ek phuseos koinonian*).[38] This 'communion of nature' is common to the three divine persons (*hypostaseis*); 'It is in the communion (*koinonia*) of the deity that the principle of unity resides.' Benoit Pruche comments that *koinonia* here has almost the sense of 'communication'.[39]

---

[33] *On the Holy Spirit*, 22 (*SC*, pp. 322–3).
[34] Compare Augustine's method in the *Confessions*, as discussed in chapter 8.
[35] *On the Holy Spirit*, 23 (*SC*, pp. 328–9).   [36] *On the Holy Spirit*, 36 (*SC*, pp. 370–1).
[37] *On the Holy Spirit*, 38 (*SC*, pp. 382–3).   [38] *On the Holy Spirit*, 30 (*SC*, pp. 352–3).
[39] *Sur le Saint-Esprit, SC*, p. 407n. *Koinonia* here comes close to the notion of *perichoresis*,

Repeatedly, Basil uses *koinonia* when he wants to speak about shared divinity: 'If we say that the Son is with the Father, we mean two things: first, that their persons (*hypostaseis*) are distinct, and second, that they are inseparably (*achoriston*) united in fellowship (*koinonia*)';[40] 'The Spirit is glorified through his *koinonia* with the Father and the Son.'[41] There is, however, a kind of reticence about his Trinitarian language because he retains a concern to protect the monarchy of the Father, but again and again, when speaking of the Spirit, he speaks of *koinonia* of or in the divine nature (*phusis*), which is his way of resisting all subordination. Already, the Council of Alexandria, presided over by the elderly Athanasius in 362, had spoken of the nature of God as 'one substance, three hypostases' (*mia ousia, treis hypostaseis*) so Basil was not innovating when he used *ousia* and *hypostasis* in this way. It is tempting to argue that he makes a distinction between *ousia* (substance) and *phusis* (nature), but very doubtful that this can be sustained.[42] What is new in *On the Holy Spirit* is the use of *koinonia* for the bond that unites the three hypostases of the triune God as one *ousia*. *Koinonia* is not something added to God. *Koinonia* is essential to God. The very being of God may be expressed as *koinonia*: the three hypostases, which are God, are united in one *koinonia*, Father, Son, and Holy Spirit.

As a footnote to this, we should note Basil's use of another term, taken from Stoicism, which has a range of meaning derived from what it means to belong to a house, to belong to a family, and so to be familiar, to make one's own, even to be suitable or be fitting. The word is *oikeiosis*, used with its immediate cognates a dozen times in *On the Holy Spirit*. S.G. Pembroke has discussed this as 'a philosophical term with a persistent reputation for being impossible to translate'.[43] Pem-

often translated co-inherence, which appears briefly in Gregory of Nazianzen, but becomes much more significant when used later by John of Damascus. On *perichoresis*, see Torrance, *The Christian Doctrine of God, One Being Three Persons*, pp. 168–202.

40 *On the Holy Spirit*, 59 (*SC*, pp. 460–1).
41 *On the Holy Spirit*, 46 (*SC*, pp. 410–11); cf. *On the Holy Spirit*, 70 (*SC*, pp. 496–7).
42 *Sur le Saint-Esprit, SC*, p. 182.
43 S. G. Pembroke, '*Oikeiosis*' in A. A. Long ed., *Problems in Stoicism* (London: Athlone Press, 1971), pp. 114–49, here p. 114; see also T. Engberg-Pedersen, *The Stoic Notion of Oikeiosis* (Aarhus: Aarhus University Press, 1990), and *Sur le Saint-Esprit, SC*, p. 327n.

broke finds the word to be applied in classical writing both to persons who were members of the household or had a blood-relationship with its members, and to those connected with it either by ties of marriage or by virtually any kind of favourable association. So it came to denote a variety of relationships which (supposedly) did not involve conflict: 'appropriateness' would be one translation. Its opposite is 'that which is alien'. Basil explains that 'the economy (*oikonomia*) of God, our Saviour, towards man, consists in drawing him back from his exile, to make him return into the *oikeiosis* of God, drawing him away from the alienation created by his disobedience'.[44] 'Entry into *oikeiosis* towards God is through the Spirit because, "God has sent into our hearts the Spirit of his Son, who cries: Abba, Father."'[45] He also talks about the *oikeiosis* of the Spirit with respect to the Father and the Son.[46] The term is vague, but it is clearly one of affinity based on the metaphor of belonging to the one household or family. In this sense, it is closely akin to Basil's notion of *koinonia*, and it makes the link with the letters in the New Testament (Galatians 6:10, Ephesians 2:19, the Pastoral Letters e.g. 1 Tim. 3:15) where the church is seen as 'the house-hold of faith' or 'the household of God'. The passage in Ephesians may be quoted in full as it brings together the metaphor of the house, and the household; the 'house of God', the Temple; Jesus Christ as the 'cornerstone' of the Christian faith; the tradition of the apostles and prophets; and the place of the Spirit. The whole sentence runs:

So then you are no longer strangers and sojourners, but you are fellow citizens with the saints and members (*oikeioi*) of the household of God, built upon the foundation of the apostles and prophets, Christ Jesus himself being the cornerstone, in whom the whole structure is joined

---

In Greek-speaking society, as far back as the world of Homer, the *oikos* was seen as a primary means of sociality. (See M. I. Finley, *The World of Odysseus*, second edition (London: Chatto and Windus, 1977), pp. 57–9.) This metaphor is extremely impor-tant for the way the 'little communities' of the early Christian church, many of which began in households and worshipped as house churches, saw themselves. It is important both for their understanding of boundaries, and of internal structure, especially leadership.

[44] *On the Holy Spirit*, 35 (my translation, based on *SC*, p. 365).
[45] *On the Holy Spirit*, 49 (*SC*, p. 421).   [46] *On the Holy Spirit*, 45 (*SC*, p. 409).

together and grows into a holy temple in the Lord; in whom you also are built into it for a dwelling place of God in the Spirit.

Basil's own experience of 'the household of faith' was four-fold: that of his own upbringing in a wealthy Christian house-hold of at least three generations; that of the monastic households he promoted and founded; that of the local church of which he eventually became bishop; that of the communion of all the churches. *Oikeiosis* for him was in each context the practical realisation of *koinonia*.

GREGORY OF NAZIANZEN

Gregory of Nazianzen is known in the East simply as Gregory the Theologian. His five *Theological Orations*, preached in Constantinople, probably in 380, provide a brilliant summary of what has subsequently been recognised as Trinitarian ortho-doxy. Before we come to those, however, we should note the explicit concern for *koinonia* expressed in some of Gregory's other writings.

When he meditates on salvation, which is for him the action of God's grace in extending the divine communion to all humanity, Gregory frequently uses the language of *koinonia*:

He that is full empties Himself, for he empties Himself of His glory for a short while, that I may have a share in his Fulness . . . I had a share in the image [of God]; I did not keep it. He partakes of my flesh that he may both save the image and make the flesh immortal. He communicates a second Communion (*deuteran koinonei koinonian*) far more marvellous than the first.[47]

In the fourth-century situation of doctrinal and political strife among the churches, Gregory saw himself as working for the concord that comes from God:

This originates in the Trinity, which has no more distinctive attribute than unity of nature and internal concord. The angelic and the divine powers, which are at peace with God and amongst themselves, participated in it; it spread to all creation, in which the cosmos is at peace; it has dwelt amongst us spiritually by pursuit of and *koinonia* in

---

[47] *Oration* xxxviii, 'On the Theophany, or Birthday of Christ', 13 (PNCF vii, p. 349); cf. *Oration* xlv, 'The Second Oration on Easter', 9 (p. 426).

the virtues, and physically by the harmonious fashion in which the members and the parties are reconciled and agree among themselves. With respect to those parties, it is indeed and is said to be both their beauty and their health.[48]

Gregory's favoured way of speaking about God is as light: salvation is enlightenment. The mission of the apostles was so that 'the Gospel might have free course everywhere, that nothing might miss the illumination of the Threefold Light, or be unenlightened by the Truth; but that the night of ignorance might be dissolved for those who sat in darkness and the shadow of death'.[49] Writing about baptism, Gregory says it is:

The aid to our weakness, the renunciation of the flesh, the following of the Spirit, the fellowship (*koinonia*) of the Word, the improvement of the creature, the overwhelming of sin, the participation of light, the dissolution of darkness.[50]

'Enlightenment' for Gregory is nothing less than human participation in the life of the Trinity, of which he writes:

No sooner do I conceive of the One than I am illumined by the splendour of the Three; no sooner do I distinguish them than I am carried back to the One. When I think of any One of the Three I think of Him as the Whole, and my eyes are filled, and the greater part of what I am thinking of escapes me. I cannot grasp the greatness of That One so as to attribute a greater greatness to the Rest. When I contemplate the Three together, I see but one torch, and cannot divide or measure out the Undivided Light.[51]

These are the words of a man who inhabits the mystery of the Trinity – which is perhaps why his theology has been found so attractive by later generations.

Though his thought is so close to that of Basil, Gregory does not habitually use the same vocabulary as Basil to speak of the Christian's participation in the life of the Trinity. In his *Theological Orations*, he makes use of neither *koinonia* nor *oikeiosis*. The link for him is light, and a favourite text for him Psalm 36:9:

48 *Oration* XXII, 'Third Eirenic Discourse' (J. Mossay ed., Grégoire de Nazianze, *Discours 20–23*, SC 270 (Paris: Cerf, pp. 252–3), 14 (my translation).
49 *Oration* XXXIII, 'Against the Arians', 11 (PNCF VII, p. 332).
50 *Oration* XL, 'The Oration on Holy Baptism', 3 (PNCF VII, p. 360).
51 *Oration* XL, 'The Oration on Holy Baptism', 41 (PNCF VII, p. 375).

The Father was the True Light which lighteneth every man coming into the world. The Son was the True Light which lighteneth every man coming into the world. The Other Comforter was the True Light, which lighteneth every man coming into the world. Was and Was and Was, but Was One Thing. Light thrice repeated; but One Light and One God. This is what David represented to himself long before when he said, In Thy Light shall we see Light. And now we have both seen and proclaim concisely and simply the doctrine of God the Trinity, comprehending out of Light (the Father), Light (the Son), in Light (the Holy Ghost).[52]

In his second theological oration, Gregory begins with a classic description of mystical experience in the tradition of Plato, Plotinus, and, later, Augustine:

I was running to lay hold on God, and thus I went up into the Mount, and drew aside the curtain of the Cloud, and entered away from matter and material things, and as far as I could I withdrew within myself. And then when I looked up, I scarce saw the back parts of God; although I was sheltered by the Rock, the Word that was made flesh for us. And when I looked a little closer, I saw, not the First and unmingled Nature (*phusis*) known to Itself – to the Trinity, I mean; not That which abideth within the first veil, and is hidden by the Cherubim; but only that Nature which at last even reaches to us.[53]

Gregory goes on to discuss the deity of the Son and the Spirit, but only in the fifth oration does he bring his understanding together in a series of classic Trinitarian statements. It is here that he goes beyond Basil in calling the Spirit *consubstantial* with the Father and the Son: 'Is the Spirit God? Most certainly. Well then, is He consubstantial (*homoousion*)? Yes, if he is God.'[54] Though Gregory here uses technical language, boldly extending its range from Christology to the realm of the Spirit, he is more at home in the powerful use of non-technical imagery:

To us there is One God, for the Godhead is One, and all that proceedeth from Him is referred to One, though we believe in Three [Persons]. For one is not more and another less God; nor is one before and another after; nor are they divided in will or parted in power; nor can you find here any of the qualities of divisible things; but the

---

[52] *Oration* xxxi, 'Fifth Theological Oration', 3 (PNCF vii, p. 318).
[53] *Oration* xxviii, 'Second Theological Oration', 3 (PNCF vii, p. 289). The roots of Palamas' theology (cf. p. 147) are plain here.
[54] *Oration* xxxi, 'Fifth Theological Oration', 10 (PNCF vii, p. 321).

Godhead is, to speak concisely, undivided in separate Persons ['those who are distinct']; and there is one mingling of Light, as it were of three suns joined to each other.[55]

The teaching of Gregory of Nazianzen on the Trinity includes a strong undertone of mystical invitation, an invitation to share in the *koinonia* that is the life of the Holy Trinity. It is this invitation which is made yet more explicit in the teaching of Gregory of Nyssa.

The distinctive contribution of Gregory of Nyssa includes a dynamic understanding of perfection in the spiritual life, whereby this could never be seen as a static 'resting', but should be seen as a continuing progress in God from glory to glory. It is to Gregory's mystical theology that we now turn.

GREGORY OF NYSSA

The starting point for Gregory's mystical and ascetic teaching is the existence of two contrasted *koinoniai*: that of light and that of darkness; that of incorruption and that of corruption; that of good and that of evil. Gregory follows Paul in stressing that between these spiritually opposed realms there can be no *koinonia*:

No way has been discovered of harmonizing things whose nature (*phusis*) is antagonistic and which have nothing in common. The Apostle tells us there is 'no communion of light with darkness', or of righteousness with iniquity, or, in a word, of all the qualities which we perceive and name as the essence of God's nature, with all the opposite which are perceived in evil.[56]

Gregory extols virginity not just because it keeps one pure like God, but as the very means by which the Christian believer may be brought into *koinonia* with God:

Now if the achievement of this saintly virtue consists in making one 'without blemish and holy', and these epithets are adopted in their first and fullest force to glorify the incorruptible Deity, what greater

---

55 *Oration* xxxi, 'Fifth Theological Oration', 14 (PNCF vii, p. 322, adapted).
56 *On Virginity* xvi (M. Aubineau ed., *Traité de la Virginité, SC* 119, Paris: Cerf, 1966, pp. 452–5), here quoted from *On Virginity* xv (PNCF v, p. 361).

praise of virginity can there be than thus to be shown in a manner *deifying* those who share in her pure mysteries, so that they become partakers of His glory Who is in actual truth the only Holy and Blameless One; their purity and their incorruptibility being the means of bringing them into relationship (*koinonia*) with Him?[57]

In his treatise *On Virginity*, Gregory repeatedly returns to the choice that has to be made by the soul between 'some adulterous participation (*koinonia*) in something evil'[58] and taking 'true wisdom as the companion (*sunoikos*) and sharer (*koinonos*) of his life'.[59]

When he concludes his memoir of his sister, *The Life of Saint Macrina*, Gregory speaks in a compressed and vivid way of the *koinonia* in his own family, in all humanity, and in the Church of God. At the moment when he comes to lay his sister in the tomb beside her parents, for a moment he fears that he will be punished should he, like Ham, the son of Noah, look on the naked body of his parents:

Before the bodies came into view when the cover of the tomb was lifted they were covered from one end to the other by a pure linen cloth. When they were covered thus with the linen, . . . I lifted that holy body from the bier and placed it beside our mother, fulfilling the common (*koinos*) prayer of both of them. For this they had asked of God all through their life, that after death their bodies should be together and that in death they should not be deprived of the [*koinonia*] they had had in their lifetime.[60]

Here is a remarkably vivid illustration of the *koinonia* that binds together the members of Gregory's family, even in death; of the *koinonia* by which all human beings share in death and in corruption; of the *koinonia* in prayer amongst Christians; and of the *koinonia* amongst all Christians who sleep in the tomb in hope of the resurrection. Most of all, the pure linen cloth, which carries the suggestion of the grave-clothes within which Christ was wrapped as he lay in the tomb, and of the pure white robes worn in the liturgy by those who were baptised into his death

---

[57] *On Virginity* I (*SC*, pp. 256–9; PNCF v, p. 344).
[58] *On Viginity* xv (*SC*, pp. 444–7; here translated by V. W. Callahan, *St Gregory of Nyssa, Ascetical Works*, FC, Washington: Catholic University of America Press, 1967).
[59] *On Virginity* xx (*SC*, pp. 500–1; FC, p. 64).
[60] *The Life of Saint Macrina* (*St Gregory of Nyssa, Ascetical Works*, FC, p. 188).

and then for the first time admitted to communion with the full congregation, all the members of his body, suggests the continuing *koinonia* in Christ which cannot be broken by death and is shared by all who participate in him.

In his *Life of Moses*, subtitled 'Concerning Perfection in Virtue', Gregory uses the biblical account of Moses typologically, so that Moses becomes a figure in whom the Christian can see exemplified Gregory's theology of dynamic participation. Early in his prologue, he alludes to Philippians 3:13 and then goes on:

We hold the divine nature to be unlimited and infinite. Certainly, whoever pursues true virtue participates in nothing other than God, because he is himself absolute virtue. Since, then, those who know what is good by nature desire participation in it, and since this good has no limit, the participant's desire itself necessarily has no stopping place but stretches out with the limitless.[61]

Participation in virtue is participation in God, and since God is infinite, participation in virtue is infinite. Taking the life of Moses to illustrate this, Gregory builds on the work of Philo, who had written two treatises on Moses, and of Origen, who had discussed Moses extensively in his *Homilies on Exodus*. Gregory has a great deal to say about participation in virtue and in God, usually using *metousia* and *metechein* with their cognates. Only twice does he use *koinonia*, but these instances are significant. He first sets out the 'history' according to the scriptural record of Moses' life; then he turns to *theoria*, contemplation. In the birth of Moses, he sees the birth of virtue. In the story of Moses putting his hand into his bosom and taking it out leprous, only to put it in again to have it healed, Gregory sees a type of the incarnation of the Son:

When he was manifested to us from the bosom of the Father, he was changed to be like us. After [the Father] wiped away our infirmities, he again returned to his own bosom the hand which had been among us and had received our complexion . . . What is impassible by nature did not change into what is passible, but what is mutable and subject

---

61 Gregory of Nyssa, *The Life of Moses*, translated by A. J. Malherbe and E. Ferguson, CWS (New York: Paulist, 1978), 1.7, p. 31.

to passions was transformed into impassibility through its participation (*koinonia*) in the immutable.[62]

By contrast, Gregory later discusses the envy that infects even
Aaron and Miriam as they look upon Moses, and Moses'
apatheia in being untouched by it:

Moses so refrained from becoming involved (*koinonia*) in their weakness that he even ministered to the condition of those who had
become ill. Not only was he not moved to defend himself against those
who caused him sorrow, but he even besought God for mercy on their
behalf. He showed through what he did, I think, that the person who
is well fortified with the shield of virtue will not be stung by the tips of
the darts.[63]

For his understanding of virtue, Gregory is indebted both to
Plato and to Aristotle. Platonic themes are evident in the
mysticism of ascent and of ascetic purification: 'The . . . person
who would approach the contemplation of Being must be pure
in all things so as to be pure in soul and body.'[64] Gregory's
conception of virtue, however, can also at times sound distinctly
Aristotelian: 'This teaching lays down that virtue is discerned in
the mean (*en mesoteti*). Accordingly all evil naturally operates in a
deficiency of or an excess of virtue.'[65] The key difference
between Gregory's conception of virtue and that of either Plato
or Aristotle is that it consists in union with God. Gregory
echoes Scripture by talking in terms of friendship (*philia*) with
God: 'We regard falling from God's friendship as the only thing
dreadful and we consider becoming God's friend the only thing
worthy of honour and desire. This, as I have said, is the
perfection (*teleiotes*) of life.'[66] Here is the Christian echo of the
Greek proverb, 'Friends have all things in common' (*hapanta
koina philois*), where the friendship is not that between two
humans bound together in virtue, but between the believer and
God. Gregory ends his treatise by saying that those things his
addressee finds in the lifting up of his understanding 'to what is

---

[62] *The Life of Moses* II.30; CWS, p. 61; cf. J. Daniélou ed., *La Vie de Moïse, SC* 1 ter (Paris:
     Cerf, 1968), p. 125.
[63] *The Life of Moses* II.261; CWS, pp. 121–2; *SC*, p. 284.
[64] *The Life of Moses* II.154; CWS, p. 92; *SC*, p. 204.
[65] *The Life of Moses* II.288; CWS, p. 128; *SC*, p. 302.
[66] *The Life of Moses* II.320; CWS, p. 137; *SC*, p. 326.

magnificent and divine' will 'most certainly be for the common (*koinon*) benefit in Christ Jesus'.[67] Gregory's understanding of dynamic participation in the life of God is presented in the *Life of Moses* in a predominantly individualistic mode but does not have to be taken that way. Set in the context of Basil's understanding of common life and his discussion of participation in the life of Trinity, together with Gregory of Nazianzen's trinitarian theology, it is clear that the Cappadocian understanding of *koinonia* is one of common participation in the life of the Trinity and the life of the body of Christ at one and the same time.

CONCLUSION: CAPPADOCIAN *KOINONIA*

In the development of Trinitarian theology and the ecclesiology of *koinonia*, the contribution of the Cappadocian Fathers was of the first importance. This has been argued strongly by John Zizioulas, who, more than any other theologian has been responsible for the contemporary, ecumenical development of a theology and ecclesiology of *koinonia*.[68] At the heart of Zizioulas' work is the consistent affirmation that, 'The being of God is a relational being: without the concept of communion it would not be possible to speak of the being of God.'[69] He claims that a momentous step was taken when the term *hypostasis* was first identified with the term *prosopon* (person), a move in which he sees the Cappadocians as central.[70] He argues that this meant there was a decisive shift away from seeing only an impersonal *ousia* or *hypostasis* as absolute. 'Personhood', as in the 'persons' of the Trinity, was now seen to be the ultimate reality of rational

---

[67] *The Life of Moses* II.321; CWS, p. 137; *SC*, p. 326.

[68] For a full bibliography of John Zizioulas' works, see P. McPartlan, *The Eucharist Makes the Church* (Edinburgh: T. and T. Clark, 1993).

[69] Zizioulas, *Being as Communion* (London: Darton, Longman and Todd, 1985), p. 17.

[70] *Ibid.*, pp. 38ff; 'The Doctrine of the Holy Trinity: The Significance of the Cappadocian Contribution' in C. Schwöbel ed., *Trinitarian Theology Today* (Edinburgh: T. and T. Clark, 1995), p. 47. Zizioulas provides little evidence to support this claim, which is, however, substantiated in the discussion by A. de Halleux, ' "Hypostase" et "Personne" dans la Formation du Dogme Trinitaire' in his *Patrologie et Oecuménisme, Bibliotheca Ephemeridum Theologicarum Lovaniensium* XCIII (Leuven: Leuven University Press, 1990), pp. 113–214.

being; and the threefold personhood of God to have its origins in the creative impulse of the Father. From the point in the fourth century when the formula '*mia ousia, treis hypostaseis*' or '*mia ousia, treis prosopa*' was adopted as an agreed way of speaking about this God, it became illegitimate theologically to think that there is first 'being' then 'person'. In the Christian understanding of God, there is no primary 'being' findable, as it were, 'behind' personhood – however much Christian theologians, especially in the West, may drift back towards this pagan or neo-platonic way of thinking. Zizioulas goes on to say, 'From an adjunct to being (a kind of mask), the person becomes the being itself and is simultaneously – a most significant point – the *constitutive element* (the "principle" or "cause") of beings.'[71] He goes on, 'Among the Greek Fathers the unity of God . . . and the ontological "principle" or "cause" of the being and life of God does not consist in the one substance of God but in the *hypostasis*, that is, *the person of the Father*.'[72]

The question of the 'monarchy' of the Father need not detain us here, except to note that it has been used to justify the ultimacy of personhood even within the Trinity. Since the Son is (eternally) begotten and the Spirit proceeds from the Father, it is the Father that is seen as the source of the differentiated divine being; the ultimate source of divine creativity lies in the free, personal being of the Father. When, however, the differentiation within the Godhead is expressed as 'three persons', and their primordial relations spoken of in terms of *koinonia*, new dangers arise. There has been in some quarters a tendency to use the language of *koinonia* not so much as a complement to the language of the divine essence (*ousia*) but as a replacement for it. This tendency may have been influenced by the approach of Existentialism in which, famously, 'existence precedes essence'. Where the existence of God as the *koinonia* of the three persons of the Trinity has been equated with an ultimately *social* understanding of God, the carefully constructed Cappadocian

---

[71] Zizioulas, *Being as Communion*, p. 39.
[72] *Ibid.*, p. 40. See the clear discussion in Lossky, *The Mystical Theology of the Eastern Church*, pp. 58ff.

balance between *hypostases* (persons) and *ousia* (essence) has been lost.

This can be further explored with the help of a fine article by André de Halleux.[73] De Halleux notes the currency of the argument that the Cappadocian Fathers, through their trinitarian theology, were responsible for a shift from what has been termed 'essentialism' to 'personalism'. He shows that, far from swinging violently to a theology of communion which privileged the three persons of the Trinity in their relatedness over their common essence, Basil and the two Gregories spoke readily of one *ousia*. As we have seen, in defence of Nicene orthodoxy Gregory of Nazianzen was prepared to extend Nicene use of the *homoousion* to the Spirit. De Halleux concludes that 'what they intended by the term intradivine *koinonia* was the common nature and not dialogic interpersonal relations'.[74] His is a moderate position: he does not reject the possibility that there could be an appropriately personalist interpretation of the 'Cappadocian formula', which would not contradict the intentions of the Cappadocian Fathers, but he does reject any attempt at an interpretation which espouses an anti-essentialism 'they would certainly have repudiated with the greatest energy'.

De Halleux utters a valuable word of caution, the more to be heeded because it is well grounded in patristic scholarship and in skilled application of that scholarship in contemporary ecumenical debate. He is right to be concerned for the preservation of the *right kind of essentialism* against an existentialist personalism that runs the risk of atomising the unity of the Trinity. His untimely death has left a gap in research at this point. In the volume of his collected essays, he does not discuss *perichoresis* as a term which begins to be found in the Cappadocians, and later developed as a key mediating term in trinitarian theology. At this point, T. F. Torrance picks up the thread:

This perichoretic understanding of the Trinity had the effect of restoring the full doctrine of the Fatherhood of God without importing any element of subordinationism into the hypostatic inter-

---

[73] A. de Halleux, 'Personnalisme ou Essentialisme Trinitaire chez les Pères Cappadociens?', in *Patrologie et Oecuménisme*, pp. 215–68.

[74] A. de Halleux, 'Personnalisme ou Essentialisme Trinitaire', p. 265.

relations between the Father, the Son and the Holy Spirit, and at the same time of restoring the biblical, Nicene and Athanasian conception of the one Being or Ousia of God as intrinsically and completely personal.[75]

A study of *perichoresis*, as used by John of Damascus (c.655– c.750) in particular, would take us too far afield. The point is that this term helped maintain the balance between 'personalism' and 'essentialism' in the way that *koinonia* was used by those who followed the Cappadocians in their trinitarian theology.

The Cappadocian achievement is, as it were, to take *koinonia* fully into the Christian understanding of God. For the Cappadocian Fathers, there is a continuity between the Church's understanding of its life as one of Christian *koinonia*, and its understanding of that *koinonia* as itself a participation in (or expression of) the life of God. Zizioulas has illuminated a further point remarkably: that in being 'partakers of the divine nature' (2 Pet. 1:4), Christians are sharing in a common essence which is *inherently relational*. In God (who is love), 'being' and 'relation' are one. We cannot say that for God and for humans, 'being' and 'relation' are united in the same manner: the 'personhood' of God is not the same as the 'personhood' of individual human beings – but for God and for humans there is nothing 'behind' personal existence, no 'essence' of divinity or humanity from which the Trinity or individual humans are derived. For human beings to be truly human, the Cappadocians teach, they must belong to the *koinonia* that is established by and in God. For God to be known truly as God, the perfect *koinonia* of Father, Son, and Holy Spirit must not only be understood, to the extent that it can, by fragile human beings; it must be entered.

---

[75] Torrance, *The Christian Doctrine of God*, p. 179.

CHAPTER 8

Augustine and the story of communion

The full and committed acceptance of Catholic Christianity by Augustine, who was baptised by Ambrose, Bishop of Milan, on Easter Eve 387, was one of the defining moments of western culture. Augustine, more than any other thinker, has been the shaping genius of western self-understanding. He developed and moulded a 'grand narrative'[1] of and for humanity with which we are still overwhelmingly engaged. It was a narrative that made sense of his own experience and the experience of the Church in history and which, through the ideological power of the Christian tradition for more than fifteen hundred years, imposed much of that sense on others.

Our task is to investigate the contribution made by Augustine to the developing understanding within the Christian tradition of all that is suggested by the Greek term *koinonia*. Greek did not come easily to Augustine. His knowledge of Platonist writings, which profoundly influenced his theological understanding, was a knowledge acquired through writers like Marius Victorinus, who translated from Greek into Latin. In Augustine, we observe a critical moment in the development of a western, Latin tradition of theological reflection on the common life. A full account of this development would attend to the history of the church in Rome, in Gaul, and in North Africa as the context of the writings of Irenaeus, who bridges the traditions of east and

---

[1] This 'grand narrative' is perhaps more accurately thought of as a series of interlocking 'grand narratives' which sometimes come into tension with each other: Plotinus' narrative of the soul's *exitus* and return (cf. R. J. O'Connell, *St Augustine's Confessions, The Odyssey of Soul* (Cambridge, Mass.: The Belknap Press, Harvard University Press, 1969)); and also the biblical narrative of the Creation, and the human 'journey' from the Garden of Eden to the New Jerusalem.

west, Tertullian, and Cyprian, but Augustine towers above all his predecessors as the synthetic genius who gave to western theology its abiding structure and themes. To say, however, that *communio* as used by Augustine sums up all that is meant by *koinonia* as used in the East would be oversimple.

There is no one Latin word that encompasses the nexus of meanings suggested by *koinonia*. The three closest are those with the same root as *communio* (communion), *participatio* (participation), and *societas* (society, fellowship). Each of these semantic families is remarkably important for Augustine. It is striking that in the *Vetus Italica*[2] New Testament the translation for *koinonia* in Acts 2:42 ('They devoted themselves to the Apostles' teaching and the *koinonia*') is *communicatio*; the translation in 2 Cor.6:14 ('For what *koinonia* have righteousness and iniquity? Or what *koinonia* has light with darkness') is first *participatio*, then *societas*; that in 1 John 1:3−7 ('Our *koinonia* is with the Father and his Son Jesus Christ') is *societas*.[3] Our investigation will concentrate on themes suggested by these three terms: communion and communication; participation; and society. With these in mind, we shall approach two of Augustine's best-known texts: the *Confessions* and the *City of God*, before exploring more broadly Augustine's theology of communion.

THE CONFESSIONS: *COMMUNIO* AND *PARTICIPATIO*

In the whole of the *Confessions*, there is only one passage where *communio* and its cognates is prominent. Augustine discusses in Book xii the interpretation of the creation narrative, maintaining that there may be a number of valid interpretations of scriptural passages and no means of adjudicating between

---

[2] Augustine would have known a variety of texts in which parts of the Bible had been translated, including elements of the Vulgate. For this chapter, I have used the Maurist edition of the Old Latin texts, edited by P. Sabatier, *Bibliorum Sacrorum Latinae Versiones Antiquae seu Vetus Italica*, 3 vols. (Remis: apud Reginaldum Florentain, 1743).

[3] Compare: 1 Cor. 10:16, 2 Cor. 8:4, 2 Cor. 9:13, 2 Cor. 13:13, Phil. 1:5, Phil. 2:1, Phil. 3:10, Philemon 6 (*communicatio*); Rom. 12:13, Phil. 4:14 (*communicantes*); 1 Pet. 4:13 (*communicatis*); Phil. 4:15 (*communicavit*); Gal. 6:6 (*communicet*); Rom.15:26 (*collatio*); Rev. 1:9 (*particeps*); 1 Cor. 10:18 (*participes*); Hebr. 2:14 (*participes*); 1 Cor. 10:21 (*participare*); Rom. 11:17, 1 Cor. 9:23, 2 Cor. 8:23, Philemon 17, 1 Pet. 5:1 (*socius*); Luke 5:7−10, 2 Cor. 1:7, Phil. 1:7, Hebr. 10:33 (*socii*); 1 Cor. 1:9 (*societas*).

them. He resists those who push their own interpretation of a text 'not because it is true, but because it is their own'. Had they loved the truth, as he himself loves the truth, they would have realised that the truth is held in common by all those who love it (*'quoniam in commune omnium est veritatis amatorum'*). Truth is not the private property of any one person but the *common* property of all, and all are called to share in the truth openly, with God giving terrible warning that we should not seek private possession of that which is to be held in common, lest it be taken away from us:

For your truth does not belong to me nor to anyone else, but to us all whom you call to share it (*ad eius communionem*) as a public possession. With terrifying words you warn against regarding it as a private possession, or we may lose it (Matt. 25:14–30). Anyone who claims for his own property what you offer for all to enjoy, and wishes to have exclusive rights to what belongs to everyone, is driven from the common truth to his own private ideas, that is from truth to a lie.[4]

The truth is above humanity and, by the grace of God, available to humanity only as human beings will share in it *together*. To grasp at truth, to set private judgement over against the judgement of other human beings, to imagine oneself to be in exclusive possession of the truth, is to have fallen out of the communion of truth into mendacity. Though in sin there may be a delusive appearance of solidarity, the sinner is ultimately alone.[5]

Augustine discusses the Fall and human frailty at length, bearing witness to this frailty again and again from his own experience. By contrast, he also talks of 'the heaven of heavens', which is in the 'intellectual' realm, above the sensible creation that human beings inhabit, with its visible heaven and earth. The 'heaven of heavens' remains above, not coeternal with God

---

4 *Confessions* XII.25. Unless otherwise stated, I have used the translation by Henry Chadwick, *Confessions* (Oxford: Oxford University Press, 1991).

5 Compare *De Libero Arbitrio* II.37 on common sharing in truth and wisdom: 'Nothing from [God's common good] ever becomes the property of a single person or of several people, but at one and the same time it is completely common to all.' In his account of the Fall, Augustine explains how the serpent persuaded the woman 'to grasp a personal and private good rather than the common and public good which is unchangeable' (*De Trinitate* XII.xii.17).

(for it is created), but participating in God's eternity ('*particeps aeternitatis tuae*').[6] This 'heaven of heavens' he also calls 'God's house', which has not wandered into the far country, but perfectly and permanently cleaves to God.[7] It is 'not made of earth, nor is it a body made from some celestial material, but is spiritual and participates in your eternity, because it is without stain forever'.[8] Thus, the soul longs that it may dwell in God's house all the days of its life. 'God's house', being spiritual, is of a different substance from that of humanity, which is carnal. Human beings, being a compound of body and spirit, can discern and long for God's dwelling place, but they cannot, while they are in the body, enter into it permanently. Augustine interweaves with what he says of the '*domus dei*' temple imagery from the psalms, together with Scriptural meditation on love for Jerusalem. Never far away is Paul's talk of 'a house, not made with hands, eternal in the heavens' (2 Cor. 5:1).

The *domus dei* participates in the *aeternitas dei*; the *famuli dei* (servants of God) together share in the *veritas dei*. The mode of this sharing or participation is perhaps the central theme of the *Confessions*, in which God is presented both as outside the individual, whether because he is far above, above even the 'heaven of heavens', or because he is the creator of all things 'in the beginning', and also as deep within, 'the life of my life' (*vita vitae meae*). Augustine presents the approach to God in three famous passages: the first two[9] of these draw on Plotinian accounts of ecstatic experience to describe how on at least one occasion he was able to ascend to God and briefly to come into touch with 'that which is' but not to sustain that communion, collapsing back into his former state of exile. Augustine describes how he entered into his innermost being ('*intima mea*') with God himself as his guide, how with the 'eye of his soul' he

---

[6] *Confessions* XII.9; cf. XII.13.   [7] *Confessions* XII.11.
[8] *Confessions* XII.15 (my translation).
[9] In discussing Augustine's experience I have drawn on the two passages of Book VII (10, 17) in which he writes in similar terms. It is not clear from the text whether he is writing in the mode of historical description, that is to say whether he experienced this mystical contact with God on one occasion or more. Augustine's second account of mystical ascent (VII.17) is closely indebted to the Platonist tradition, which goes back to the classification of knowledge according to Plato's vertically 'divided line' in Book VI of the *Republic*. Translations have been slightly adapted.

was enabled to 'see', above his seeing and above his mind, the immutable light, which was above any light that humans may know on earth. 'It was superior because it made me, and I was inferior because I was made by it.' Augustine's immediate reaction was to know himself distant from this light: 'I found myself far from you "in the realm of unlikeness" ', though he heard a voice which said to him: 'I am the food of the fully grown: grow and you will feed on me. And you shall not change me into yourself like the food your flesh eats, but you shall be changed into me.' The relational language is extraordinary in its tension. Augustine is drawn away from the things of earth, he sees the invisible light in which God dwells, knows himself to be one who dwells in the region of *unlikeness* (the prodigal son's 'far country', where he was so hungry he would have eaten pigfood) and is promised that God himself will be the food of his soul and he will be at one with the Father. The account concludes with direct reference to the Burning Bush and direct address to God: 'You cried from afar, "I am who I am" ' – a voice that spoke to Augustine in his heart – and all doubt was swept away. In this remarkable account, at one and the same time Augustine is drawn close to God and shown his distance from God; he is addressed by a God who is other than himself, and yet the address comes from deep within him.

This experience, as retold by Augustine, preceded his final acceptance of Catholic Christianity, the hearing of '*tolle, lege*', and his baptism. Within the narrative, it opens the way for a discussion of the meaning of the Incarnation over against anything that could be found in the books of the Platonists, the religion of Plotinus, 'the flight of the alone to the Alone'.[10] After telling of his baptism, Augustine speaks of an ecstatic experience, shared with his mother Monica, at Ostia.[11] Augustine relates how, when he and his mother were engaged in spiritual conversation,

Our minds were lifted up by an ardent affection towards eternal being

---

[10] Cf. *Enneads* VI.9.11. For discussion of Plotinian and Augustinian mysticism, see A. Louth, *Origins of the Christian Mystical Tradition* (Oxford: Clarendon, 1981), pp. 36–51, 132–58.
[11] *Confessions* IX.10.

itself. Step by step we climbed beyond all corporeal objects and the heaven itself, where sun, moon, and stars shed light on the earth. We ascended even further by internal reflection and dialogue and wonder at your works, and we entered into our own minds. We moved up beyond them so as to attain to the region of inexhaustible abundance where you feed Israel eternally with truth for food. There life is the wisdom by which all creatures come into being, both things which were and which will be. But wisdom itself is not brought into being but is as it was and always will be . . . And while we talked and panted after it, we touched it in some small degree by a moment of total concentration of the heart . . . That is how it was when at that moment we extended our reach and in a flash of mental energy attained the eternal wisdom which abides beyond all things.

Much of the *Confessions* to this point discusses forms of human relating and the ambiguities of human love, both as something God-given and as a temptation to opt for the carnal in preference to the spiritual. Here, Augustine shares in true *communion* at a number of different levels. He is reconciled with his mother (and with Mother Church) in their shared Catholic Christianity. This is a chaste unity, with true love but without sexual desire.[12] They share together in a dialogue in which they transcend the realms where language is sequential communication in time with an alienated other. They rise beyond the realm of the mind to that realm from which Israel is forever fed 'with truth for food'. As with the earlier vision, the moment of contact with God is attained 'in a flash',[13] but a 'flash' that opens the vista of eternity. After this vision, Monica makes it clear that with the conversion of her son all she has hoped for in this life has been completed and she is now ready to die. The one thing she asks is that Augustine should remember her at the Lord's altar, wherever he may be.[14] For Monica, this represents continued communion in the Lord's Body through her son's sacramental participation in the same Body at the eucharist. In

---

[12] There are strong echoes here of Plato's *Phaedrus*.

[13] The word '*ictus*' is the same as that used in 1 Cor. 15:52 for 'the *twinkling* of an eye'. Immediately after Augustine's use at IX.10 of *ictus* (which he also uses at VII.17 to speak of his momentary attainment of communion with God), he makes explicit reference to 1 Cor. 15:51.

[14] When Augustine describes Monica's pious visits to the memorials of the martyrs (VI.2), he talks of the '*communicatio dominici corporis*' (VII.2). Compare *CD* 20.ix.

this way, Monica, when removed from body, time, and earthly ties, will continue in *communion* with her son and, by his communication, with those who read his *Confessions*.[15]

This communication of mother and son, within the communion of saints, depends upon Augustine's basic belief in a God who makes himself known in the communication of love. Throughout the *Confessions*, Augustine addresses God in prayerful response to that love. Though he tells his own life story chronologically as that of his search for God, it is clear that at a deeper level, the story is that of God's search for Augustine, who has become lost in the 'far country', the 'land of unlikeness'. We need to go back for a moment to examine the process by which Augustine came to believe in a God with whom it was possible to *communicate*. It is clear that one major step along the way, a step vital for his experience of communion, is the shift that took place when he ceased to think of God as physical substance of some kind, locatable in space, but as 'spiritual substance' accessible in space though without spatial, that is physical, location.

For the young Augustine, the reading of Aristotle's *Categories*, probably in translation, had been vital to his developing understanding.[16] Augustine was captivated by the clarity of Aristotle's classification of objects in the world. Looking back on his ready acceptance of Aristotle's analysis, Augustine criticised his own uncritical application of the language of substance not only to God's creation, but also to God. He lamented the fact that he had at that stage conceived of God as *a being*, with 'substance', like any other being. He says at the beginning of Book VII that he could not yet think in terms of 'spiritual substance' which was not distributed through space, whether that space be in the world or above the world:

I conceived even you, life of my life, as a large being, permeating infinite space on every side, penetrating the entire mass of the world, and outside this extending in all directions for immense distances

---

[15] See the final paragraph of *Confessions* IX.13, where Augustine appeals for the prayers of his readers for his mother and father.

[16] *Confessions* IV.16.

without end; so earth had you, heaven had you, everything had you, and in relation to you all was finite; but you not so.[17]

Augustine thought of God as being like the sunlight, which fills all the air, both in the heavens and on earth.[18] Ridiculous though the implication of this was, there was more of God in an elephant than a sparrow.[19]

Clearly, this wouldn't do. A major shift came when Augustine began no longer to see God as distributed through space. The 'substance' of God was in some way different: it was 'spiritual'.[20] He uses the memorable image of an infinite sea in which there floats a finite sponge, thoroughly permeated by the water of the sea: 'This is the kind of way in which I supposed your finite creation to be full of you, infinite as you are.'[21] Here was a material creation saturated with God, which could only be possible if God were something other than corporeal. Augustine had come to see God in Plotinian terms, as spiritual and therefore not constrained by space and time, but not yet as a God to whom one could relate.

A further shift in Augustine's understanding, whereby he found God to be the object of *relation*, is not traced clearly, though a number of contributing shocks are recorded. There was the shock of reading the books of the 'Platonists' and the discovery there, not in the precise words of the prologue to John's Gospel, but in outline that,

In the beginning was the Word and the Word was with God and the Word was God. He was in the beginning with God. All things were made by him, and without him nothing was made. In that which was made was life; and the life was the light of men. And the light shone in the darkness, and the darkness did not comprehend it.

What, however, Augustine did not find in the 'Platonists' was

---

[17] *Confessions* VII.1.
[18] The analogy is difficult for a modern reader, because we think of light as a form of energy. Augustine thought of sunlight as having 'substance' – rather as we might imagine 'particles' of light.
[19] In *CD* 4.xii Augustine argues strongly against the motion of Jupiter as *animus mundi* ('soul of the world'), which would entail the self-evidently blasphemous belief that 'nothing at all remains which is not a part of God'.
[20] Augustine speaks of 'spiritual substance' at *Confessions* V.14, VI.3, and contrasts this with 'corporeal substance' at VII.1.
[21] *Confessions* VII.5.

the message that the word became flesh; or that the Son took the form of a servant and humbled himself to death, even death on a cross; or that the Father did not spare his only Son but gave him up for us all. Augustine distinguishes clearly between his preliminary understanding of the spiritual presence of God, and his later conversion to a recognition of a God who was known to him in *relation*. The first ecstatic experience, as discussed above, marks the point at which Augustine knew himself addressed by God, invited to grow and to feed off him. 'And you cried from far away: "Now, I am who I am." I heard', he says, 'in the way one hears within the heart, and all doubt left me.'[22]

Augustine came to believe in a God who spoke, a God one could hear, and to whom one could be close for a moment, but not yet a God with whom one could be in sustained relation. For that, yet further steps were needed. First was the acceptance of the incarnation: *verbum caro factum est*. For Augustine, the incarnation brings *communion* between God and man in a new way. He talks of the participation (*participatio*) of Christ in our 'coat of skin'.[23] With his acceptance of a God to whom one could relate came his acceptance of Scripture as a book that spoke the word of God directly to humans, as opposed to the books of the Platonists in which 'No one . . . hears him who calls "Come to me, you who labour"'.[24] The truth he had encountered in those books he now found reformulated by Paul in the language of personal address, 'with the commendation of your grace'. The most striking example of Scripture speaking was, of course, the words from Romans that he read in response to the command, '*tolle, lege*': 'Not in riots and drunken parties, not in eroticism and indecencies, not in strife and rivalry, but put on the Lord Jesus Christ and make no provision for the flesh in its lusts.' (Rom. 13:13–14) Then, and only then, was he ready to respond to God's call, by accepting baptism into the communion of the Church.

---

22 *Confessions* VII.10.
23 Though being careful to differentiate his position from the Apollinarian heresy that in Christ God took a 'covering' of flesh, but not a human soul (VII.18–19).
24 *Confessions* VII.21.

We could go on at this point in our discussion of the *Confessions* to consider in greater depth Augustine's interwoven ecclesiology, his deep understanding of the sacraments as a means of spiritual *communication*, his ready use of Scripture to the same end, his lively appreciation of the communion of saints. All of these are present in his remarkable text, but they are more fully worked out elsewhere. What distinguishes the *Confessions* is the way in which the whole text is itself a prayerful and reflective conversation with God. The book is written in intimate dialogue, in *communion*, with a loving creator. In this respect it is like no other book of early Christian literature. It is written with God as interlocutor, so that the whole of Augustine's life, his whole vision of the world, from the creation, on which he meditates extensively, through his continuing narrative of his own place within that creation, to the consummation of all things in God, is seen in the light of God's personal presence and activity.

The most obvious influence on Augustine at this point is the psalms, which he read repeatedly from the period before his baptism to the end of his life. Amongst the many references to all parts of Scripture, reference to the deep, trusting, conversational and confessional tone of the psalms is pervasive. Augustine himself tells what an impression the psalms made on him in the days he was at Cassiciacum waiting for baptism: 'My God, how I cried to you when I read the Psalms of David!'[25] The primary form of address throughout the *Confessions*, before there is any address to the reader, is address to God, rehearsing *coram deo* the story of Augustine's life as the story of God's mercy to his prodigal son, just as the psalms beginning '*Confitemini domino*' (e.g. Pss. 105–7)[26] confess God's mercy to a wayward people. Augustine constantly interweaves quotation from the psalms with his own comment. For example, 'Lord hear my prayer' is a direct quotation from the opening of Psalm 61, to which Augustine adds 'that my soul may not suffer exhaustion [fail] in confessing to you your mercies'.[27] A similarly beautiful instance occurs where Augustine begins, 'What shall I render to the

---

[25] *Confessions* IX.4.   [26] Coverdale's translation is in each case, 'O give thanks. . .'
[27] *Confessions* I.15.

Lord?', a direct quotation from Psalm 116:12, where the psalmist continues 'for all his bounty to me'. Augustine, however, continues: 'who recalls these things to my memory, but my soul feels no fear from the recollection'.[28] Recollection before God is at one and the same time a means of confession, of reclamation of the past, and a form of thanksgiving. His use of the psalms is wonderfully allusive, setting up an intertextual dialogue in the creation of his own text, and through this with the putative experience of the psalmist through which Augustine is 'reading' and 're-reading' his own life.

A psalm such as Psalm 138 expresses a number of the themes which are central to the *Confessions*. It begins '*Confitebor tibi, Domine in toto corde meo*' ('I will give thanks unto thee, O Lord, with my whole heart'[29]), announcing the themes not only of confession, but of praise with the undivided heart. It continues with recognition of the mighty acts of God, '*quoniam magnificasti super omnia nomen tuum sanctum*' ('for thou hast magnified thy [holy] name above all things'). The *magnificat* themes continue later: '*excelsus Dominus, et humilia respicit: et alta de longe cognoscit*' ('For though the Lord be high, yet hath he respect unto the lowly: as for the proud, he beholdeth them afar off'). Augustine's own pilgrimage is seen as a triumph of grace bringing him from his proud and distanced isolation to the point of humbly calling upon God. Throughout the *Confessions*, Augustine praises God for his open access to God in prayer, and for God's drawing his soul into the path of virtue: '*In quacunque die invocavero te, exaudi me: multiplicasti me in anima mea in virtute tua*' ('When I called upon thee, thou heardest me: and enduedst my soul with much strength'). His book is written that others may be drawn into the pattern of confession and praise: '*Confiteantur tibi Domine omnes reges terrae: quia audierunt omnia verba oris tui*' ('All the kings of the earth shall praise thee, O Lord: for they have heard the words of thy mouth'). As a summing up of what Augustine has to 'confess', the last words of the psalm could

---

28 *Confessions* II.7.
29 For the text of this psalm I have followed the *Vetus Italica*, which differs from the Vulgate and that in Augustine's *Enarrationes in Psalmos*. For the English translation, I have used Coverdale's version in the *Book of Common Prayer*.

hardly be bettered: '*Domine, misericordia tua in saecula*' ('Thy mercy, O Lord, endureth for ever'), together with the prayer, '*opera manuum tuarum non omittas*' ('Despise not then the works of thine own hands'). As the themes within the psalter are deliberately repetitive, one could doubtless choose other psalms which would similarly encapsulate central themes on which Augustine is meditating. Psalm 138 is simply taken here as an example to show the source in the psalms of much that he interweaves with the narrative of his own life to make sense of his experience and, more than that, to expound the intimate communion with God which is central to the *Confessions*.

The narrative of the *Confessions* finishes at the end of Book IX with the death of Monica. Through Books X to XIII Augustine presents a theological reflection on his own, earthly existence, which he uses still further to deepen his reflection on communion with God. First, he seeks the dwelling-place of God within himself, questing for that 'place' in his memory where God is now to be found: 'You conferred this honour on my memory that you should dwell in it.'[30] Yet there is no 'place' within memory where God is to be located, for God transcends memory: 'You remain immutable above all things, and yet you have deigned to dwell in my memory since the time I have learnt about you.' Just as memory provides access to God but does not contain God, so time offers access to God. God dwells in an eternal present but when, through his Word, he created all things, he created time. We measure time in our minds as we observe sequential change in the world but within the mind we can also know from the beginning to the end, as when we remember a psalm word by word, but know that we hold the whole psalm in our mind from beginning to end. It is in the mind, within ourselves, that our transcendence of time becomes a reality, and within the mind that we find one route of access to God. This, however, is a route for the individual. Augustine is just as interested in how we *together* share access to God, and for this he turns to discussion of Scriptural interpretation, in which we may differ but may *together* find access to God's truth. 'If both

[30] *Confessions* X.25.

of us see that what you say is true and that what I say is true, then where, I ask, do we see this? I do not see it in you, nor you in me, but both of us see it in the immutable truth which is higher than our minds.'[31] Though there may be individual access to truth, truth is not the property of any one individual. It is not 'possessed' either individually or corporately. It dwells in us, and we, if we accept such indwelling, in truth. It would be better to say, *he* dwells in us and we in *him*, that is to say in God, who is the truth. Central to Augustine's theology of earthly life is communion with one another and with God, in the reading of Scripture and in the sacramental life of the Church. This is why he concludes the *Confessions* with discussion of the Trinity – the place for our restless hearts of eternal communion and rest.

THE CITY OF GOD: *PARTICIPATIO* AND *SOCIETAS*

It has been said that the City of God is 'an application of the theme of Augustine's own development, as described in the *Confessions*, to the broader, less immediate, canvas of man and destiny'.[32] This is an attractive, but misleading view. Like the *Confessions*, though to a lesser and less intense extent, the *City of God* is doxological, but it is not, or at least not directly, about conversion. There is in this long book remarkably little about the passage from membership of the earthly to membership of the heavenly city. There is a givenness about the cosmological scenario of the two cities, which issues in praise to God who has ordained things in this remarkable way, but there is a complete absence of invitation to apply for membership of the heavenly city. Who does this, how and why, is lost to human view in the mystery of God. The clearest statement of the theme of the *City of God* is located in Augustine's earlier writing, when Augustine writes of two loves: 'The one social, the other private; the one looking to the common advantage for a supernal fellowship, the other seeking to bring even what belongs to the community into

---

[31] *Confessions* XII.25.
[32] J. J. O'Meara, Introduction to *The City of God* (Harmondsworth: Penguin, 1984) p. 1. Unless otherwise stated, this is the translation I have followed.

its own power for the sake of an arrogant domination; the one submissive to God, the other God's rival.'[33]

Augustine, writing as a theological interpreter of history, traces the story of these two loves. His immediate purpose is to take issue with those who blame Christianity for the fall of Rome, to refute the accusations of those who say the ancient gods should never have been neglected either for what they have to offer in this life or in the life to come. For this he has to engage with the history of Rome and the Roman gods, to show that they were neither morally nor religiously superior to the deity the Christians worshipped, and that they were by no means better at their job of protecting Rome before they were overtaken by the advent of Christianity. Through the ten books of this polemic, Augustine's major theme of the 'two cities' is sketched but not developed systematically. In his last twelve books, he turns from an aggressive and polemical reading of secular history to an exposition of sacred, that is to say biblical, history, bringing it into chronological relation with secular history, but maintaining a clear distinction between the two. Thus, he is keen to expound what God did through Noah or Abraham or David. He is prepared to follow Scripture and discuss what God did through Pharaoh or Nebuchadnezzar or Cyrus, even Pontius Pilate, but he doesn't follow this through to any sustained discussion of God's action in the political history of Rome, in the Gracchi or Augustus or Constantine.[34] The nearest he comes is an intense engagement with what God has been saying through philosophical and poetic thinkers, especially in the tradition of the Platonists: Plato, Plotinus, and other Greek thinkers such as the Stoics. Behind much of what

---

[33] *De Gen. ad Litt.* XI.xv.20, quoted J. Burnaby, *Amor Dei* (London: Hodder and Stoughton, 1938, pp. 120–1); cf. P. Brown, *Augustine of Hippo* (London: Faber and Faber, 1967), pp. 319–20.

[34] There are exceptions. For example, he writes of Rome, 'It was God's design to conquer the world through her, to unite the world into the single community of the Roman commonwealth and the Roman laws, and so to impose peace throughout its length and breadth' (18.xxii) and notes that 'The Sibyl of Erythraea certainly recorded some utterances which are obviously concerned with Christ' (18.xxiii). Augustine's more usual strategy is to fend off too close an identification between the action of God and events in non-biblical history, though he remains interested in showing how the one has been the context or the backdrop for the other.

he writes lies the *Republic*, mediated by Cicero in *de Respublica*, and also, with respect to cosmology, the *Timaeus*. Augustine's supreme respect for Virgil among the Latin poets is evident in his frequent, though critical, quotation from the *Aeneid*. All of this, however, does not add up to a philosophy of history. Augustine's is a *theology* of history, which remains remarkably hesitant, even agnostic, about attributing to God specific involvement in actual political events, notably the Fall of Rome to the Goths in 410.

Augustine's aim is thus limited and elusive. He says himself that he wants to write about the two cities, their origin, development, and destined ends. Here, on earth, their identity is confused, '*permixtum*', but in the final judgement they will be decisively separated: 'These two cities are interwoven and intermixed in this era, and await separation at the last judgement.'[35] Augustine's two cities are the earthly and the heavenly, Babylon and Jerusalem. In Roman society, though Christianised, the two are thoroughly interwoven: 'While the City of God is on pilgrimage in this world, she has in her midst some who are united with her in participation in the sacraments, but who will not join with her in the eternal destiny of the saints . . . At one time they join [God's] enemies in filling the theatres, at another they join with us in filling the churches.'[36] Augustine is keen to pre-empt any over-simple identification of Christianised Rome either with Babylon or with Jerusalem.[37]

For the purposes of our investigation, the *City of God*, on which Augustine worked for perhaps fourteen years between 413 and 427, is of vital importance because he is concerned throughout to establish the inalienably social nature of the Christian faith. He did this by drawing extensively on the tradition of thought which can be traced from the Greek *polis* and the thinkers of the *polis*, beginning with Plato and Aristotle, blending this with Roman reflection on the *respublica*, especially in the work of Cicero. The City of God is for Augustine both

---

[35] *CD* I.xxxv.   [36] *CD* I.xxxv.
[37] For clarification of Augustine's aim in writing *City of God*, see the marvellous discussion in R. A. Markus, *Saeculum: History and Society in the Theology of St Augustine* (Cambridge: Cambridge University Press, 1970), e.g. pp. 53–71.

the true *respublica* and the heavenly Jerusalem, where the 'Jerusalem experiment' of holding goods in common (cf. Acts 2:42) has been fulfilled: 'There the public treasury needs no great efforts for its enrichment at the cost of private property; for there the common stock is the treasury of truth.'[38] Central to Augustine's exposition of the social nature of Christian faith are terms like *participatio, societas, communicatio,* and their cognates, but to these should be added *respublica* and *civitas,* used with power and resonance to transmute the best of thought about the Roman 'commonwealth' and the privilege of Roman citizenship into a theological and Christocentric register. What was novel about Augustine's approach was that he weighed in the balance the whole history of Roman society, setting it in the cosmic context of biblical judgement on other societies and showing how within the history of Rome there was being worked out a greater story of two cities whose destiny is manifest in every human society.

Augustine strongly supports the philosophers in their commendation of the common life: 'How could [the City of God] have made its first start, how could it have advanced along its course, how could it attain its appointed goal, if the lives of the saints were not social (*socialis*)?'[39] Such social life is realised in the city: 'The life of a city is inevitably a social life.'[40] A city is nothing other than 'a number of people bound together by some tie of fellowship (*societatis*)'.[41] Not all human aggregations fulfil this social ideal. Augustine speaks disparagingly of the '*multitudo*' that lacks the *vinculum* or bond by which it might attain the unity of the '*populus*'. Twice he suggests what might be the *vinculum* which constitutes a *populus.*[42] The first time, following Cicero's Scipio, he says a 'people' is bound together by consent to law and common interest' (*iuris consensu et utilitatis communione sociatum*').[43] Later, he speaks of 'the association (*coetus*) of a multitude (*multitudo*) of rational beings united by a

---

[38] *CD* 5.xvi.   [39] *CD* 19.v.   [40] *CD* 19.xvii.   [41] *CD* 15.viii.

[42] Here we should think not only of the *populus Romanus,* but also of the *populus Hebraeus,* constituted *a people* (rather than a *multitudo,* or 'rabble') by God. In the case of the Hebrews, the *vinculum* could be said to be the covenant (outwardly) and the love of God (inwardly).

[43] *CD* 2.xxi (translation amended); cf. *CD* 19.xxiii.

common agreement on the object of their love'.[44] He follows Cicero's Scipio in arguing that for there to be a 'republic' there must be both a 'people' and justice: 'Where there is no justice there is no republic.'[45] This is true of all political authority and rule: 'Remove justice, and what are kingdoms but gangs of criminals on a large scale?'[46] Justice, of course, is never the property of individuals. It is the great common political virtue. Justice is the central theme of Plato's *Republic* and central to Aristotle's *Ethics*. 'Justice is that virtue which gives to each his due'[47] and the place where such justice will be found truly and without fail is in that Republic whose founder and ruler is Christ.[48]

The members of any integrated group are not then merely a *multitudo;* they are a *societas. Societas*, for Augustine, is a keyword that he applies both to angels and to men, to the heavenly city, which the unfallen angels inhabit, and to the earthly. He talks of '*duae . . . civitates, hoc est societates*' ('two cities, or communities'),[49] of which 'the one is a community of devout men, the other a company of the irreligious, and each has its own angels attached to it'.[50] There is, however, an inherent contradiction in talking about a *societas* of those who have given way to wilfulness and egocentricity. Augustine's mature thought about the fulfilment of the social nature of angels and men centres on the image of joyful and peaceful participation in the heavenly city, by contrast with which he demonstrates to what depths the earthly city has fallen.

Fundamental for him is the difference between God and his created beings: 'To be a partaker of God is not the same thing as to be God.'[51] God stands alone as the plenitude and source of all being. However, in creating beings, he has endowed them with *participation* in his own divine being. This is a theme to which Augustine returns again and again. He distinguishes absolutely between creator and creation, but he stresses equally the continuing bond between them. The nature of that bond he leaves largely undefined and unexplored, neither defining participation nor speculating on degrees or modes of participation.

[44] *CD* 19.xxiv.   [45] *CD* 19.xxi.   [46] *CD* 4.iv.   [47] *CD* 19.xxi.
[48] *CD* 2.xxii.   [49] *CD* 12.i.   [50] *CD* 14.xiii.   [51] *CD* 22.xxx.

It is, however, basic to his thought on union with God. In a key chapter on Christ the Mediator,[52] he expounds how the beatitude of angels and men consists in participation in the one God[53] and the misery of the evil angels consists in deprivation of this participation. Later in the discussion, when distinguishing angels from demons, he talks of the angels *participating* in the eternity of the Word of God and, by *participation* in the Spirit of God, knowing the will of God.[54] If this is the unbroken joy of the angels, this is precisely what the demons (and fallen humans) lack. It is the destiny of the redeemed, through the mediation of Jesus Christ, to share with the angels in the blessing of *participation* in the divine Trinity: 'For in liberating us from mortality and misery it is not to the immortal and blessed angels that he brings us, so that by participation in their nature we also may be immortal and blessed; it is to that Trinity, in which the angels participate, and so achieve their felicity.'[55]

What makes this possible, indeed what could only make this possible, is the double participation of the Mediator both in divinity and in humanity: 'God himself, the blessed God who is the giver of blessedness, became partaker of our human nature and thus offered us a short cut (*compendium*) to participation in his own divine nature.'[56] The use of *participation/participare* suggests precisely what we have seen all along in discussing *koinonia*: a way of speaking of genuine unity (unitedness) whilst maintaining differentiation (distinction). Augustine is not interested here in defining further what that might mean. What concerns him passionately is that mediation between divinity and humanity, first by the action of God in Christ and then in the communion of the Church, is a God-given reality, and therefore to be trusted in the vicissitudes of history.

The story of communion is told in terms of the heavenly city, from the creation of the angels, the fall of certain angels and the

---

[52] *CD* 9.xvi. Compare 21.xv, where he repeats that it is precisely by *participation* in Christ 'the immortal and just one' ('*eius inmortalis et iusti participatione*') that we are saved.

[53] Augustine uses the word *multitudo* here. It is clear that what makes of a 'multitude' a body (*coetus, societas, populus*), which is bound together, is shared participation in some uniting goal or activity, some good constituting a common bond, or, conversely, some evil that constitutes the parody of a common bond.

[54] *CD* 9.xxi, xxii.   [55] *CD* 9.xv.   [56] *CD* 9.xv.

fall of man, to the restoration of a society of men and angels which populates the heavenly city: This is 'the most glorious City of God, which knows and worships one God. It is proclaimed by holy angels, who have invited us into the society (*societas*) of that City, and have desired us to become their fellow-citizens in it.'[57] What God establishes in the heavenly city is peace, 'the tranquillity of order'. Augustine's vision of peace is comprehensive. It is at the same time individual and social, historical and eschatological. How the eschatological engages with the historical remains, as we have seen, ultimately a mystery, and, when Augustine addresses the history of Rome, unclear, but he affirms that it does, and not only in the life of the Church. For him, every experience of true peace within history is a participation in the eschatological peace which is the life of the heavenly city:

The peace of body and soul is the duly ordered life and health of a living creature; peace between mortal man and God is an ordered obedience, in faith, in subjection to an everlasting law; peace between men is an ordered agreement of mind with mind; the peace of a home is the ordered agreement among those who live together about giving and obeying orders; the peace of the Heavenly City is a perfectly ordered and perfectly harmonious fellowship (*societas*) in the enjoy-ment of God, and a mutual fellowship in God; the peace of the whole world is the tranquillity of order (*tranquillitas ordinis*) – and order is the arrangement of things equal and unequal in a pattern which assigns to each its proper position.[58]

This is the *pax dei* in which the Church already participates: 'But we, in our measure, are made partakers of his peace; and so we know the perfection of peace in ourselves, peace among ourselves, and peace with God, according to our standard of perfection.'[59] This is the *pax dei* which belongs to no individual, and is shared with all those who are members together of the heavenly city. It is known within the Church now, but the Church is a 'mixed body', struggling to be faithful amidst the conflicts of earthly life. The 'tranquillity of order' and the peace of God will be known in its fullness within the heavenly Jerusalem, the true city of God.

---

[57] *CD* 10.xxv. [58] *CD* 19.xiii. [59] *CD* 22.xxix.

AUGUSTINE'S THEOLOGY OF COMMUNION

In the *Confessions* Augustine gives us a theological history of his own communion with God, embedding it within the story of all communion from the Creation to the end of time. In the *City of God* he tells the story of two 'loves' or two communions, the one a negative parody of the other. In both texts, his aim is ultimately doxological: the very act of writing is grounded in worship of the trinitarian God, whose spiritual essence is nothing less than *communion*.

Augustine often stresses the difference between *participation* in the life of God and the being of God himself, which is eternal life: 'For we too are made partakers of this eternal life and become, in our own measure, immortal. But the eternal life itself, of which we are made partakers, is one thing; we ourselves, who by partaking of it shall live eternally, are another.'[60] There is no confusion between creator and creation, between the life of the Trinity and the life with which created beings, angels and human, are endowed. The life of created beings is social;[61] the Trinity is not *a society* as such. However, the bond between members of the society that God brings into being, the Church, is the bond of love, love which is a participation in God the Holy Spirit. Within the trinitarian life of God, the Holy Spirit is the 'bond of love' ('*vinculum caritatis*').[62] In concluding *De Trinitate*, Augustine calls the Spirit 'the *communion* of both Father and Son, in some way consubstantial' ('*communio quaedam consubstantialis Patris et Filii amborum Spiritus*').[63] The Holy Spirit, who is God ('*consubstantialis*') is both the

---

[60] *De Trinitate* 1.x.

[61] 'By virtue of human nature, each human being is social' (*De Bon. Conjug.* 1).

[62] Cf. Burnaby, *Amor Dei*, p. 174.

[63] *De Trinitate* 15.l. Augustine speaks forcefully of the Spirit as the *communio* of Father and Son (cf. *De Trinitate* 5.xii) which is love, but he has often been criticised for the analogies that he uses in *De Trinitate* to illustrate the triune nature (Books 9–10) of humans and of God; first, the mind, the knowledge by which the mind knows itself, and the love with which it loves both itself and its own knowledge; second, our memory, intellect and will. Both analogies reflect too strongly the unity of the threefold 'modes' of being within the Trinity, failing to do justice to the *persons* in their *relatedness*. Augustine is not at all comfortable with social analogies for the Trinity (cf. *De Trinitate* XII.9). When Augustine speaks of the nature of God, however, he speaks of *substance*, *communio* and *love*: 'In that simplest and highest nature,

love that passes between Father and Son, and the gift of that love to humanity:

Through that which is common to the Father and the Son, They have willed that we should have communion with one another and with Them, that we should be brought together into one through That one Gift, which is of Them Both – the Holy Spirit, God and God's Gift. By that Gift are we reconciled to the Divine and made to delight therein.[64]

By the gift of the Spirit God brings into being the Church, which is the Body of Christ. In this life, human beings, who are intrinsically social, are scattered and competitive, but Christians, who are members of the Body of Christ, experience reconciliation and unity in Christ:

There are many Christians but only one Christ. The Christians themselves along with their Head, because he has ascended into heaven, form one Christ. It is not a case of His being one and our being many, but we who are many are a unity in Him. There is therefore one man, Christ, consisting of head and body.[65]

This image of the body of Christ recurs through his sermons, in which he repeatedly stresses the need for unity. One well-known passage brings together a number of favourite themes: unity, participation in the sacraments, and the gift of the Spirit:

If you are the body and members of Christ, your mystery (*sacramentum*) is placed upon the table of the Lord: you receive your mystery. To that which you are you respond 'Amen', and by responding you give your assent . . . Why then is (Christ) in bread? Let us not put forward any teaching of our own, but listen to the repeated teaching of the Apostle; for, he says, speaking of this sacrament, 'We, being many, are one bread, one body.' Understand and rejoice: unity, truth, goodness, love. 'One loaf.' What is that one loaf? . . . Remember that the bread is not made from one grain of wheat but many. When you were exorcised, you were, in a manner, ground; when baptised, you were, in a manner, moistened. When you received the fire of the Holy Spirit, you were in a manner cooked. Be what you see, and receive what you are.[66]

substance should not be one thing and love another, but . . . substance itself should be love, and love itself should be substance, . . . and yet the Holy Spirit should specially be called love.' (*De Trinitate* 15.xxix (PNCF III, p. 216); cf. 15.l).

[64] *Sermon* 71.18, quoted Burnaby, *Amor Dei*, p. 177.   [65] *Enarr. in Pss.* 127.3.

[66] *Sermon* 272, cf. *Sermon* 227. See E. Mersch, *The Whole Christ* (London: Dennis Dobson, 1938), pp. 412–40.

Burnaby stresses how, for Augustine, 'God has made men apt to find their completion in communion, because such communion is a likeness of (he might have said "participation in") the mutual love in which and through which Three Persons are One God . . . What St Augustine's doctrine of the Holy Spirit means is that the perfection of love is spiritual *koinonia* or fellowship.'[67] This is what Christians experience now within the communion that is the Body of Christ.

This communion constitutes the Church as Augustine experienced it and knew it ought to be in all the world. Loyalty to this communion, over against those who would break it, is what he stood for as a bishop in the turbulent North African church, which had a history of rigorism and schism. In the clarity of his thinking about the unity of the Church as the unity of communion, Augustine was indebted to Cyprian, whose view of the importance of unity in the Catholic Church was uncompromising,[68] but Augustine was a thinker of a later age, who, though he shared Cyprian's concerns in the face of rigorist opposition, recognised that the Church as it is known in the world is a '*corpus permixtum*'. We can never be sure about the ultimate perseverance and destiny of any particular person or group, though we can be sure about the perseverance in communion of the Church as a whole, through the activity of the Holy Spirit. In Augustine's time the concern of the Church was no longer survival in the face of persecution by hostile authorities, but recovery from the long-term effects of that persecution, including the Donatist schism, and steadiness in a period when the *pax Romana* was in a state of terminal collapse. He was passionately concerned to teach and to exemplify the way in which God sustained the distinctive life of the Church, urging his fellow-members to live more fully as what they were, members of the Body of Christ. It was not their business, in this

---

[67] Burnaby, *Amor Dei*, p. 306.

[68] Cyprian's influential *De Catholicae Ecclesiae Unitate*, is the first theological treatise on this subject. Whilst Augustine agreed with Cyprian on the essential unity of the Body of Christ and the vital role of bishops, both individually and collegially, in maintaining that unity, he disagreed with Cyprian's rigorist stance towards schismatics like the Novatianists and (later) the Donatists. Augustine worked forcefully for reconciliation but he did not insist on the re-baptism of schismatics.

world of wheat and tares, to expect absolute clarity in dis-
cerning who was living faithfully and who was not, but to
concentrate on living in the unity of communion. Who would
ultimately be in and who out was better left to God.

Augustine saw the Catholic Church as a worldwide communion, maintained in truth and love by the Holy Spirit. His own
experience of church life was much more localised as he
devoted himself single-mindedly to the care of his diocese at
Hippo and the common life of the monastic community in
which he lived. Hence the importance for his theology of
communion of his sermons and his community rule.[69] Augustine's rule is patently written by the same man as the one who so
exposed his soul in the *Confessions*. The aim is unity: 'to live
harmoniously (*unianimes*) in the house and to have one heart and
one soul seeking God'. In one phrase Augustine echoes Psalm
68:6, '*Deus qui inhabitare facit unianimes in Domo*' ('God who makes
those of one mind to dwell together in one house')[70] and Psalm
23:6, '*ut inhabitem in domo Domini, in longitudine dierum*' ('that I may
dwell in the house of the Lord for ever'). Such a life in
community is the practical realisation on earth of the life of the
heavenly Jerusalem and echoes Acts 4:32, 'Now the company of
those who believed were of one heart and soul, and no one said
that any of the things which he possessed was his own, but they
had everything in common.' Augustine writes that, 'Those who
owned anything in the world should freely consent to possess
everything in common in the monastery.' In the monastery, the
divisive consequences of the Fall are overcome. Humans live in
community, realising on earth something of the heavenly life for
which we are ultimately intended.

This is Augustine's ideal of communion, a communion realised but not consummated in history. His telling of the story by
which this communion has been realised in history gave to the
West the shape of history itself. It was the brilliant insight of
Augustine which showed history to be in its essence the story of
communion.

---

[69] See G. Lawless, *Augustine of Hippo and his Monastic Rule* (Oxford: Clarendon Press, 1987).

[70] Here I have followed the Old Latin for Psalm 68:7.

CHAPTER 9

Ecumenism and the practice of communion

The starting point for this study was the recognition that the term *koinonia* has been used almost universally in current ecumenical discussion: in bilateral discussions like those of the Anglican–Roman Catholic International Commission and the Roman Catholic–Orthodox dialogue, and in multilateral discussions like those of the World Council of Churches' Baptism, Eucharist, and Ministry process, and the Fifth World Conference on Faith and Order, whose report was entitled *On the Way to Fuller Koinonia.*[1] Within the Roman Catholic Church there has since Vatican 2 (1962–5) been a striking convergence around the self-understanding of the Church as *communion.* There has also been a new recognition of the communion that already exists, though in various ways impaired, between the Roman Catholic Church and other ecclesial bodies. This willingness to recognise the ecclesial life of churches not in communion with the Bishop of Rome has brought Roman Catholicism much more fully into the ecumenical movement.

If the churches have been discovering each other afresh in *koinonia,* this has by no means been simply a process of convergence. It has also been a process in which boundaries, such as those marked by the ordination of women to the priesthood and episcopacy, and episcopacy itself, are being drawn more sharply. In this sense, the facing of new issues and new social situations is causing churches to review, and in some cases to

---

[1] T. F. Best and G. Gassmann eds., *On the Way to Fuller Koinonia,* Faith and Order Paper 166 (Geneva: WCC, 1994).

define more sharply, the limits to communion.[2] There are real tensions here, which are far from being resolved.

It has been my intention in this study to contribute towards a theory and practice of *koinonia* in the strength of which the Christian churches will be able to draw closer together, despite the tensions they experience as they seek to do so. Only if churches can deepen their *koinonia* in the midst of the tensions that threaten to pull them apart can they truly exercise their ministry of reconciliation in a divided world.

The first task was simply to survey the ecumenical scene, showing how widespread is the use of the term *koinonia*, and the number of ecumenical issues that are raised by examining its use within bilateral and multilateral ecumenical discussions. We then turned to Plato because it is not always realised among theologians how central to Plato's philosophy was his understanding of *koinonia*, nor is it always realised to what extent Christian doctrine, especially ecclesiology, has been interpreted through a kind of received platonism. The point here is that the novelty of the Christian understanding of *koinonia* emerged not over against, nor above, nor beside, but within a baggy tradition of largely platonic philosophical thought, an understanding of which is as necessary to our understanding of the mystery of the Church as an understanding of Second Temple Judaism is to the mystery of Jesus Christ.

No one has identified more sharply the dangers in Plato's thought than Karl Popper, whose *The Open Society and its Enemies* still sounds a grim warning against all naive platonism: 'There was an Inquisition; and, in another form, it may come again.'[3] The dangers of identifying any human society, sacred or secular, with some utopian vision (such as that of Plato) cannot be stated too strongly. Popper, who showed how Plato presented a vision of Athens which incorporated some of the most repressive features of the life of Sparta, argued passionately that community of wives and children in a male-dominated society, strict

---

[2] The statement by the Roman Catholic Bishops of Britain and Ireland, *One Bread, One Body* (London: CTS, 1998) has been drawn up expressly for this purpose.
[3] K. R. Popper, *The Open Society and its Enemies*, 2 vols. (London: Routledge and Kegan Paul, 1945), vol. 1, p. 104.

regulation of the educational programme, and restriction of artistic activity to the edifying and ideologically correct, would be too high a price to pay for the humane society that Plato wished to construct. Even the questioning wisdom of Socrates, which readily deconstructs received understandings, is ultimately, as the circumstances of his death show, presented by Plato as deeply loyal to the state. Plato's understanding of political *koinonia* is fundamentally conformist and in a century of terrible conformism, we need to ask of any *koinonia* what it does to its Socratic dissidents. In Plato's *Republic* the issue is raised in terms of the artists: if they do not produce work that is sufficiently edifying, they are to be expelled. Here *koinonia* comes to mean something like enforced consensus, and its instrument to be censorship in the hands of those who claim the power to discern what that consensus is or should be. This is the threat personified by that servant of earthly *koinonia*, Dostoyevsky's Grand Inquisitor.

No less than Plato, Aristotle believed that it is possible within human society to discern and hold onto the Good. His hierarchy of *koinoniai*, from the male–female bond, through the village, to the *polis*, is also a hierarchy of social bonds in which each person has to learn how to live according to virtue. Unlike Plato, he leaves it to citizens to recognise and cultivate virtue as best they can within the possibilities and constraints of their life in the *polis*. Aristotle is much more sensitive than Plato to the ambiguities of the structured co-operation and participation that this requires, something that has in recent years given rise to lively discussion.[4] The problem we identified with Aristotle's use of *koinonia* comes in another area: that of ontology. Aristotle's account of being is central to his whole philosophy and enormously influential for later Christian theology. It is developed in critique of Plato, particularly Plato's view of this world as but a pale shadow of an 'ideal' world. Aristotle is always concerned to illuminate the way *this* world is. He applies himself to this by his study of particular entities in his *Physics*, by his accounts of natural history, and by his studies of human

---

[4] The seminal text is A. MacIntyre, *After Virtue*, second edition (London: Duckworth, 1985), especially pp. 256–63.

societies in his *Ethics* and *Politics*. One might think that because of his inductive approach, which moves from observation of discrete entities (each of which is what Mackinnon calls a 'nuclear realisation of being')[5] to what they have in common, from 'primary' to 'secondary' substance, that he would view society as an aggregate of individuals, but he does not. Human *society* in all its forms is for Aristotle a foundational reality. 'Man' is the *koinonikon zoon*, the animal made for *koinonia*, or, elsewhere, the *politikon zoon*, the animal made for life in the *polis*.

Aristotle is more of a realist than Plato. He recognises that *poleis* are not going to be perfect and that, given the way we function, we have to look for the best kind of constitution we can actually live with. This is prudent and attractive. When he says, in outlining what makes for the best possible state, 'A city can be excellent only when the citizens who have a share in the government are excellent . . . let us then enquire how a man becomes excellent',[6] he goes on to develop an account of education as a process which is in principle lifelong. His philosophy of belonging to the state is in some ways remarkably similar to Plato's: 'Neither must we suppose that any one of the citizens belong to himself, for they all belong to the state, and are each of them a part of the state, and the care of each part is inseparable from the care of the whole.'[7] The debt to Plato is obvious, but so is the development away from a monolithic understanding that places great weight on a 'philosopher king' to rule, guardians to act as an elite, common ownership of women, children, and property, and a social blueprint in the heavens.

Aristotle's humane social vision is not, however, adequately linked to his metaphysics of substance. He gives no account of what we might call 'the substance (or being) of relation'. Thus, when Christian writers began to ask metaphysical questions about the *koinonia* of human beings with each other, or with God, or within God, it was all too easy to see the primary realities as those of individual human beings, or the Father and

---

[5] S. W. Sykes and J. P. Clayton eds., *Christ, Faith and History* (Cambridge: Cambridge University Press, 1972), p. 281.

[6] *Politics* VII.13; 1332a. 33–5.   [7] *Politics* VIII.1; 1337a. 27–30.

the Son, and subsequently to consider the Spirit, or relation, as the necessary, secondary bond between pre-existent entities.

One of the most creative modern attempts to rethink ontology, giving priority to the Spirit, is Geoffrey Lampe's Bampton Lectures, *God as Spirit*.[8] Lampe is notably unsympathetic to the development of trinitarian doctrine: he finds in the tradition of Christian writing about relations within the Trinity attempts to define differences without real distinctions, and so he offers a monism of Spirit, concluding that, 'The Trinitarian model is in the end less satisfactory for the articulation of our basic Christian experience than the unifying concept of God as Spirit.'[9] Lampe's emphasis upon the being of God as the being of Spirit is to be welcomed, but not his lack of Trinitarian differentiation, which does away with the need for actual *relating* in God. To say that *God relates to us* as Spirit is not the same thing as to say that *relation is of the essence of God*. The first is the position taken by liberal Protestant theologies of communion (such as that of Schleiermacher); the second is that taken by Trinitarian theologies of communion such as those of the Cappadocians, Augustine, and most contemporary ecumenical agreed statements.

To understand the 'life-world' of the early Christian communities, it was necessary to look not only at the Hellenistic background suggested by the use of the very word *koinonia*, but also at the Jewish tradition in which Jesus and the early Christians were formed, which was a tradition of covenant. This is a tradition of 'belonging' quite different to anything in Hellenism, for the Jews see themselves as the descendants of one man, Abraham, to whom a son was born by the action of God when he and his wife were no longer fertile. Through this promise, the sign of which is borne by every circumcised male Jew, and this event, from which all Jews trace their descent, and through a series of other such specific divine actions, as with Moses at Sinai, there was sealed a specific covenant bond between God and his people, and therefore among the people themselves. At every point in life, in birth, puberty, marriage,

---

[8] Geoffrey Lampe, *God as Spirit* (London: SCM, 1977).   [9] *Ibid.*, p. 228.

and death, in the weekly and yearly cycle of time, in eating, and sleeping, and waking, the Jew is reminded of this bond. The point to note here is that this covenant-bond was constituted by divine initiative, by election, but that this election carried with it the responsibility of faithfulness, and the expectation that this faithfulness would be a blessing to all people. There is about the Jewish understanding of covenant both an exclusiveness (when the Jews are faithful to the covenant there is complete clarity about who belongs to the community and who does not) and an inclusiveness (the blessing to Abraham is ultimately to be a blessing to all the nations). What the Jews brought to the Hellenistic world was an understanding of sustained divine–human relation: a personal God inviting his people into *koinonia*, or covenant, with himself, and so into *koinonia* with each other, *koinonia* constituted by their being 'children of Abraham'.

The understanding of *koinonia* here is focused on the specific choice of a community, which carries with it the specific ethical and ritual demands involved in that choice. We have to be careful, however, of being simplistic about our understanding. Though the horizon for the whole of Jewish understanding was one of covenant, the form that this covenantal experience took was by no means uniform. We saw how at the time of the Maccabees the outward signs of covenantal belonging, circumcision, keeping of dietary laws, and sabbath-keeping, took on a new symbolic significance, and how a sectarian community like that of Qumran could see itself in an exclusive way as that of the 'community of the everlasting covenant' over against the rest of Israel. What it meant to observe the demands of the covenant, what it meant to keep the law, was a matter of lively debate which continues even today. There was nothing simple or monolithic about Second Temple period covenant belief and practice.

This understanding of covenant, and of election, was carried over into the life of the New Testament communities. The ethical and ritual demands of the relation between the believers and Christ were similarly seen as implicit in the fundamental relation which constitutes the community. This is captured by Paul's use of the term 'in Christ'. To be 'in Christ', or to be 'a member of the body of Christ' is to be in relation with Christ and with other Christians. The use of the term *koinonia* in the New Testament suggests some of the characteristics of this relational matrix as it was experienced within the early Christian communities. In Paul's writing, there is the emphasis on the bread and the wine of the eucharist as a *koinonia* in the body and blood of Christ, on the sharing of goods through the collection for the Jerusalem Christians, on mutual sharing of sufferings, of comfort, and in all this the repeated imperative of unity. At various points it is clear that there is a *koinonia* between the members of the community which is brought about by and in the Spirit, which is the Spirit of Jesus Christ. The beginning of Acts gives a picture of the Jerusalem community having all things in common, and of the members of the community devoting themselves to the *koinonia*, to the common life, an ideal to which early Christian writers return again and again. In the letters of John, this *koinonia* is seen as a sharing in or with the Father and the Son, and as bringing with it the clear ethical demand to walk in the light and to abstain from sin. In 2 Peter 1:4, Christians are called 'partakers (*koinonoi*) of the divine nature'. When these scattered and unsystematic uses of *koinonia* and its cognates are put together, we have a picture of the common life in little Christian communities that experienced themselves as communities of the new (or renewed) covenant, constituted by their sharing in Christ and the Spirit.

It was vital for their survival that these little Christian communities developed means of staying in touch with one another, and of deciding which other communities were to be recognised as authentic. There is abundant evidence of conflict within and around the earliest churches, and of lively struggles amongst various groups who wished to be seen as within the *koinonia*, or to determine who else could be similarly recognised. In the New Testament, there is witness to sharp discrimination as to who is in and who is out, and to the emergence of criteria by which authoritative pronouncements relating to boundaries, to inclusion and exclusion, can be made in succeeding generations. The need for a succession of recognised leaders, who would make provision for the authentic continuance of the community according to the tradition that had been received, was paramount. In both the letters to the Corinthians, in the letters of John and in the Acts of the Apostles, conflicts and struggles for power, focusing on the authentic transmission of the tradition, and the recognition of leaders, can be seen as the presupposition for the writing of the texts. The continuing question for the body of Christ is not whether there will be conflict within the body, but how it will deal with the conflicts that inevitably arise.

The question of tradition is thus one that is central to the life of the churches. Terry Eagleton has written of 'that tangle of crimes, blunders, oversights and off-chances . . . which goes by the name of tradition',[10] a description which implies salutary warning against too purist an understanding of what is a messy and conflictual dynamic. The politics of tradition, which are the politics of the *reception* of tradition, are central to the identity of the Christian Church. In any process of transmission, the question of tradition – of what to receive and what not to receive, and who makes the decision on what grounds – will be a matter of continuing and lively debate, that is to say a matter of dialogue and conflict. Stephen Sykes has drawn attention to Gallie's discussion of the 'essentially contested concept', by which he means a term such as 'justice' or 'democracy' which is used repeatedly in discussion and which gives rise to a chronic series of disputes. It is *characteristic* of the term to give rise to such disputes, so we should not be surprised at their recurrence. Sykes suggests that Christianity is an 'essentially contested concept' and that what Christian unity amounts to is 'contained diversity'.[11] He characterises Christian identity in dynamic terms: 'Christian identity is . . . not a state but a process; a process, moreover, which entails the restlessness of a dialectic, impelled by criticism.'[12] For Sykes, it is imperative that the community in which this process is worked out is a community held in unity by common worship. This is where the ecumenical question has to be pressed: how diverse can 'contained diver-

10 Terry Eagleton, *The Crisis of Contemporary Culture* (Oxford: Clarendon Press, 1993).
11 S. W. Sykes, *The Identity of Christianity* (London: SPCK, 1984), pp. 262, 11.
12 *Ibid.*, p. 285.

sity' be in the community that celebrates the eucharist, and how is that decision to be made? Churches and theologians may be able, in creeds, confessions, and joint agreed statements to bring the heartland of Christianity into reasonably sharp *verbal or conceptual* focus. The problem remains as to how sharp and how extensive that focus needs to be before we can properly enter or re-enter the *koinonia* of the eucharist.

To pursue this line of 'contained diversity' a little further, we turn to Chrétien Duquoc, whose *Provisional Churches*[13] is a polemic against platonist assumptions in ecclesiology. Duquoc begins from the givenness of *diversity* amongst the churches, and rejects all assumptions about an original or an ideal unity:

> Far from needing to be marginalized in an unfortunate accident of our history, on the contrary the fact that there are many churches forms the starting-point for theological and ecclesiological thought. If we forget this empirical multiplicity we tend towards an idealistic way of thinking: and in that case the church that is spoken of is no longer our historical church, as we find it, but its ideal. And it is not far from thinking in ideal terms to imposing norms on concrete reality, or from the imposition of norms to repressive measures . . . So I consider that it is necessary to abandon the classical approach to ecclesiology.[14]

For Duquoc, the churches are 'provisional societies', whose provisionality consists in 'the condition of innovation, of continual creation, of presence in changing situations'. He finds that it is 'in the positive acceptance of plurality that the churches, by their capacity for communion, bear witness to the ultimate'.[15] Duquoc's scepticism (going beyond even that of Walter Bauer) about an original unity in the churches, and his emphasis upon innovation, are challenging, but when he appeals to 'communion', the question of the *limits* to diversity, and of the *integrity* of a 'Church of churches', has once more to be faced. Where Sykes puts great weight on *common worship* to maintain unity, Duqoc stresses *communion*, without spelling out how that communion is to be recognised, or what structures are required for the maintenance of communion in love and in

---

[13] C. Duquoc, *Provisional Churches: An Essay in Ecumenical Ecclesiology* (London: SCM, 1986).
[14] *Ibid.*, pp. vii–viii.   [15] *Ibid.*, pp. 91, 110.

truth. By refusing adequately to face the historical question of communion, Duquoc begs the central question of ecumenism.

The central, continuing task for the Christian Church is the contemporary appropriation of a common life which has over many generations been mediated by classic texts and actions (the Scriptures, the creeds, patterns of ministry, the sacraments, ethical action). To speak in this manner of a hermeneutic of tradition or traditions is to imply that the faithful interpreters must actually participate in the common life, in this case the *koinonia* that is grounded in the life of God, and that this participation will condition their theological interpretation. Christian theology is a dimension of the common life; participation in the common life is a precondition for specifically Christian theology.[16] Commitment to the *koinonia* within and between the churches is thus a commitment to faithful interpretation of tradition and the agonised debates this causes. It is a matter of faith, that when those debates become deadlocked, in the very activity of mutual dialogue there will emerge a deeper and more truthful *koinonia*. Here we have to argue against the premature foreclosing of debates, against comfortable *koinonia* (the ecclesiastical equivalent of 'the neighbourhood watch'), the illegitimate manufacture and imposition of consensus that is ultimately a failure of faith in God the Holy Spirit to lead God's people through the wilderness into all truth; but this study has repeatedly shown that there must be limits to diversity, and it is the central theological task of ecumenism to agree upon them.

When we came to the Cappadocians we entered a very different world of discourse. It was the Cappadocians who took the language of Greek philosophy and used it in a *theological* register to support and develop a new and creative statement of

---

[16] This is not at all to say there is nothing to be learnt from theological critiques that come from outside Christianity. Attention to such critiques is vital to the health of the churches. The point is different: Christian theologians have to reckon with, and accept, the properly ideological nature of their own activity in the service of the *koinonia* of the Word and of the Spirit. There is *no* critique which operates without presuppositions rooted within the tenets and life of specific communities. In this respect Christian theology as such is no more compromised than other less obviously ideological forms of critique.

Trinitarian orthodoxy. The struggle at the outset of the Arian controversy in the first quarter of the fourth century had been to find a way both of speaking of the unity of the Son with humanity in the incarnation and the unity of the Son with the Father in the fullness of deity without token participation in humanity and without subordination of the Son to the Father. The solution in both respects was to speak of identity of *ousia* whilst in other respects differentiating between the only-begotten Son and created human beings, and the only-begotten Son and the unbegotten Father. The part played by the Spirit in the life of God remained theologically undeveloped until the third quarter of the fourth century. We have seen that Basil, though returning again and again to the deifying role of the Spirit, avoided using the word '*homoousios*' for the unity of the Spirit with the Father and the Son, preferring to speak in terms of '*koinonia*'. The Spirit engenders *koinonia* with the Father and the Son because the Spirit shares in *koinonia* with the Father and the Son. In the light of Basil's acceptance of the formulation that in God there is 'one substance; three hypostases' ('*mia ousia; treis hypostaseis*'), it is clear that for him the Spirit is the co-equal third member of the Trinity, and that the threefold hypostases cannot be understood without unity of substance, nor the unity of substance without the threefold hypostases.

It is Gregory of Nazianzen who makes this plain. The 'Cappadocian formula' of '*mia ousia; treis hypostaseis*' is carefully balanced to give priority neither to unity nor diversity. It is a moot point, given the stress upon the *arche* of the Father as the originating principle of deity, how successfully this is sustained, but the formula itself is carefully balanced. When the Cappadocians took into their Trinitarian understanding of divinity the language of *koinonia*, they were careful to maintain this balance, neither atomising the unity of the godhead, so it became a prototypical society of three entities, nor coalescing the relation of persons within the Godhead so the unity took precedence over the three distinct 'modes of relation'. Beyond this, in speaking of the nature of the Trinity, we cannot go, but we can usefully enter a *caveat*.

For the Cappadocians especially, the mystery of God was

expressed only with utter poverty through the medium of language. The language was merely an invitation to enter into what they variously spoke of as the divine darkness and the divine light to experience union with God. The 'Cappadocian formula' is far less a linguistic theorem than a dynamic paradox, like the paradox of the bush which burnt with living fire and yet remained the same, because it was not consumed. If the nature of God is *koinonia*, then divine *koinonia* is a living and burning reality in which there is constant renewal and still there is perfect identity. This is not, however, a self-enclosed *koinonia*. The believer is invited to participate in the very life, the *koinonia* of God, made known in Christ, by the Spirit.

At this point it is not really possible to drive a wedge between Augustine and the Cappadocians. Augustine returns again and again to our participation in the divine life, but also to the distinction between ourselves and God: as he puts it in the *City of God*, 'It is one thing to be God; another to participate in God.' ('*Alium enim esse Deum; alium particem Dei.*')[17] Participation for Augustine is the key to the Incarnation. He says of Christ, 'God himself . . . became partaker of our human nature and thus offered us a short cut to participation in his divine nature.'[18] On human participation in the life of God, human communion with God, he has a great deal to say that is excellent, but, like the Cappadocians, he struggles to find terminology to speak of the divine tri-unity:

For, in truth, as the Father is not the Son, and the Son is not the Father, and that Holy Spirit, who is also called the gift of God, is neither the Father nor the Son, certainly they are three . . . Yet when the question is asked, What three? human language labours altogether under great poverty of speech. The answer is given, three persons, not that it might be spoken, but that it might not be left unspoken.[19]

It is Augustine's intuition that the 'spiritual substance' of God is love, and that the believer *participates* in this love without becoming consubstantial with God. Once more we return to the point that the being of God is relational, and that human beings are invited to enter into relation with God. Augustine

---

[17] *CD* 22.xxx.   [18] *CD* 9.xvi.   [19] *De Trinitate* 5.x.

tells the story of his own communion with God by setting it in the context of all communion in God. His account of the love that he knows leads him back to its ground: the love that is within the Trinity. Those who share in the communion of the Church of God share in the communion of God, the communion that is God. This is why for Augustine sacramental communion and unity are indivisible manifestations of the one divine reality.

It was the fragility of human communion that awakened in Augustine the quest for communion that could not be broken. What the Christian tradition asserts, ultimately from the story of Jesus, is that no breakdown of *koinonia* is ever finally irretrievable, even though reconciliation may come beyond the grave. Thus within every human meeting there is an implicit hope of unbroken *koinonia* (compare Habermas' 'ideal speech situation') even though this is not our experience now. In any account of *koinonia* that is true to the reality of our experience, we have to look at what actually takes place within the flow of time, which is an experience of *koinonia* as memory, as hope, and perhaps, for a moment in time, as experience, but never as unbroken and unbreakable possession. It is the longing within time for this possession, which could only be realised outside time, which is expressed so eloquently by Augustine, when he speaks out of the experience in the 'land of unlikeness' of a shared communion with God that can be traced in him back to the beginning of time and forward to its ending. When we speak of *koinonia* between or among humans we are speaking of a process which involves conflict, reconciliation, and risk. When we speak of *koinonia* between members of churches or between churches, exactly the same dynamics are present, but they are explicitly set against an eschatological horizon of unbreakable communion, that is to say the unbroken coinherence of the Trinity.

The paradigm of earthly conflict, risk, and reconciliation must for Christians be the self-giving of Jesus in his ministry and death, a ministry characterised by conflict with his family and his disciples, who failed to understand him and at times sought to prevent him doing what he perceived to be the will of God, and conflict with the religious authorities who sought to have him silenced. The agony in the garden is an agony of self-commitment to the will of the Father, to sustained *koinonia*, and it is in the strength of this sustaining *koinonia*, but otherwise alone, that Jesus faces the risk of annihilation entailed by his own death. The cry of dereliction, 'My God, my God, why hast thou forsaken me?' is the cry of broken communion; it is the point at which communion can only be sustained as it were 'one-sidedly', whether by the fidelity of God to the one who experiences no communion, fidelity demonstrated in the resurrection, or even, as has been explored in post-Holocaust Jewish theology, by the fidelity of the forsaken to the God who forsakes.

What this means for the Church can only be spelt out in terms of a practice which incorporates a doctrine, not a doctrine from which a practice can be derived. The nature of Christian knowing is participatory; it never operates according to some disengaged ideal of 'scientific' knowing. The paradigm for such knowing is the activity of the Christian in worship. To gather with others for worship is to be united explicitly in communion (*epi to auto*) for a brief space. The form of liturgy will for this brief space both obviate conflict, and take up into itself (e.g. in the prayers) conflicts experienced within the life of the Church. The paradigm of worship for the local church is the eucharist ('Holy Communion'), the central symbolic action of the Christian faith, in which the conflict and the risk in Christ's dying is incorporated within the wider liturgical affirmation of the resurrection. In the sharing of the bread and the wine of the eucharist there is an *anamnesis* of the giving of the body and the blood of Christ. The eucharist is always an action of hope because within it the annihilation of the crucifixion is transcended in the *koinonia* of the living body, united at worship.

The unity of the churches will not come through the steady flow of ecumenical agreed statements that spell out the virtues of *koinonia*, though they have their part to play. The way forward must include the practice of a common life, which provides a context for the continuing theological debate. Building unity in all its dimensions, whether through joint action, through common study of the Scriptures, through shared intellectual engagement with complex issues, through prophetic action, or prayer, is the continuing task of the churches, who recognise themselves as already, inalienably in *communion*. The starting point remains that the Christian churches see themselves as already bound by a unity (a communion) of Word and Spirit, of baptism and shared, if fractured, tradition, which reaches forward towards the hope of a yet more inclusive unity at the eucharist. It is vital that when the moments of discouragement, of apparently irreconcilable difference, come, that the effort to build *koinonia* continues, which in the short term means a preparedness to face conflict and the risk (even the experience) of separation. What makes such risk-taking possible is the presence of the Spirit, for the substance of relation is the substance of the Spirit, and it is the presence of the Spirit in each human encounter, whether between individuals or communities, whether for a moment or miraculously sustained, whether in agreement or disagreement, which makes each such encounter a moment of new creation and a fresh occasion of hope. It is the activity of the Spirit that generates the common life; it is the hearing of the Word and the sharing of the sacraments, to the fullest possible extent, that distinguishes the common life of Christian churches as a participation in the life of Jesus Christ; it is the worship of the Father and the service of the world that bears witness to this common life as a *koinonia* in the life of the triune God.

Select bibliography

Anglican–Roman Catholic International Commission, *The Final Report* (London: SPCK/CTS, 1982)

Annas, J. *An Introduction to Plato's Republic* (Oxford: Clarendon Press, 1981)

Apostolicity and Succession, House of Bishops' Occasional Paper (London: General Synod of the Church of England, 1994)

Aristotle, *Categories* and *De Interpretatione*, translated and edited by J. L. Ackrill (Oxford: Clarendon Press, 1963)

Eudemian Ethics, translated by H. Rackham, LCL 285, revised edition (Cambridge, Mass.: Harvard University Press, 1952)

Nicomachean Ethics, translated by H. Rackham, LCL 73, revised edition (Cambridge, Mass.: Harvard University Press, 1934)

The Politics, translated with notes by E. Barker (Oxford: Clarendon Press, 1948)

The Politics, edited by S. Everson (Cambridge: Cambridge University Press, 1988)

The Politics, translated by H. Rackham, LCL 264, reprinted with corrections (Cambridge, Mass.: Harvard University Press, 1944)

Armstrong, A. H. (ed.) *The Cambridge History of Later Greek and Early Medieval Philosophy* (Cambridge: Cambridge University Press, 1967)

Athanasius, *The Life of Antony*, translated with an introduction by R. C. Gregg, CWS series (London: SPCK, 1980)

Augustine, *City of God*, translated by H. Bettenson, Penguin Classics (Harmondsworth: Penguin, 1972)

Augustine, *La Cité de Dieu*, text from fourth edition of B. Dombart and A. Kalb, introduction and notes by G. Bardy, *Bibliothèque Augustinienne*, 5 vols. (Paris: Desclée de Brouwer, 1959–60)

Les Confessions, text from edition of M. Skutella, introduction and notes by A. Solignac, *Bibliothèque Augustinienne*, 2 vols. (Paris: Desclée de Brouwer, 1962)

Confessions, translated by H. Chadwick, World's Classics (Oxford: Oxford University Press, 1992)

Confessions, translated by R. S. Pine-Coffin, Penguin Classics (Harmondsworth, 1961)

Confessions, translated by William Watts, LCL 26–7, 2 vols. (Cambridge, Mass.: Harvard University Press; London: Heinemann, 1912)

La Trinité, vol.1 translation and notes by M. Mellet and T. Camelot, introduction by E. Hendrikx, vol. 2 translation by P. Agaësse, notes by J. Moingt, *Bibliothèque Augustinienne*, 2 vols. (Paris: Desclée de Brouwer, 1955)

On the Trinity, translated by A. W. Haddan, PNCF III (Edinburgh: T. and T. Clark, 1993)

Banks, R. *Paul's Idea of Community*, revised edition (Peabody, Mass.: Hendrickson, 1994)

Baptism, Eucharist and Ministry, Faith and Order Paper 111 (Geneva: WCC, 1982)

Baptism, Eucharist and Ministry 1982–1990, Report on the Process and Responses, Faith and Order Paper 149 (Geneva: WCC, 1990)

Barker, E. *Greek Political Theory* (University Paperbacks edition, London: Methuen, 1960)

Barnes, J. *Aristotle* in *Founders of Thought* (Oxford: Oxford University Press, 1982)

(ed.) *The Cambridge Companion to Aristotle* (Cambridge: Cambridge University Press, 1995)

(ed.) *The Complete Works of Aristotle*, Bollingen Series LXXI.2, 2 vols. (Princeton: Princeton University Press, 1984)

Barr, J. *The Semantics of Biblical Language* (Oxford: Oxford University Press, 1961)

Basil de Caesarée (Basil of Caesarea), *Sur le Saint-Esprit*, edited by B. Pruche, *SC* 17 bis (Paris: Cerf, 1968)

Basil of Caesarea, *The Ascetic Works of Saint Basil*, edited by W. K. L. Clarke (London: SPCK, 1925)

Letters and Select Works, PNCF VIII (Grand Rapids: Eerdmans; Edinburgh: T. and T. Clark, 1996)

Basil the Great (Basil of Caesarea), *On the Holy Spirit* (Crestwood, New York: St Vladimir's Seminary Press, 1980)

Bauer, W. *Orthodoxy and Heresy in Earliest Christianity* (Philadelphia: Fortress Press, 1971)

Bernstein, R. J. *Beyond Objectivism and Relativism: Science, Hermeneutics and Praxis* (Oxford: Basil Blackwell, 1983)

Best, T. and Gassmann, G. (eds.) *On the Way to Fuller Koinonia* (Geneva: WCC, 1994)

Bockmuehl, M. and Thompson, M. B. (eds.) *A Vision for the Church* (Edinburgh: T. and T. Clark, 1997)

Bolgar, R. R. *The Classical Heritage and its Beneficiaries* (Cambridge: Cambridge University Press, 1954)

Bonhoeffer, D. *Sanctorum Communio* (London: Collins, 1963)

Breslauer, S. D. *Covenant and Community in Modern Judaism* (New York: Greenwood Press, 1989)

Brown, P. *Augustine of Hippo* (London: Faber and Faber, 1967)

Brown, R. E. *The Churches the Apostles Left Behind* (London: Geoffrey Chapman, 1984)

The Community of the Beloved Disciple (London: Geoffrey Chapman, 1979)

Burnaby, J. *Amor Dei* (London: Hodder and Stoughton, 1938)

Burtchaell, J. T. *From Synagogue to Church* (Cambridge: Cambridge University Press, 1992)

Campbell, J. Y. 'Koinonia and its Cognates in the New Testament', reprinted from *Journal of Biblical Literature* 51 (1932), 352–82 in *Three New Testament Studies* (Leiden: E. J. Brill, 1965)

Catechism of the Catholic Church (London: Geoffrey Chapman, 1994)

Chadwick, H. *Augustine* (Oxford: Oxford University Press, 1986)

Christiansen, E. J. *The Covenant in Judaism and Paul* (Leiden: E. J. Brill, 1995)

Clarke, W. K. L. *St Basil the Great, a Study in Monasticism* (Cambridge: Cambridge University Press, 1913)

Collingwood, R. G. *An Autobiography* (Oxford: Oxford University Press, 1939)

Confessing the One Faith, Faith and Order Paper 153 (Geneva: WCC, 1991)

Cornford, F. M. *Plato and Parmenides* (London: Kegan Paul, Trench, Trubner, 1939)

Plato's Theory of Knowledge, The Theaetetus and the Sophist of Plato (London: Routledge and Kegan Paul, 1935)

Courcelle, P. *Recherches sur les Confessions de Saint Augustin*, nouvelle edn (Paris: Editions de Bocard, 1968)

Crick, B. *In Defence of Politics*, fourth edition (London: Penguin, 1993)

de Halleux, A. *Patrologie et Oecumanisme* (Leuven: Peeters, 1990)

de Vaux, R. *Ancient Israel*, second edition (London: Darton, Longman and Todd, 1965)

Douglas, M. *Natural Symbols* (Harmondsworth: Penguin, 1973)

Dunn, J. D. G. *The Partings of the Ways* (London: SCM; Philadelphia: Trinity Press International, 1991)

The Theology of Paul the Apostle (Edinburgh: T. and T. Clark, 1998)

Duquoc, C. *Provisional Churches: An Essay in Ecumenical Ecclesiology* (London: SCM, 1986)

Elert, W. *Eucharist and Church Fellowship in the First Four Centuries* (Saint Louis, Missouri: Concordia, 1966)

Esler, P. F. *Community and Gospel in Luke-Acts* (Cambridge: Cambridge University Press, 1987)

Evans, G. R. *Augustine on Evil* (Cambridge: Cambridge University Press, 1982)

   The Church and the Churches (Cambridge: Cambridge University Press, 1994)

   Method in Ecumenical Theology (Cambridge: Cambridge University Press, 1996)

Ferrari, G. R. F. *Listening to the Cicadas, a Study of Plato's Phaedrus* (Cambridge: Cambridge University Press, 1952)

Figgis, J. N. *Churches in the Modern State* (London: Longmans, 1913)

Finley, M. I. *The World of Odysseus*, second edition (Harmondsworth, Penguin, 1979)

Flannery, A., O. P. (ed.) *Vatican Council II, The Conciliar and Post Conciliar Documents* (Dublin: Dominican Publications, 1975)

Gadamer, H.-G. *The Idea of the Good in Platonic–Aristotelian Philosophy* (New Haven: Yale University Press, 1986)

   Truth and Method, second, revised edition (London: Sheed and Ward, 1989)

   Wahrheit und Methode, revised edition (Tübingen: J. C. B. Mohr, 1986)

Gager, J. D. *Kingdom and Community* (Englewood Cliffs, New Jersey: Prentice-Hall, 1975)

Gassmann, G. (ed.) *Documentary History of Faith and Order 1963–1993* (Geneva: WCC, 1993)

Grégoire de Nazianze (Gregory of Nazianzen), *Discours 27–31 (Discours Théologiques)*, edited by P. Gallay, *SC* 250 (Paris: Cerf, 1978)

Gregory of Nazianzen, *Select Orations and Letters*, PNCF VII (Grand Rapids, Eerdmans; Edinburgh: T. and T. Clark, 1996)

Grégoire de Nysse (Gregory of Nyssa), *La Vie de Moise*, edited by J. Daniélou, *SC* I troisième edition (Paris: Cerf, 1968)

   Traité de la Virginité, edited by M. Aubineau, *SC* 119 (Paris: Cerf, 1966)

Gregory of Nyssa, *Ascetical Works*, translated by V. W. Callahan, FC series (Washington: Catholic University of America Press, 1967)

   The Life of Moses, translated by A. J. Malherbe and E. Ferguson, CWS series (New York: Paulist, 1978)

   Select Writings and Letters, PNCF V (Grand Rapids: Eerdmans; T. and T. Clark: Edinburgh, 1994)

Griffiss, J. E. and Martensen, D. F. *A Commentary on 'Concordat of Agreement'* (Minneapolis: Augsburg; Cincinnati: Forward Movement Publications, 1994)

Guthrie, W. K. C. *A History of Greek Philosophy*, volume 4, 'Plato, the Man and his Dialogues: Earlier Period' (Cambridge: Cambridge University Press, 1975)

  A History of Greek Philosophy, volume 5, 'The Later Plato and the Academy' (Cambridge: Cambridge University Press, 1978)

Habermas, J. *Knowledge and Human Interests*, second edition (London: Heinemann, 1978)

  The Theory of Communicative Action, 2 vols. (Boston: Beacon Press, 1984, 1987)

Hainz, J. *Koinonia, 'Kirche' als Gemeinschaft bei Paulus, Biblische Untersuchungen* 16 (Regensburg: Pustet, 1982)

Hamilton, E. and Cairns, H. (eds.) *The Collected Dialogues of Plato*, Bollingen Series LXXI (Princeton: Princeton University Press, 1963)

Hartman, D. *A Living Covenant* (London: Collier Macmillan, 1985)

Hebblethwaite, P. *Synod Extraordinary* (London: Darton, Longman and Todd, 1986)

Hengel, M. *Judaism and Hellenism* (London: SCM, 1974)

Henry, P. *La Vision d'Ostie* (Paris: J. Vrin, 1938)

Hill, C. and Yarnold, E. (eds.) *Anglicans and Roman Catholics: The Search for Unity* (London: SPCK/CTS, 1994)

Hooker, M. D. *The Gospel According to Mark*, Black's New Testament Commentaries (London: A. and C. Black, 1991)

Horrell, D. G. *The Social Ethos of the Corinthian Correspondence* (Edinburgh: T. and T. Clark, 1996)

Jeremias, J. *The Eucharistic Words of Jesus* (London: SCM, 1966)

  Jerusalem in the Time of Jesus (London: SCM, 1969)

  New Testament Theology, part one (London: SCM, 1971)

Josephus, *The Jewish War*, Books I–III, translated by H. St. J. Thackeray, LCL 203 (Cambridge, Mass.: Harvard University Press, 1927)

Kee, H. C. *Christian Origins in Sociological Perspective* (London: SCM, 1980)

  Community of the New Age (London: SCM, 1977)

Kenny, A. *The Aristotelian Ethics* (Oxford: Clarendon Press, 1978)

Klibansky, R. *The Continuity of the Platonic Tradition during the Middle Ages* (London: Warburg Institute, 1939)

Kraut, R. (ed.) *The Cambridge Companion to Plato* (Cambridge: Cambridge University Press, 1992)

LaCugna, C. M. *God For Us* (New York: HarperCollins, 1991)

Lakeland, P. *Theology and Critical Theory, The Discourse of the Church* (Nashville: Abingdon Press, 1990)

Lampe, G. *God as Spirit* (London: SCM, 1977)

Latin American Bishops, Second General Conference *The Church in the Present-Day Transformation of Latin America in the Light of the Council, Conclusions*, second edition (Washington DC: USCC, 1973)

Third General Conference *Puebla, Evangelisation at Present and in the Future of Latin America, Conclusions* (Slough: St Paul Publications, 1980)

Lawless, G. (ed.) *Augustine of Hippo and his Monastic Rule* (Oxford: Clarendon Press, 1987)

Lieu, J., North, J. and Rajak T. (eds.) *The Jews Among Pagans and Christians in the Roman Empire* (London: Routledge, 1992)

Lloyd, G. E. R. *Aristotle: The Growth and Structure of his Thought* (Cambridge: Cambridge University Press, 1968)

Lohfink, G. *Jesus and Community* (London: SPCK, 1985)

Lohse, E. *Die Texte aus Qumran*, second edition (Darmstadt: *Wissenschaftliche Buchgesellschaft*, 1971)

Long A. A. (ed.) *Problems in Stoicism* (London: Athlone Press, 1971)

Lossky, V. *The Mystical Theology of the Eastern Church* (Cambridge: James Clarke, 1957)

Louth, A. *The Origins of the Christian Mystical Tradition, From Plato to Denys* (Oxford: Clarendon, 1981)

MacIntyre, A. *After Virtue*, second edition (London: Duckworth, 1985)

Whose Justice? Which Rationality? (London: Duckworth, 1988)

Macmurray, J. *The Self as Agent* (London: Faber and Faber, 1957)

Persons in Relation (London: Faber and Faber, 1961)

McPartlan, P. (ed.) *One in 2000?* (Slough: St Paul's, 1995)

Markus, R. A. *Saeculum: History and Society in the Theology of St Augustine* (Cambridge: Cambridge University Press, 1970)

Meeks, W. A. *The First Urban Christians, The Social World of the Apostle Paul* (London: Yale University Press, 1983)

The Moral World of the First Christians (London: SPCK, 1987)

The Meissen Agreement, Texts, Occasional Paper 2 (London: The Council for Christian Unity of the General Synod of the Church of England, 1992)

Meredith, A. *The Cappadocians* (London: Geoffrey Chapman, 1995)

Mersch, E. *The Whole Christ* (London: Dennis Dobson, 1938)

Meyer, H. and Vischer, L. (eds.) *Growth in Agreement* (Geneva: WCC; New York: Paulist Press, 1984)

Milbank, J. *Theology and Social Theory: Beyond Secular Reason* (Oxford: Basil Blackwell, 1990)

Mitchell, M. M. *Paul and the Rhetoric of Reconciliation* (Tübingen: J.C.B. Mohr, 1991)

Musurillo, H. (ed.) *From Glory to Glory* (London: John Murray, 1962)

Neusner, J. *Torah Through the Ages, A Short History of Judaism* (London: SCM, 1990)

Nicholson, E. *God and his People* (Oxford: Clarendon Press, 1986)

Nietzsche, F. *Twilight of the Idols and The Anti-Christ* (Harmondsworth: Penguin Books, 1968)

Nock, A. D. *Conversion* (Oxford: Oxford University Press, 1933)

    Early Gentile Christianity and its Hellenistic Background, Harper Torchbooks Edition (New York: Harper and Row, 1964)

Nussbaum, M. C. *The Fragility of Goodness* (Cambridge: Cambridge University Press, 1986)

O'Connell, R. J. *St Augustine's Confessions, the Odyssey of Soul* (Cambridge, Mass.: Belknap Press, Harvard University Press, 1969)

Palmer, R. E. *Hermeneutics* (Evanston: Northwestern University Press, 1969)

Plato, *Gorgias*, translated by W. R. M. Lamb, LCL 166 (Cambridge, Mass.: Harvard University Press, 1967)

    Laws, translated by T. J. Saunders (Harmondsworth: Penguin, 1970)

    Phaedo, translated with an introduction and commentary by R. Hackforth (Cambridge: Cambridge University Press, 1955)

    Phaedrus, translated with an introduction and commentary by R. Hackforth (Cambridge: Cambridge University Press, 1952)

    The Republic, translated by F. M. Cornford (Oxford: Oxford University Press, 1941)

    Symposium, translated by W. R. M. Lamb, LCL 166 (Cambridge, Mass.: Harvard University Press, 1967)

Popper, K. R. *The Open Society and its Enemies*, volume 1, 'The Spell of Plato' (London: Routledge and Kegan Paul, 1962)

    Unended Quest, An Intellectual Autobiography (Glasgow: Fontana, 1976)

Pouchet, R. *Basile le Grand et son Univers d'Amis d'Après sa Correspondance, une Stratégie de Communion, Studia Ephemeridis 'Augustinianum'* 36 (Rome: Institutum Patristicum 'Augustinianum', 1992)

Rigal, J. *L'Ecclésiologie de Communion* (Paris: Cerf, 1997)

Rowland, C. *Christian Origins* (London: SPCK, 1985)

    The Open Heaven (London: SPCK, 1982)

Rorty, A. O. (ed.) *Essays on Aristotle's Ethics* (Berkeley: University of California Press, 1980)

Rosenthal, J. M. and Currie, N. *Being Anglican in the Third Millennium* (London: Morehouse, 1997)

Ross, D. *Plato's Theory of Ideas* (Oxford: Clarendon Press, 1951)

Rousseau, P. *Basil of Caesarea* (Berkeley: University of California Press, 1994)

Pachomius, The Making of a Community in Fourth-Century Egypt (Berkeley: University of California Press, 1985)

Sanders, E. P. *Jesus and Judaism* (London: SCM, 1985)

Paul and Palestinian Judaism (London: SCM, 1977)

Schürer, E., new English edition, revised and edited by Vermes, G., Millar, F. and Black, M. *The History of the Jewish People in the Age of Jesus Christ* (Edinburgh: T. and T. Clark, 1979)

Segal, A. F. *Rebecca's Children* (Cambridge, Mass.: Harvard University Press, 1986)

Stambaugh, J. E. and Balch, D. L. *The Social World of the First Christians* (London: SPCK, 1986)

Steiner, G. *Real Presences* (London: Faber and Faber, 1989)

Sweet, J. P. M. *Revelation* (London: SCM, 1979)

Sykes, S. W. *The Identity of Christianity* (London: SPCK, 1984)

Sykes, S. W. and Clayton, J. P. (eds.) *Christ, Faith and History* (Cambridge: Cambridge University Press, 1972)

Tappert, T. G. (ed.) *The Book of Concord* (Philadelphia: Fortress Press, 1959)

Theissen, G. *The Social Setting of Pauline Christianity* (Edinburgh: T. and T. Clark, 1982)

Thornton, L. S. *The Common Life in the Body of Christ*, third edition (London: Dacre Press, 1950)

Tillard, J.-M. R. *Eglise d'Eglises, L'Ecclésiologie de Communion* (Paris: Cerf, 1987)

L'Eglise Locale (Paris: Cerf, 1995)

Together in Mission and Ministry (London: Church House Publishing, 1993)

Torrance, A. J. *Persons in Communion* (Edinburgh: T. and T. Clark, 1996)

Torrance, T. F. *The Christian Doctrine of God, One Being in Three Persons* (Edinburgh: T. and T. Clark, 1996)

The Truth Shall Make You Free, The Lambeth Conference 1988 (London: Church House Publishing, 1988)

Turner, H. E. W. *The Pattern of Christian Truth* (London: Mowbray, 1954)

Ut Unum Sint (Vatican City: Vatican Press, 1995)

Vanderkam, J. C. (ed.) *The Book of Jubilees, Corpus Scriptorum Christianorum Orientalium, Scriptores Aethiopici* 88 (Louvain: Peeters, 1989)

Veilleux, A. (ed.) *Pachomian Koinonia, the Lives, Rules, and other Writings of Saint Pachomius and his Disciples*, 3 vols., Cistertian Studies Series 45–7 (Kalamazoo: Cistertian Publications, 1980–2)

Vermes, G. *The Dead Sea Scrolls in English*, revised and extended fourth edition (Sheffield: Academic Press, 1994)

von Ivanka, E. *Plato Christianus* (Einsiedeln: Johannes Verlag, 1990)

Walsh, M. J. (ed.) *Commentary on the Catechism of the Catholic Church* (London: Geoffrey Chapman, 1994)

Williams, R. D. *Resurrection* (London: Darton, Longman and Todd, 1982)

(ed.) *The Making of Orthodoxy* (Cambridge: Cambridge University Press, 1989)

Women in the Anglican Episcopate (Toronto: Anglican Book Centre, 1998)

Wright, N. T. *The New Testament and the People of God* (London: SPCK, 1992)

Zimmerli, W. and Jeremias, J. *The Servant of God* (London: SCM, 1957)

Zizioulas, J. D. *Being as Communion* (London: Darton, Longman and Todd, 1985)

Index

Abraham, 101–4, 111, 112n, 184, 198, 199
Academy, 78, 88
Acts of the Apostles, 56n, 124–8, 129, 130, 133n, 143, 148, 151–4, 172, 193, 200, 201
Alexander the Great, 76, 83, 97
Alexandria, 99, 101, 135n, 140, 149, 158
Allchin, A. M., 146–7
Ambrose, 171
Anglicans, Anglicanism, 12, 19, 20–8, 33, 40
Anglican-Roman Catholic International Commission (ARCIC), 20–1, 194
Antioch, 116, 127, 135, 140, 144
Antiochus Epiphanes, 104–5
Antony, 150–1
Apocalypse, Book of the, 46, 138–9, 144
'apostolic succession', 25–8, 38
Arendt, H., 13
Arianism, 64n, 151, 204
Aristotle, 2, 5, 10, 11, 14, 17n, 46, 47, 48n, 49, 51, 71, 72–96, 97, 98n, 125n, 153, 166, 177, 185, 187, 196–8
  Categories, 93–4, 177
  Ethics, Eudemian, 78–9, 82, 92n, 94–5, 187, 197
  Ethics, Nicomachean, 79, 82, 92n, 94–5, 187, 197
  Metaphysics, 90
  Physics, 196
  Politics, 78, 80–6, 197
  Soul, on the, 90
Athanasius, 150–1, 155, 158, 170
Athens, 14, 49, 50, 55, 56, 67, 69, 76, 78, 83, 97, 98, 129, 149, 195
Augustine, 2, 10, 46, 47, 98, 157n, 162, 171–93, 198, 205–6
  City of God, 172, 183–9, 190, 205

Confessions, 157n, 172–83, 190, 193
Monastic Rule, 193
On the Trinity, 173n, 190–1, 205
Sermons, 191

baptism, 20, 26, 36, 42, 44, 154, 161, 165, 179, 180, 208
Baptism, Eucharist and Ministry (BEM), 25, 42–3, 44, 194
Barnabas, Epistle of, 114
Barth, K., 115n, 147
Basil of Caesarea, 148–60, 161, 169, 204
  On the Holy Spirit, 156–9
Bauer, W., 140–2, 202
Benedict, 13
Berlin, I., 76n
Bernstein, R., 13
bishop, bishops, 12, 21, 22, 23, 24, 25, 27, 28, 29, 30, 33, 37, 38, 45, 144–5, 149, 154, 156, 192, 194
Bonhoeffer, D., 8
Brown, R. E., 120n, 135–6, 138
Burnaby, J., 192
Burtchaell, J. T., 101, 116n, 135n

Calvin, J., 32
Canberra, 44–5
Cappadocian Fathers, 2, 10, 47, 146–70, 198, 203–5
Catechism of the Catholic Church, 32–3
Chadwick, H., 142n, 173n
Chalcedon, Council of, 65n
Church of England, 20n, 24, 25, 27
Church of Norway, 26
Church of Sweden, 26
Cicero, 185, 186–7
Clement, First Epistle of, 129, 135n, 140
Clement of Alexandria, 149

218

15172877R00137

Printed in Great Britain
by Amazon.co.uk, Ltd.,
Marston Gate.